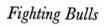
Fighting Bulls

Antonio Bienvenida, who restored honour to the bullfight

ANGUS MACNAB

Fighting Bulls

AN ACCOUNT OF THE
BULLFIGHT

NEW YORK

HARCOURT, BRACE AND COMPANY

first American edition 1959

Published in England in 1957 under the title *The Bulls of Iberia*

Library of Congress Catalog Card Number: 59-6422

Printed in the United States of America

CONTENTS

v

ILLUSTRATIONS

ILLUSTRATIONS

BRINDIS

Por Mogs, quien se hizo aficionada
en una sola tarde de toros

Por Manuel Alvarez
diestro de solera clásica
gran director de lidia y sin par estoqueador
quien nació fuera de su época
y
Por Antonio Megías 'Bienvenida'
el torero más largo de la posguerra
quien resuscitó la fiesta ya en trance de muerte
y le añadió glorias nuevas e inmarcesibles

¡Va por vosotros!

DEDICATION

To Mogs, who became an aficionada
in one afternoon

To Manuel Alvarez
matador of classic mould
grand director of ringcraft and peerless swordsman
who was born out of his period
and
To Antonio Megías 'Bienvenida'
the 'longest' torero since the Spanish war
who resuscitated the fiesta when at the point of death
and gave it new and imperishable glories

To you I dedicate this faena

Preface

After twenty-five years, Mr. Ernest Hemingway's *Death in the Afternoon* remains the standard work of literature in the English language on the subject of bullfighting, and it is difficult to see how it could well be dislodged from that position. No doubt it is an easy book to raise secondary objections to, but on the permanent, unalterable things Hemingway has said what was to be said, once and for all. Anything else is a matter of individual taste, viewpoint or emphasis, or else a question of brute fact like yesterday's Stock Exchange prices.

However, Hemingway's book was published in 1932, it deals chiefly with events before 1930, and its outlook is that of before 1928. These last two dates are crucial, for in 1928 the horse-protector came in, and in 1930 the five-year-old bull went out. These two events brought about far-reaching, unsuspected and radical changes in the bullfight, quite comparable to those introduced into warfare by the use of firearms. From 1750 to 1928 the bullfight had been fundamentally unchanged. From 1930 onwards (and even more, from 1939 when the Spanish War ended and bullfights were regularly held again all over the country), the difference was so great that it is astonishing to find any continuity at all. Naturally the names of the things remain unaltered and so does the routine form of the spectacle; but the mutual relationship of the parts, their relationship to the whole, the composition and reactions of the audience, the grounds for criticism of the bullfight, and the type of men who engage in it, have all undergone profound transformation; in short, the original elements, themselves largely altered, have combined to form a completely different pattern.

Thus *Death in the Afternoon* is still valid as literature and as history, but in its utilitarian aspect as a guide to current bullfighting it is simply out-of-date; and that is really my chief excuse for producing this book, which seeks to give information, and perhaps some entertainment, but has no literary pretensions, much less anything beginning with 'psycho-' or 'socio-'. I have no case to put, no thesis to propound, no '-ology' to nourish; there is no 'symbolic meaning' or 'interpretation of life' or anything like that. It is just an account of what happens in the bullring, with some hints on how to get the best out of what you see and how to distinguish the good stuff from the fake. Being human, I have naturally added my personal comments whenever there seemed to be something worth saying, but I do not claim to be 'objective' or 'impartial', for I have lived long enough, and seen enough of objectivity and impartiality, to have a deep distrust of both. However, as a matter of plain fact I solemnly declare that the general attitude taken in these pages is such as would be endorsed by the more solid Spanish *aficionados*, especially those known as *toristas* because their primary interest is in the Bull rather than the Bullfighter, and those whose memories go back (as mine, alas, does not) to the days of Joselito and Belmonte at the end of the First World War. For that reason, I trust, no one will find the ideas in this book very 'original', for in something like bullfighting, which depends on permanent canons, anything really and truly original is simply false.

One feature that I think is new in books of this kind is the reports of important bullfights of recent years, written up not from vague impressions, but nearly always from my own notes scribbled down in the *plaza* at the time. Here the trouble was what to leave out, and I was obliged, with great regret, to cut what I had already written down to half, so as to balance the claims of the newcomer who wants basic information, and those of the *aficionado* who prefers taurine journalism.

The absence of another feature, too, may be greeted with relief: while naturally condemning abuses in the bullfight today, and supporting those who have tried, with some success, to clean them up, I have entirely omitted the general moralisings which nearly every writer in English seems to regard as obligatory. I am here as witness, not as counsel. Once anyone knows what a bullfight is and what it is not, he will certainly make up his own mind, if he wishes to, about such questions, in so far as they still exist—for those which appear so clearly in *Death in the Afternoon* hardly arise today, and if they do, they must be posed in the opposite sense. I believe that everyone will here find such facts as are needed to form a judgment; and the only thing I would add is that no sound judgment of any kind, moral or otherwise, about modern bullfighting on foot can be formed unless it is clearly grasped that the thing is not in any way a sport—nor even, *pace* a distinguished English journalist who has written with considerable knowledge of it, a 'pastime'. If, as he suggests, bullfighting were the 'Spanish national pastime', then Spain would be an even more remarkable country than it is.

The bullfight is in fact a public performance or spectacle, to entertain the people on holidays or festivities, whether it is organised by official authorities, or by an impresario for private profit like a theatrical show. In itself, it partakes of the nature of the drama—the death of the fighting bull, a tragedy in three acts—and at heart there are also appreciable elements of ritual warfare and sacrifice.

It takes place regularly nowadays in integral form in Spain (whence it has spread to southern France and to

Morocco) and in the Spanish-speaking lands of Mexico, Peru, Colombia, Ecuador and Venezuela; irregularly in other parts of the former Spanish empire; and in a truncated form in Portugal and her colonies.

A certain amount of the material in this book has been condensed, expanded or otherwise adapted from my weekly talks on bullfighting broadcast from 1949 to 1955 in English, by the Spanish National Radio, to which my acknowledgements are due. I must also express my gratitude to don Benjamín Bentura ('Barico'), editor-in-chief of *El Ruedo*, and to Messrs. Editorial Revista de Occidente, for their kind permission to reproduce in translation the passages quoted on pages 64 and 109 respectively.

Santo Tomé, Toledo, 1955   A. M.

Fighting Bulls

PART ONE

What and How

CHAPTER ONE

Introducing *Bos Taurus Africanus*

I

If there is one truly Spanish institution in the world, it is bullfighting, and naturally enough Spanish has numerous bullfighting technical terms which are untranslatable in English. But oddly enough it has no single term for either 'bullfight', meaning the spectacle, or 'bullfighting', meaning the art or science and all that goes with it.* Now, when this occurs in a language, it means one of two things: either the idea is a purely foreign one (for example, 'baseball'), or else the conception of the thing is different. The latter is the case here. The Spanish do not say 'a bullfight', they say 'a running of bulls'; and when they speak of 'bullfighting' in general, they simply say 'the bulls'.

In the opposite way, when American ranchers speak of land suitable for cattle raising, they call it 'cow country'. Notice that they do not call it 'bull country' or 'steer

---

* *Toreo* and *lidia* will not do, for they strictly refer only to the preparation for the kill, and exclude the kill itself. The only really adequate word is *tauromaquia*, but that is a 'learned' word simply picked straight out of the Greek dictionary, and does not correspond to any popular need. Nor does it really cover all that is meant by the English word 'bullfighting'. The latter word, when an adjective, is in Spanish simply *taurino*, 'taurine', a fact which reinforces what has been said above. The headline 'Taurine News' in a paper means bullfighting news and nothing else, and *un taurino* means not 'a taurine man', but 'a man connected with bullfighting'.

3

country': *cow* is the essential word. So also in Spanish: the expression for the livestock of a ranch is 'cow-cattle', not 'bull-cattle'. All the Far West was once part of New Spain; the language has changed, but the ideas remain the same.

The conclusion of all this is as follows: in the Spanish mind, the word 'bull' has a special connotation. 'Cow' suggests milk and meat (the Spanish have no word for beef, they simply call it 'cow'), but 'bull' does not merely mean the male of the cow. It means, in the first place and above all, the bull that is a fighting animal, not a meat producer. Added to this, the shape of the country on the map resembles a bull's hide, and the bull is the Spanish emblem or totem, like the British lion or the American eagle. The sight of a fine bull stirs deep emotion in the Spaniard. I know one torero who actually shed tears of reverential joy in the ring one day, when he saw the magnificent, inspiring bull that came out for him to fight.

But this Spanish fighting bull is a long way removed from the Hereford or the Jersey, or even the Texas Longhorn. You can let cattle run loose on the open range for generations until they are complete 'outlaws', but they will never turn into what the Spanish call *toros bravos* or fighting bulls. The reason is that the race is different. So the first thing of all, before we even begin to think about how a bull is fought, is to know a little about the Spanish *toro bravo* himself. With your permission, then, I will introduce you to him.

There is no need to be afraid. He will not attack us as we ride slowly on our horses out to the pasture where he is grazing. Out there, unless we startle him by some foolish action, we are safer than we should be with an ordinary farmer's bull. The fighting bull is not savage, he is brave, and normally attacks only when provoked or cooped up. No one is so mild and peaceful as a good soldier when not on the battlefield. He is not truculent or vicious. Neither is the true nobleman or aristocrat. And Señor Toro Bravo is

C. Fighting Bulls (BW)

Scientist (vi) (Eng)

G

distinguished for his nobility. He is indeed an aristocrat: his pedigree is the oldest in the world and still often perfectly pure, as it was in the days of the Pharaohs, for in actual fact, we are told, he is an ancient Egyptian aristocrat.

Cattle are said to have reached ancient Spain in two ways, by land and sea. The first lot came overland from Asia with the Celts, and were pretty well domesticated and had little or no fighting qualities. The second kind were those of North Africa, already thoroughbred in Egypt, and were introduced into Andalusia, it is said, by the Carthaginians and the Berbers. They were only slightly domesticated and, as they roamed the vast ranges of south and central Spain, more or less wild, they quickly reverted to type.

So in Spain today there are two races of native cattle, apart from modern foreign importations: the domesticated ones, some with a bit of wild blood perhaps, and the fighting bull, whose full name is *Bos Taurus Africanus*. He is a descendant of *Bos Primigenius* or the Primordial Bull, that is, the giant aurochs of antiquity. The aurochs became extinct some centuries B.C. in most parts, but a few herds lingered on in the German forests, and were even hunted by Julius Cæsar. Cæsar, always a sober and restrained writer, describes them thus: "In size they are a little less than elephants; in species, colour and shape, they are bulls." In fact, the aurochs stood about six feet six at the withers; but any torero will tell you that bulls have a way of doubling their apparent size when you come to fight them. The last surviving aurochs was alive in 1712 in the King of Prussia's zoo; the famous Leibniz got the king to have it painted from life, and a representation of the picture still exists.*

But let us get back to *Bos Taurus Africanus*. We are told that he was first introduced into Spain by the Carthaginians.

* For all this, see Ortega y Gasset's epilogue to *El Arte del Toreo* by the famous matador Domingo Ortega (publ. *Revista de Occidente*, Madrid, 1950, in book form; originally a lecture before the Madrid Athenaeum).

That is what the official scientists say; but I have a suspicion that he was there long before that, and I will say why.

The typical habitat of the fighting bull (who, as we shall see later, is today entirely of the 'Andalusian' caste or sub-variety) is the great valley of the Guadalquivir in Andalusia, especially the marshy lands near its mouth. Near that river mouth stood the ancient city of Tartessos with its dazzling civilisation—the Tarshish of the Bible. Now, Tartessos is a typically Minoan word, and the traditional sport or spectacle of Minoan Crete was the leaping over the horns of a charging bull, as can be seen from the representations in the Palace of Minos. We all know the Greek legend of Theseus and the hostages and the Minotaur, but I do not believe that the hostages were thrown to a fabulous monster half man and half bull. I believe they got themselves killed in the ring when trying to execute this terribly difficult and dangerous hazard. Plutarch, in his life of Theseus, implies almost in so many words that Ariadne fell in love with Theseus from the moment she first saw him in the bullring. This sounds like a sentimental novel of the last century about southern Spain. And if you compare the women's costumes of ancient Crete and modern Andalusia, the resemblance is most striking. The Spanish one is decidedly more modest by our standards, but the long skirt of many flounces is just the same as it was four thousand years ago. My own view is that Tartessos was a Cretan colony and that the Minoans brought the fighting bulls with them. Even the very bull-leaping still exists today, though not in Spain, but only in the Landes in southern France, presumably derived from the known Cretan colonies there (the emblem which appears on French coins of the Pétain régime in 'unoccupied France' after 1940 is precisely the *labrys*, or sacred double-headed axe of Minoan Crete).*

---

* For the aurochs (Lat. *urus*) as a sacrificial victim in ancient Crete, see Leonard Cottrel, *The Bull of Minos*, page 155 (Pan Books, London,

At any rate, whether it is Crete or Egypt, our Spanish bull can take his pedigree back much further than even the Emperor of Japan. And if you hold the view, as some do, that both those civilisations originated from Atlantis, you can take him back seven thousand years more. Certainly Plato in the *Critias*, when quoting the Egyptian priests' description of Atlantis, tells us of something not unlike a bull-fight which took place there. All these considerations make it likely that our *Bos Taurus Africanus* should be something rather different from the ordinary cattle tribe. It is therefore time to abandon speculation about his origin, and to say something about him as he is today.

2

The fundamental characteristic of the fighting bull is bravery. But, as was said, 'brave' does not mean merely savage, like a domestic bull that suddenly attacks you without provocation. Bravery implies disregard of risk or pain. All tame cattle will give some sort of a charge if you wave a red (or any other coloured) cloth at them. But suppose that the man they charged at was riding a horse; and suppose that instead of galloping away, he stood fast and jabbed a spear into the withers of the charging animal. What would occur? The bull or cow would give a bellow of pain and surprise, and would turn and make off, and would not charge that man again in a hurry. Now, that is precisely the test of bravery, which fighting cattle of both sexes are given when they are calves, and which also forms the first part of a proper bullfight in the ring.

In Spain there do exist animals of mixed race, called

1956). I would add that the bull depicted on the Knossos frescoes, quite apart from its enormous size, has horns exactly similar to those of the Prussian aurochs of A.D. 1712.

moruchos, half fighting blood and half tame blood of the Salamanca area. These animals look quite handsome, they charge in a more spirited way than domestic cattle, and in village cape-fights they put up a good show, because there is no bravery test. But if they ever appear in a fight with picadors, they will seldom charge the horse a second time, because they have not the caste and the bravery, and they 'can't take it'.

The genuine fighting bull of pure caste, when he is a good one, is different. He may not always charge very hard the first time; but as soon as he feels the pic he will come back all the harder for more. When his blood is up, he ignores pain altogether, and probably, like a soldier in the heat of battle, does not even feel it. The more he is punished the braver he gets and the harder he charges. Not all breeds are pure or free from degeneration, but it would be easy to name a dozen in which most of the bulls, if they were allowed to, would go on recharging against the pic until they fell down dead.

Again, the bull of caste is completely fearless. His bravery in this sense has been very well described by Hemingway as "something quite unearthly". In the last century, bulls were sometimes put up to fight against panthers, bears, lions and tigers, sometimes against two at once, and always killed them immediately and looked around for more. Bulls have even fought elephants, though of course they could not actually kill them. But the last time, in 1898, the bull charged the elephant again and again, and on the twelfth charge overthrew it and gored away to its heart's content. Bulls have been known to charge motor-cars, and sometimes trams and even trains.

The elephant story brings us to the power of the bull. Compared with big beef animals like the Hereford or Aberdeen Angus, the fighting bull looks small. But he is more like a racehorse than a huge draught animal. His

8

skeleton is not massive, and his hocks and fetlocks are so slender and dainty that you wonder how they can bear his weight. You wonder still more when you see how even a four-year-old bull, not fully mature, can lift up a horse, covered with a mattress-like protector weighing as much as 200 pounds,* mounted by a corpulent picador on a heavy high-cantle saddle with large bucket stirrups of plate iron, and wearing steel greaves and iron-shod boots, and throw the whole outfit four feet in the air. Any massiveness or coarseness in the legs of a fighting bull is a sure sign of impure blood and low caste. The actual weight on the hoof of a good average bull of today, with four years completed, is seldom much over half a ton: 500 kg. or 1,100 lb. is a very fair specimen. Some breeds come a bit larger, notably Pablo Romero, Miura, and Tulio and Isaias Vázquez, famous breeds about which we shall hear some more later.

However, bulls in Spain are normally reckoned, not by gross weight but by net weight *en canal*; this means the weight of meat and bone left after skinning, beheading, gutting and removal of the feet. Thus, the net weight represents useful bone and muscle only, or power without dead weight; and here lies the secret of the fighting bull's extraordinary strength. In ordinary Spanish cattle this net weight is only fifty per cent of the gross or live weight; but in the fighting bull the average net weight is something over sixty per cent, and in the best breeds it works out at between sixty-three and sixty-six per cent. These figures speak for themselves: just as in the racing car as against the tourer, the secret of 'performance' lies in the power-to-weight ratio. Considered *en canal*, a bull is regarded as well-grown when it exceeds 300 kg.; 320 is large, 345 is the classic old-time

---

* The regulation weight is sixty-six lb., but this regulation was never adhered to, and the overweight protector was one of the chief abuses in the pic act. The authorities restored the regulation protector in May 1957.

weight of 'thirty *arrobas*'. The biggest bulls I remember
seeing myself were a Pablo Romero of about 375 in 1946, a
string of Miuras which *averaged* 345 in 1947, and a Tulio and
Isaias Vázquez of 357 in 1951; but a bull of 403 was fought in
Madrid in 1952 (of poor caste, a substitute), and the biggest
of all was a Pablo Romero of 424 at Almagro in 1948. Anything over 375 can be reckoned a monster by present-day
standards; this last bull, allowing a sixty-two per cent yield,
would work out at about 1,415 lb. on the hoof.

As regards the bull's speed, that is another question, and
here breeds vary very considerably. Those of the Arranz
breed—one of the best from the Salamanca area—are rather
light-boned, and charge like racehorses at the picadors,
sometimes from fifteen or twenty yards in spectacular style.
Heavier bulls naturally tend to be slower in general; yet that
string of Tulio and Isaias Vázquez in 1951, which averaged
327 and were therefore a very big string, were also some of
the fastest I have ever seen, and the combination was truly
formidable.

The other great quality of the fighting bull, apart from
bravery, is what is called *nobleza*. I have freely used the word
'nobility' in this book, but perhaps a better translation
would be 'honesty'. The degree of honesty varies greatly
from bull to bull and breed to breed; but all bulls have
some, otherwise they would be unfightable. Most of them
have a good deal; but an excess of it means a bull that is
docile to the point of silliness, and this is not desirable, for
such animals will be deficient in fire and aggressiveness and
will be very nearly tame. It may sound odd to the newcomer, but what the matador wants, and also the audience,
is an aggressive bull that charges hard. Why this is so will
become clear later.

Nobility or honesty consists in innocence and absence of
craftiness: in other words, a bull that gives a frank, straight
charge, directed at the coloured cloth lure rather than the

man's body. All bulls will go for the coloured cloth at first, because they have never seen such a thing before, and it excites them. But after a while they start learning to distinguish the cloth (which they took for a solid object) from the body. Some breeds, such as Miura, learn quickly, and unless the man knows his stuff properly ('gives correct *lidia*' is the technical expression), he is apt to find himself hanging on a horn. Other breeds, particularly the purest strains of the Vistahermosa caste, tend to remain noble and honest to the end (unless spoilt by excessively bad *lidia*), and are thus much less difficult to fight, and more popular with matadors since they provide good opportunities for brilliant work; an example of this is the bulls of Urquijo, the celebrated Murubes of old.* Again, a bull that is very noble may scorn to gore at a man whom it has tossed or knocked down, whereas a bull of *sentido*, that is, a craftier one, will not spare him. In general, bulls of up to four-and-a-half years are much more noble than older ones, but bad *lidia* can spoil the noblest bull. The bull's state of mind does not remain the same from start to finish, but goes through different psychological stages, which we shall have to discuss later on.

---

* The blood of the T. and I. Vázquez bulls is virtually identical with the Murubes, yet you hardly ever see them fought by matadors of standing. The reason is that, although noble, they have that frightening combination of exceptional speed, power and stamina, and a tremendous effort is needed to dominate them.

CHAPTER TWO

The Primary Element:

Castes and Breeds of Bulls

This book contains the boiled-down results of ten years'
experience in seeing, discussing, and reporting bullfights.
It has been rewritten more than once, for the more you learn
the more you realise you are ignorant of. The present
chapter did not appear at all in the first draft, and has been
completely recast, cut and streamlined, and brought up to
date, from the second. To the newcomer, it will inevitably
appear dull, and my advice to those who have not seen any
bullfights, or have no previous knowledge, is to skip it until
they have at least read through all the rest of the book. But I
assure them that it is nevertheless quite elementary, and the
information in it is common knowledge to all real *aficionados*.

Why, then, include it? The best answer is to refer to
personal experience, for if I have arrived at any real knowledge of the subject—starting naturally from nothing, like
anyone else born outside Spain—then the process will be
similar for others. I will therefore say this, and no italics or
capital letters could sufficiently convey the importance of the
next few paragraphs:

When you see your first few bullfights, your sole interest,
once you have got the hang of it, lies in the men and what
they do. The bull is just a bull. It is clear that some bulls are
larger, more powerful, or better-armed than others. But all
you see the first few times—some people never see any more,

and these are the ones who frequently complain that the fights are no good, for superlatively 'brilliant' and spectacular shows are not too common—is that matador A seemed to do very well, he gave a lot of beautiful passes to his bull, he stood firm and did not seem to go on the defensive or run away, and the crowd applauded him heartily; on the other hand, matador B was constantly on the move, he did not appear at all confident, his passes were not at all beautiful, and the audience whistled at him. But then, matador C does a number of things that do not look very attractive or spectacular either, one feels no desire to take a snapshot of any of his work, and yet he receives a quite unexpected ovation in the middle, and is loudly applauded at the end. All this is very puzzling.

As time goes on, the new spectator begins to sort the chief men out. X is fine with the cape, but clumsy when it comes to the kill; Y's cape is not worth anything, but his *faena* or solo work with the red cloth is beautiful. Z is just workmanlike until it is time for the sword, and then he pulls out the big organ-stop and does something that stirs you to the depths. And after, say, two dozen major fights, one has the men classified by what each can do, or at least what one has seen them do.

That is just the moment when, I am sorry to say, the new enthusiast must be on his guard. He knows just enough to be aware, if he is modest, of his own ignorance. He has so far been paying little or no attention to anything but the men. But the men—although of course they fill the ignorant spectator's eye, and are always the same whereas the bulls are new every time, and their personalities are ventilated a good deal in newspapers and conversation—are not the primary element in the *fiesta*. And after the first flush of satisfaction in being able to describe a fight, to discuss it with Spanish friends, to recognise and even appraise the different *suertes* or hazards, to give a reasoned opinion why one fighter is better than another (or was better last week), one begins to get more and more interested in the primary element in the *fiesta*—the bull.

After a year or two, in fact, in which some leading matadors have retired and new stars have arisen, the *aficionado* will realise that what was just said about the men being the same and the bulls different each time is not true at all. It is the matadors that come and go, and the bulls that are always the same—not individual animals, of course, but the various breeds. Some go off, and either become degenerate or are pulled together again, others retain their position; but when due allowances are made for this, the bulls are the permanent element, and one can compare the abilities of two matadors who were not contemporaries by their known performances with certain breeds of bulls. When this stage has been reached, the *aficionado* will willingly travel a good distance, at times, to see certain breeds of bulls fought by competent though second-class men, whereas he will stay away from a much-boomed star fight in the capital or wherever he lives, simply because, given the breed of bulls advertised to be fought, he knows in advance it is any odds the show will not be worth seeing, however famous the stars on the programme. (In 1953, I was visited in Spain by a well-known London journalist and writer, who had never seen a bullfight, and he asked me to take him to one of the big shows of the year in Madrid which was held during his few days' stay. I managed to get out of it and he never went; he thus remains in simple ignorance of bullfighting, instead of getting a totally false impression, for that show was a disgrace, as I knew it would be, simply from the breed of bulls to be fought.) He will also begin to derive much more pleasure, of an intellectual rather than a purely emotional kind, from seeing really intelligent and valiant work done to certain bulls, without any 'apotheosic triumphs', than from *faenas* to certain others which send the public delirious.

All the above is by way of explanation. As I said, it may seem dull to many, and what follows may seem duller still. But if anyone is going to see bullfights over any period of time, or if he wants to get more out of them than just the obvious appeal of a few superlative pieces of work, I assure him that this chapter, little as he may have enjoyed it at first reading, is the one that he will perhaps value most in the end, even if only because it will probably have saved him from wasting several times the price of the book on going to indifferent shows, and perhaps helped him towards getting the best out of his opportunities to see good ones, when the question of a choice has arisen.

No bull, no bullfight. In other words, if the animal is too small or too young, if its horns are too short or too inward-curving so that the danger is reduced to a minimum, or worst of all—as often used to occur until the end of 1952 in the provinces, though not very much in Madrid—if the horn-tips had been artificially blunted or shortened at the dictates of some influential matadors and their managers, then there is no longer any emotion, except repugnance: the thing is a 'carve-up', and all interest vanishes except the æsthetic appeal of the pretty colours and what might be called the 'ballet' element. Conversely, with a big powerful bull of five years, or four if well grown, weighing over half a ton and with respectable horns, which really dominates the *plaza* with its personality and 'seriousness', and may even 'sow panic' among the subordinate foot fighters, then indeed there is emotion and interest, and the attitude of the audience will be very different. When really large and tough bulls, such as those of Pablo Romero, are in the ring, the change in the spectators is most striking: every little bit of good work will be duly applauded, and if the man is unlucky without cowardice, they will be sympathetic. Fantastic feats—not too difficult for a man who knows his stuff and is facing a 'silly' three-year-old that hardly knows how to use its horns—

will not be expected. Valour will get its proper reward, and if the animal is a really nasty customer and an accident looks likely, the crowd will freely shout to the man to "kill it now!", and not expose himself uselessly where no brilliance is possible. And scientific *lidia*, or the general art and strategy of the fighting, will be keenly appraised and rightly rewarded, at least in Madrid. After a little time, the fashionable, spectacular, but sadly standardised work palls terribly unless the bull is one commanding real respect; and I have often saved myself money and boredom by giving a miss to a fight that aroused great public keenness—among people who took no account of the first item on the programme.

In reporting a fight (as distinct from writing a literary chronicle of one), the reporter always begins by stating the programme, that is, first the number and breed of the bulls to be fought, and then the names of the matadors booked. After that, when writing for a non-Spanish public, as for instance in my bullfighting broadcasts to North America since 1949, I usually make some observations about the bulls: what caste they belong to and its degree of purity, the general reputation of the ranch in question, and whether these bulls in fact behaved in accordance with that reputation. Only then do I go on to describe the fighting, or part of it, in detail.

The use of the word 'caste' calls for some explanation, because it is used both generally and technically. Used generally, it means something similar to 'class' in race-horses, but in bulls it refers not to speed but to bravery. Examples of such usage are statements such as the following: "The bulls today were of poor caste"; or, "The caste has gone off badly in that herd"; or, "A bull of real caste gets braver the more he is punished". This general meaning explains itself. But there is quite another technical meaning, namely the various 'castes' that exist among thoroughbred fighting bulls of different ranches.

In this sense, the word refers, not to goodness or badness, bravery or lack of it, but to differences of blood as a simple biological fact. Whole books have been written on the subject, but I am now dealing with the spectator's practical angle only, and will try to make the introduction brief, though not, I hope, altogether uninteresting, for the Spanish fighting bull is an animal unique in the world, and one which arouses enthusiasm readily as soon as one gets to know a little about him.

I have already spoken of the aurochs and the race *Bos Taurus Africanus*. The aurochs was probably extinct in Spain by the time of Hannibal, but his typical feature, the lighter brownish stripe running down the spine, continues to appear with great frequency in black bulls, especially of the Vista-hermosa caste, and bulls bearing it are known as *listón*.

However that may be about the aurochs, the modified African bull may now be called the Iberian bull, and the word *castes* is commonly used to denote the different regional sub-types that developed. The Andalusian, the Navarrese, and the New Castilian or Colmenarenian are the best-known of these sub-types. Perhaps, however, 'sub-varieties' would be a better word than 'castes', at any rate for our present purpose, and then we can reserve the word 'castes' for something else, which is an important and quite visible factor in the breeding and even the fighting of bulls today. I will come to this as quickly as possible.

Of the above three regional sub-varieties (I omit the lesser known ones), the Andalusian is today universal and the rest have disappeared. Of the others, the New Castilian type were large, tough, big-horned, rather coarse, very powerful, and very difficult to fight because of their lack of what is called 'nobility'. These were the 'Castilian bulls' that the famous matadors Pepe-Illo and Costillares wanted to get banned from the royal fights in 1779, to the astonishment and disgust of Pedro Romero, who undertook to kill any bull that ate grass in a field. However, this 'caste' eventually died out, in view of the superior fighting qualities of the Andalusian. Likewise the Navarrese 'caste' died out, the reason being their excessively small size, though their bravery was all that could be desired. It has however left its mark, as we shall see. Thus, for all practical purposes, all modern bulls belong to the Andalusian 'caste' or sub-variety.

Now we come to the more restricted, but more practical, meaning of 'caste'. During the eighteenth century, serious selective breeding for fighting purposes began, and by 1800 certain herds showed clearly marked characteristics, from which, either alone or in combination, there emerged a number of biological bull types which are today clearly recognisable. Thus, by 1800, there were several such castes: the Jijona, dating back to long before, and all red of various shades; the Gallardo, dating from about 1750; the Cabrera, about 1770; the Vistahermosa, black or grey or piebald; and the Vázquez, dating from 1780. The names are those of the first ranchers who assembled a herd of more or less uniform animals clearly distinguished by certain features of appearance or temperament. Some castes consisted of a mixture of others: the Vázquez, for instance, contained blood of Vistahermosa and Cabrera. The Gallardo is particularly interesting, because it originated from a cross between the small Navarrese bulls and the big Andalusian cows, the result being a tall animal of great bravery and power, which retained its faculties to the end. This strain is preserved today, to an appreciable extent, in one breed and one only, namely the famous Pablo Romeros, which also contain Cabrera, Vistahermosa, Jijona and Vázquez blood (mainly Vázquez), and are therefore perhaps the most biologically interesting of all the breeds at present being fought, with the possible exception of the Miuras.

The Jijona caste, the oldest, is today extinct. The bulls were notable, but long before the Civil War the blood was running thin, and one Jijona rancher after another was obliged to refresh, or rather cross, his herd's blood with a stud bull from the dominant Vistahermosa caste. The last pure-bred Jijona animals left were a few red cows which Don Manuel Aleas preserved in hiding from the Communists during the Civil War; but today a pure Jijona bull is non-existent, and the blood has been almost entirely absorbed by Vistahermosa.

The same cannot be said of Cabrera. It is true that no Cabrera bulls now exist as such, but the caste lives on, through the admixture of the Cabrera blood that survives in the two most famous breeds of modern times, the Pablo Romeros and the Miuras. The Miuras have much more Cabrera blood than the Pablo Romeros. The Vázquez caste survives, pure, in the Concha y Sierra herd, and partly mixed with Vistahermosa in several more. Apart from these, it can be said that all fighting herds now in existence consist of Vistahermosa blood, either totally pure, or with small admixtures of other strains. How good the bulls will be, of course, depends partly on which line of Vistahermosa it is, and chiefly on the care and interest which the rancher has put into the selection of stud bulls and brood cows; but the Vistahermosa features will be dominant.

The reason for the supremacy of Vistahermosa is not far to seek. The characteristics of the caste are: bravery to a remarkably consistent degree and without intractable violence; good but not exorbitant size; rapid, even precocious development; and above all, 'nobility', that is, absence of craftiness, and slowness to learn how to distinguish the man's body from the coloured cloth. When added to great physical beauty and fineness like that of a racehorse, this clearly provides the type of bull *par excellence* with which brilliant artistic work can be done. A typical example of main-line Vistahermosa in complete purity today is the famous Murube herd, now owned by señor Urquijo; these bulls enjoy a well-deserved favouritism with both bullfighters and audiences.

On the other hand, the Pablo Romeros and Miuras, each with their proportion of Cabrera blood, are bulls which call for a torero who above all knows his science thoroughly. A Cabrera characteristic quoted by a well-known expert is the following: "Great height, heavy without exaggeration, long, greyhound-like, hard on their feet, strong, brave, but cunning or suspicious when badly fought." The last-named feature was so marked in the old Miuras that they gained a sinister reputation owing to the accidents (several fatal) which they caused to toreros who took liberties with them. Today, the proportion of 'noble' Vistahermosa blood has been increased by crossing, and the bulls are not notoriously difficult, yet they do provide a most interesting object-lesson in the hands of a skilful matador, while the unskilful or unsound man, however brave, is apt to fail ignominiously.

After this very sketchy account of 'caste', we now come to individual breeds or herds, and here, although the Andalusian sub-variety is universal, as stated, and the Vistahermosa caste virtually so, the difference in performance, even between breeds almost identical in blood, is enormous. Much can be attributed to the factors of selection and care by the rancher, already referred to. But there is still another factor, namely the geographical, and when the bulls are of pure caste and the breeder scrupulous, this factor is decisive.

The districts where fighting bulls are bred are conventionally grouped into three regions: Salamanca, Centre with Extremadura, and Andalusia. Andalusia is self-explanatory; Salamanca includes some neighbouring provinces such as Zamora; and the rest of Spain forms the third group, which is much more uniform than might be expected, other things being equal, though in my opinion the Extremadura bulls are a good deal better than those of the Centre proper; I have never seen a really poor string of bulls from that region, they are always hard and strong on their feet, and their good specimens are equal to the best of Andalusia, though the proportion of really good bulls is not so high; they also tend to be *bronco* and call for more domination.

The inferiority of Salamanca bulls is not disputed by anyone. Obviously a good brave bull (or string of bulls) from there is better than a bad one from the South; but other things being equal, the presence of Andalusian bulls on the programme is an attraction, while it will be a drawback if one sees the names of three first-class matadors on the poster, with only Salamanca bulls to test their powers. There are very few Salamanca breeds that can stand comparison with those of the Centre and South; in my opinion, only four, and even these are not equal to the best of Extremadura and Andalusia. These four breeds are those of Arranz, Atanasio Fernández, Garci-Grande, and Graciliano Pérez Tabernero; they are the equal of all but the best Andalusian breeds, and not only are scrupulously selected, but seem on the whole to have escaped the prevailing Salamanca characteristics, possibly through some local peculiarity in pastures near the River Yeltes. For, even apart from the commercialised methods of some of the bigger Salamanca breeders whose bloodstock itself is of the best origin, and the lowering of caste in other herds where inferior cows have been used in the past, there really does seem to be something fatal in the mere geographical area, which sooner or later robs the bulls of some of their fire and vigour, and even their size and horn development, to say nothing of making them weak on their feet. Possibly the soil is deficient in calcium; I cannot say. But Hemingway comments on the same fact, and I can endorse all he says, today. More than a quarter of a century has passed since he noted the same facts; there has been no change except for the worse, and I doubt if there ever will be. People have bought cattle from the best Andalusian herds and transferred them to Salamanca, but after so many taurine generations the typical Salamanca characteristics make their appearance; or, if you like, the Andalusian characteristics get watered down. On the other hand, when animals of Andalusian origin but bred in Salamanca are transferred back to the South, they can recover what they had lost. These considerations do not apply to Madrid province, Toledo, and other parts of the Centre, even when quite near Salamanca itself; nor to Cáceres in Extremadura, which borders on Salamanca province.

There are at present about 180 ranches officially recognised by the Sub-Group of Breeders of Fighting Bulls as qualified to supply full-grown bulls for major fights, together with many others who supply *novillos* (young bulls) for junior ones. To qualify for ascent from the second group into the first, a breeder must, within three years, have six successive strings fought with picadors without a single animal being 'fired' (see Chapter 7 on *banderillas*) or rejected for manifest tameness. Four must be in different rings of at least the second class (provincial capitals) and two in first-class rings which must be either both in Madrid, or one in Madrid and one in Seville. Finally, he must submit one string of full-grown bulls under the same conditions in Madrid or Seville.

The following is a list of some of the better-known fighting ranches, with comments which indicate my view of them as at the outset of the 1956 season. In accordance with the existing Spanish division, I have classed them into three groups: Salamanca area, Centre with Extremadura, and Andalusia.

I *Salamanca area*

I ARRANZ, MANUEL. Pure Vistahermosa. Fast, brave, handsome bulls, occasionally weak on feet. Light-boned, should not exceed 500 kg. gross for best results. Generally black with white belly.

2 FERNÁNDEZ, ATANASIO. Pure Vistahermosa, Ibarra line. Large, heavy, powerful, often formidable, sometimes *bronco*, need dominating. Good.

3 GARCI-GRANDE, VISCOUNT. Ibarra, as above. Brave and noble.

4 PÉREZ-TABERNERO, GRACILIANO. Generally excellent; nervous bravery more like Andalusian bulls. Pure mainline Vistahermosa. Black.

The above four breeds are in my opinion superior to all others of Salamanca, with the possible exception of No. 13. Of the rest, some of the best-known are:

5 BERNALDO DE QUIRÓS, LUIS. Vistahermosa caste with some Pablo-Romero blood. Irregular; sometimes good.

6 COBALEDA, JUAN. Not to be confused with No. 15. Vistahermosa caste. Generally good. The famous 'Civilón' (see under *indultar* in Index-Glossary) was of this breed.

7 GALACHE, WIDOW OF. Uneven in size and bravery. Poor till recently, improved in 1954–5. Black or piebald. Not much recommended.

8 LAMAMIÉ DE CLAIRAC, HEIRS OF. Grand Vistahermosa-Parladé caste, but gone off badly now.

9 MONTALVO, HEIRS OF. The last remains of the famous Martínez breed (red Jijona cows crossed with black Vistahermosa). At four years, apt to be flabby; at five, hard and difficult but interesting to see. Generally piebald black-and-white.

10 MURIEL, VICENTE. Size and appearance satisfactory, caste and performance poor.

11 PÉREZ, ANTONIO, of San Fernando. Famous breed, nearly always black, heavier than they look. The ranch has about the largest output in Spain. Noble, often brave, but little real fire; do not give the sensation of danger. Often weak on feet. The standard-model 'medium bull' of Salamanca. Seldom really *bad*, often very good, but . . . Very popular with matadors.

12 PÉREZ-TABERNERO SANCHÓN, ALIPIO. Very noble, generally brave, not much power; little emotion. Light skeleton, run out of gas soon if over 500 kg. on hoof. Always black.

13 RODRÍGUEZ GARCÍA, DIONISIO. New herd. Excellent results so far: at least one *toro de bandera*. Highly recom-

mended; might be added to my 'four Salamanca exceptions' in a year or two, if all goes well.

14 SÁNCHEZ, IGNACIO. Two herds. The blacks are Vistahermosa, the light colours are of Trespalacios origin (Vázquez caste). Both lots are large, sluggish and inferior.

15 SÁNCHEZ COBALEDA, ARTURO (also Jesús, Ignacio, etc., and sometimes fought under name of ranch as 'Barcial'). Origin, a straight cross between Veragua cows (Vázquez caste) and a Santa Coloma bull (pure Vistahermosa), and for some time gave the 'ideal' animal for the matador: very noble, brave but with little power, slow-charging and docile. Now bred down so much that caste has degenerated completely. Soft, flabby, very weak on feet, 'horned doughnuts' which deflate at the first pic. Faces like cart oxen, coarse thick feet, look like *moruchos*, but like them have very big horns, which disguise other defects. Mostly piebald. Very popular still with flash stars for reasons stated. Headed list of fines for underweight for years and years. A fight with these animals is a caricature; latest string fought at Barcelona, autumn 1956, nearly caused a riot. Just occasionally, at five years, one animal of the six will be really first-class, with very high net weight; but most are flabby.

16 SÁNCHEZ FABRÉS, HERMANOS. Irregular, make no appeal to me.

17 TABERNERO DE PAZ, ALICIO. Origin, cross between Nos. 6 and 15. Till 1954, just plain bad. Owner has purged herd; improving now; the strain of No. 6 goes back to Count of la Corte and is good. But there is still a long way to go.

18 VILLAGODIO, HERMANOS. Light, often underweight (twice thrown out in Madrid by vets, even under relaxed regulations before 1953). Flabby and short of bravery in general. Avoid.

2 *Centre with Extremadura*

19 ALBARRÁN, ARCADIO (Badajoz, Extremadura). Good, brave, powerful.

20 ALBAYDA, MARQUESS OF (Old Colmenar, Madrid).

Fine-drawn, brave, nervous, great caste (pure Vistahermosa). Small herd, half-destroyed in Civil War. Very good, but not easy meat, need dominating.

21 ALVAREZ, JUAN ANTONIO (Cáceres, Extremadura). Origin same as No. 27. Small herd, all descended from a bull-calf whose mother died on a cross-country trek and who was brought up on a baby's bottle. Good on the whole, tough. Mixed colours and sizes.

22 ARAUZ DE ROBLES, JOSÉ M. (Madrid). Good-lookers, poor caste. Avoid.

23 'BATANEJOS' (name of ranch) (Segovia). A mixed lot, mostly poor.

24 'CASTILLO DE HIGARES' (ranch), bred by Pedro Gandarias (Toledo). Large, powerful, well-armed, very brave, excellent bulls but too tough for 'phenomenons'. Appearance, origin and performance similar to No. 67.

25 CEMBRANO (SONS OF) ANTONIO (Cáceres, Extremadura). Very good and brave, pure Vistahermosa (Parladé). Recommended.

26 CORTE, COUNT OF (Badajoz, Extremadura). Excellent, brave, noble, great caste; but one or two in each string are generally undersized.

27 ESCUDERO CALVO, HERMANOS (Cáceres, Extremadura). Tough, powerful, sometimes brave and noble, sometimes *bronco*. The *old* Albaserradas, pure Vistahermosa. Parent herd of 'Zamarrito' (see page 154). Need dominating.

28 GARCÍA-ALEAS, MANUEL (Old Colmenar, Madrid). Large, powerful, very good. (See Chapter XIV, 1).

29 GARRO Y DÍAZ GUERRA, HERMANOS (Madrid). Of various origins. Not recommended.

30 GONZÁLEZ, MANUEL (Madrid). Poor caste.

31 MARTÍNEZ ELIZONDO, ANTONIO (Navarre). Very good, brave.

32 MORENO YAGÜE, JOSÉ M. (Escorial and Toledo). Herd in reconstruction; has been excellent and may be again.

33 OLIVEIRA, MARIA TERESA (Escorial). Splendid reputation, only one indifferent string in several years. By bad luck I saw that one. Recommended.

34 ORTEGA, DOMINGO, the matador (Madrid and Segovia). Origin Vistahermosa-Parladé. Good on the whole, but some recent lapses.

35 PINOHERMOSO, DUKE OF (Escorial). Was very good; then one bad lapse. Duke now rebuilding herd. Good results so far.

36 RUISENADA, COUNT OF (Toledo). Bad. Undersized, flabby, *manso* and not even good-looking.

37 'SAMUEL HERMANOS' (Don Samuel Flores) (Albacete). Pure Vistahermosa. Brave, noble, highly recommended.

38 SANCHO, FRANCISCA, WIDOW OF ARRIBAS (Escorial). Poor, avoid.

39 TOVAR, HEIRS OF DUKE OF (Madrid). Once a grand herd under the old Duke, now gone all to pieces. Magnificent façade with nothing behind.

3 *Andalusia (always Seville unless otherwise stated)*

40 ALBASERRADA, MARQUESS OF. Not to be confused with No. 27. New herd, made very bad start, lately some improvement.

41 ARELLANO, RICARDO. New herd, apparently a reconstruction of the famous breed of Gamero-Cívico, origin Ibarra-Parladé, superlative caste. The Arellanos are very large and brave but extremely noble. A string of them at Valencia in 1955 *averaged* 352 kg. net (over 1,250 lb. on hoof); too big for the flashy stars, but the second-raters who fought them did extremely well. Highly recommended.

42 BARTOLOMÉ, FELIPE. Origin No. 46. Very good, won recent bravery prize in Madrid.

43 BELMONTE, JUAN, the famous ex-matador. Bad; in ten years I cannot recall one brave string, in a major fight.

44 BENÍTEZ CUBERO, JOSÉ. Large, heavy, sluggish, poor caste.

45 BOHÓRQUEZ, FERMÍN (Cádiz). Origin Murube (No. 65). Excellent blood; Manolete's favourite cattle. Said to have

been bred down too much so as to suit him. Were weak on feet for some years; now recovered; very good indeed.

46 BUENDÍA, JOAQUIN. The old Santa Colomas, pure Vistahermosa main line. Generally very good indeed, with exceptionally high yield *en canal*.

47 CALDERÓN (SONS OF) J. E. (Cádiz). Origin No. 26. Good.

48 CHICA, FRANCISCO (Jerez). Once part of royal herd. Now very poor. Avoid.

49 CONCHA Y SIERRA, C. DE LA. Very ancient ranch. Vázquez caste. Imposing-looking, especially when grey. Often very large and heavy. Old-fashioned bulls; caste degenerated, generally tame and dangerous now. Difficult to dominate and unpropitious for brilliant work.

50 CONRADI (SONS OF) J. B. Another ancient ranch, also Vázquez caste, but still more degenerate, even in size. Worthless.

51 COVA, ENRIQUETA DE LA. Large, imposing, brave, often very tough. At five years, formidable.

52 DOMECQ, J. P. (Jerez). Very good, practically always brave. See under *indultar* in Index-Glossary.

53 FLORES ALBARRAN, HEIRS OF (Jaén). Founded by Gil de Flores in eighteenth century (Jijona caste). Mostly Vistahermosa today. Very good.

54 GUARDIOLA, SALVADOR. Nearly always very good indeed in recent years. Won bravery prize in Madrid, 1956.

55 MARÍN, EUGENIO (Jaén). Brave, good reputation.

56 MIURA, EDUARDO. The most famous herd of all time. Unique bulls, nothing quite like them. Mixture of Vázquez, Gallardo, Vistahermosa and Cabrera castes. From the last, get their long necks and suspicious nature. Sinister reputation grew up around them after deaths of Espartero, Dominguín I., and Posada; the legend was about spent when revived by death of Manolete, also killed by a Miura (with artificially blunted horns too) in 1947. Always interesting to see fought. Often very large and powerful, often very brave, especially the Vistahermosa types (black and grey), but never easy to fight; get wised up rapidly by poor *lidia*. Had bad epidemic of foot-and-mouth, which kept them away from Madrid for some years. Reds,

especially the classic Cabrera type with red circle round eye (*ojo de perdiz*) are splendid-looking but usually sluggish or tame, being throw-backs.

57 MORENO ARDANÚY, FELIX. Old-established breed, fine reputation but irregular recently.

58 NÚÑEZ, CARLOS (Cádiz). Origin Vistahermosa-Parladé, grand caste. Irregular: generally very good, but occasionally awful.

59 PABLO ROMERO, JOSÉ L. Gallardo-Vázquez caste. The leading breed for very many years. Magnificent looking, very large, and superb bulls when brave, which is generally; a falling-off in 1956, when a string of handsome *mansos* in Madrid disappointed everyone.

60 PÉREZ DE LA CONCHA (SONS OF) TOMÁS. Origin is No. 49. Vázquez caste, but crossed with Santa Coloma (Vistahermosa). Quite good.

61 PRIETO DE LA CAL, TOMÁS (Cádiz). Origin is Miura crossed with Vistahermosa; herd almost destroyed in the Civil War; expanded 1945 with animals of Vázquez caste. Results pretty irregular. Largely used as substitutes in Madrid, not a good sign. Often *jabonero sucio* (colour of milk chocolate); do not appeal to me.

62 RAMOS PAÚL, LUIS. Derived from No. 68 and have suffered similarly.

63 SOTO, JOSÉ M. Poor: once popular with Madrid management as cheap substitutes, and were regularly 'fired'. May perhaps have got less bad recently, but are very second-rate stuff.

64 TASSARA, CLEMENTE. Poor for years, some improvement 1954–5. Acceptable.

65 URQUIJO, ANTONIO. The famous Murubes of old. Principal herd of main-line Vistahermosa. The 'Rolls-Royce' of taurine breeds. Excellent; the name on the programme is a guarantee in itself. They are *always* good.

66 VÁZQUEZ, IGNACIO. Distinguish carefully from No. 67. Large, heavy, sluggish, poor caste.

67 VÁZQUEZ, TULIO and (the late) ISAIAS. Frequently mentioned in this book. For me, these are the best bulls in the

world; but you hardly ever see them decently fought, though they are nobler than the Pablo Romeros. Origin Ibarra-Parladé, main-line Vistahermosa.

68 VILLAMARTA, MARQUESS OF (Cádiz). Origin, same as No. 58. Once superlative, but have got very flabby in recent years and cannot be recommended at present.

In the above comments, any adverse criticism is intended to apply to the breed in question when fought at four-and-a-half years and upwards as full-grown bulls in a major fight. At under four years, when fought in a minor fight as *novillos*, many animals of such breeds give decidedly better play. Even the notorious Sánchez Cobaledas are often satisfactory in junior fights, because they are then more agile and less quickly exhausted, for their naturally light skeletons are not burdened with the excessive meat needed to enable them to draw the necessary minimum weight, and they will not have been hog-fattened for the purpose. There is no minimum weight for *novillos*, which may be almost any size, and of age 'over three and under six' according to regulations. Strictly, therefore, no full-grown animal of four-and-a-half years, which cannot draw the minimum weight without artificial fattening, should ever be fought except in junior fights.

CHAPTER THREE

The Plaza de Toros

I

Before actually dealing with what happens in the arena, something must be said about the *plaza de toros* or bullring building itself, and the preliminary operations before the fight. Bullfights of one kind or another are held in almost every Spanish town of any importance, and even in village squares, suitably barricaded. However, I shall deal only with regular rings, and particularly that of Madrid.

Of proper masonry rings there are roughly two types. The smaller ones are cheese-shaped, and have either a single bank of seats (*tendido*) running all round, or else a main bank and a gallery (*grada*) as well. Such rings will accommodate between 5,000 and 10,000 people, except for that of Seville (12,500). The other type is taller, more like a cylinder than a disc; the biggest of these are the 'Monumental' Plazas of Madrid and Barcelona, each holding about 23,000. The largest in the world is the new monster one in Mexico City, which holds more than twice as many, but 25,000 is about the limit, if one is to see decently from everywhere.

In these larger rings, the main *tendido* is divided into upper (*tendido alto*) and lower (*tendido bajo*), each sub-bank containing about eighteen rows. This *tendido* is open to the sky and contains the bulk of the audience. Above the back row of the upper part, there is a first gallery or *grada*, covered in, with about half a dozen rows, and above it in turn a second gallery (*andanada*) which is a repetition of it. Part of the *grada* is divided into boxes (*palcos*), and one of these, in the portion permanently in the shade, is reserved for the President, the official who directs the fight. He is thus some way off in the big rings; but you see details much more clearly from a high seat, and you get a joint view of the action as a whole, which, by an odd illusion, appears to happen more slowly when seen from above. Newcomers who insist on taking expensive ringside seats (*barreras*) or row 2 (*contrabarreras*) for their first few fights make a great mistake, and get only a confused or fragmentary impression of what goes on; the *grada* or upper *tendido* is far better for them, at a fraction of the price. The front row (*delantera*) of the *andanada* (no other row) is also excellent, above all if you want to view the fighting critically and dispassionately. It is the best place in the ring from which to detect faking, or shoddy work with the sword, and the *banderilla* act takes on quite a new aspect from there.

Now, if we descend to the ringside, the front row (*barrera*) is still seven or eight feet above ground level. The spectators in it have a stout wooden parapet, chest-high, in front of them, resting on masonry below. In front of this, a circular alleyway (*callejón*) runs all round, and a circular inner wall (*barrera*) of wood separates it from the actual ring. The floor of this alley, which is between six and nine feet wide, and of the ring itself, is of fairly soft sand—soft enough for men and animals to run on easily, but not so loose as to clog their movements. The sand of the ring is watered before the fight and also generally at half-time; otherwise, any wind will raise clouds of dust and make fighting difficult and very dangerous.

The two circular wooden walls are not solid all the way round. There have to be a number of openings, and the position of these varies, so I shall describe those of Madrid only.

Imagine yourself sitting in the President's box, high up above the arena. There are ten numbered blocks of seats (each block including everything from ringside to upper gallery), and this box is exactly at the division where Block 10 ends and Block 1 begins. Looking round anti-clockwise to your right, you can distinguish Blocks 10, 9, 8, 7 and so on. The first opening you see is a big one, between Blocks 8 and 7. There are double doors in the inner barrier and corresponding ones in the outer, whence a short passage leads out to the main gate in the street. This gate is more or less ceremonial, and is used in the fight only when the show starts with the entrance of the two mounted constables (*alguaciles*) in seventeenth-century dress. The next opening, similar in size, is between Blocks 4 and 3 and here, the covered passage leads to the horse-yard (*patio de caballos*) and stables. Through this pair of gates the parade of bull-fighters enters at the beginning, and later the picadors ride in through it, and out again when Act 1 is over. Then, in the centre of Block 3 itself, there are two small separate doors in the outer barrier, with a partition between, corresponding to two others in the ringside barrier. Set back a little from these pairs of doors are those of the bullpens (*toriles* or *chiqueros*). When a bull is to be let out into the ring, the attendant first opens the doors in the two barriers, which exactly fit across the alley and thereby block it both ways, and then he opens the bullpen door (with himself behind it), leaving a short passage open into the ring for the bull. Once it is out, the barrier doors are closed again and the alley is free. If a bull should jump into the alley, it can be diverted back into the ring again by the reopening of one of these various doors, which automatically blocks the alley and gives exit into the ring. Lastly, between Blocks 2 and 1, there is another large pair of doors, behind which is the passage leading to the butchery department (*desolladero*). When a bull is dead, a team of three mules comes out, the bull's horns are hitched to the towing harness, and they gallop briskly out through this passage. In a few minutes the bull's carcass is weighed, skinned, cleaned, and cut up for meat. This meat, by the way, is of very good quality, but it still has the blood in it and is dark in colour, and most people do not care for it much. The best way is to treat it as game and cook it with spices.

That is about all you would see from the President's box. But what happens behind those two small doors in Block 3 is of considerable interest, though it concerns preliminary organisation rather than the actual fighting.

2

Seen from outside the main entrance, any bullring looks circular. But if you walk round it you will always find that there is a big square bulge sticking out for nearly a quarter of the circumference. This is the part where all the preliminary operations take place, and they are more complicated than might be supposed.

When a spectator watches his first fight, he just sees six bulls come out, a new one after the last one is dead, and it all looks quite simple. But in fact the new bull is not just any one of the string. The matador who is to kill it knows in advance which one it is: its branded number, colour, size or shape of horns, and approximate weight. It is 'his' bull, one of the two that he has drawn by lot. He is due to fight those two bulls and no others of the string, assuming it is an ordinary fight with six bulls and three matadors.* So that if a mistake is

* Unless one of his companions gets injured, in which case the senior remaining matador must kill the injured man's outstanding bull; if both are outstanding, the junior matador kills the other one. If the injured man had first made an attempt to kill his first bull, the turn does not pass and the senior matador must finish off that one and also kill the other. The injured man receives his full pay just the same.

made, as does occasionally occur, and the wrong bull is let out, then it must be fought by the matador to whom it rightly corresponds, even if it is not his turn. Now, supposing that the six bulls are penned up waiting for the fight, let us see how they got there.

The first job, of course, is to get the bulls to the *plaza* at all. Bullrings are either in a town or on the outskirts. Formerly, the bulls travelled on their own feet, and there is still a regulation in force which specifies that this must be done between 2 and 4 a.m., and mentions other precautions that must be taken. But nowadays they are nearly always transported in solid crates on motor lorries, from the ranch if fairly close, from the railway station if they have been railed from a long distance. How the bull is got into the crate on the ranch, we shall see later on. But let us assume that the six bulls, in their crates, are being delivered to the *plaza* on a lorry.

The end panels of the crates can be slid up, and the bull is then free to emerge, down a ramp, into a corral attached to the *plaza*, in part of that square bulge already mentioned. This operation must take place at least three days before the fight, if the animals have come any distance, for they get cramped in the crates, their feet swell, and they emerge dispirited and dejected. They need three days of rest and good food to recover their fine appearance and their proper faculties.

A big *plaza* like Madrid has several corrals and can accommodate thirty-odd bulls (bulls of different herds must not be mixed or they will start fighting and killing one another). But any ring must have at least two open-air corrals, together with some indoor apartments which we shall come to in a minute. The minimum of two corrals are for the bulls and the trained steers (*cabestros*) respectively. These steers play a most important part and are indispensable for the handling of fighting bulls, above all in enclosed

34

places. The bulls may prod the steers about a bit and occasionally gore at one, but normally they will follow the intelligent old fellows about like lambs. The steers have carried out the same operations over and over again for years and know their job backwards.

The day before the fight, the official vets look the bulls over to see if any are diseased or crocked or otherwise unfit to fight. That however is not enough; they must also decide whether the animals appear to be of the requisite minimum age (four years rising five for a major fight), and whether they seem adequate in build, horns and general set-up, and comply with the minimum weight demanded by regulations.* Scrawny or shabby animals, or those with inadequate horn development or other defects can be thrown out by these officials, and often are. If the management has any doubts, it will have substitutes ready, or the fight will not be authorised.

On the morning of the fight, the examination is repeated, and after the official formalities have been complied with, the bulls are divided by agreement into three lots of two, after some haggling between the matadors' representatives— generally confidential peones or capemen; it is very rare for the matador himself to attend. The lots are made up so that they are roughly equal: for instance, the biggest bull and the smallest, and so on. Once agreement is reached, the bulls' numbers, two and two, are written on three cigarette-papers and drawn by lot from a hat. Then each peon returns to his matador to tell him what he has drawn.

* Fines inflicted after the event for underweight bulls will never stop this abuse. The public always pays the fine in the end, in increased seat prices. The only sound way is that used in Mexico: weigh the live bull in its crate, subtract known weight of the latter, and ban the underweight bull in advance. Maybe it will draw the right weight next year. A leading Madrid critic is agitating for the adoption of this method in Spain. It would remove a whole constellation of abuses, save bulls, and cheapen seat prices. But vested interests are against it.

After this, at noon sharp as a rule, comes the *apartado* or sorting-out, to which the public are admitted on payment of a small fee. It consists in the transferring of the bulls from the open corral, where they can mill about at their ease, into their six separate pens behind the doors leading to the ring.

Under cover, in the part of the outbuildings nearest to the pens, there is a small labyrinth of narrow passages and tiny corrals the size of a room, all connnected by doors. A public gallery runs round above the whole layout, and this operation is well worth a visit. The intelligent spectator, in any case, wants to have a look at the bulls in the open corrals. No two bulls are quite alike, and it is most interesting to form one's opinion beforehand and then see how it works out in the ring. In some cases, a visit to the *apartado* will tell you whether the afternoon's fight is worth going to see or not; this is especially true of *novilladas* or junior fights, where there is no stipulated weight, and the animals may be of almost any size or age.

When all is ready, the door into the bulls' corral is swung open from above by pulling on a rope, and the steers troop in, round up the bulls, and lead them under cover through the labyrinth to the small indoor corrals. The bulls pad along after them like children playing follow-my-leader. But the final door shuts in the last bull's face, and it remains alone in one of the small corrals. Now the *plaza* herdsman swings open another door, leading through a dark passage to the bullpens. He calls out to the public "Third!" or "First!" or whatever is the order in which this bull will be fought. Cattle are inquisitive creatures, and generally the bull will wander off down the passage to the waiting pen, by itself. If not, the herdsman prods it on the rump with a long pole and that does the trick. Bulls dislike being confined, and will go through any door that seems to lead to the open. The passage is too narrow to turn in, and when the bull gets

36

into the pen left open at the rear end, the door slams shut behind it.

The same process is repeated for the other five bulls, and generally within fifteen minutes the whole six are in their respective pens. It is dark and cool in there, which has a calming effect, and each bull waits quietly, with no more food or water now, until its turn comes, five or six hours later, to emerge into the blazing sun and fight its last battle on the sand.

CHAPTER FOUR

The Life of the Bull

The life of the fighting bull lasts upwards of four years, but the incidents in it, from our point of view, nearly all occur in the last week, and above all in the last twenty minutes. That ultimate 100-thousandth part of his existence is the real subject of this book, but some mention must be made of the remaining 99.999 per cent of it.

The bull's life, from calfhood to maturity, is one of almost unbroken peace in a state of nature, with the best pastures reserved for him, and latterly a good ration of corn, beans and root vegetables as well.

The calf is born during the winter and lives on his mother's milk until the new spring grass comes and he begins to eat that as well. He will eat his 'second grass', therefore, soon after his first birthday; so that a bull of, say, 'four grasses' means a three-year-old going on for four. At about eight months the calf is weaned and separated from the mother, a process calling for plenty of skill from the cattlemen, who have to evade the charges of the cow. The fighting cow is just as brave as the bull and more agile, although smaller. This weaning is generally done in a closed corral, with the aid of one or two trained steers. If the cow should die in giving birth, or become diseased and unable to feed the calf, the latter is put to a tame cow if he will accept her; if not, an artificial mixture has to be given him, or else cow's milk in a feeding-bottle. The small but brave herd of Juan Antonio Alvarez, of Badajoz, is all descended from a bull-calf that was bought when still a suckling, because its mother had abandoned it on the road during a cross-country migration. The future sire of a fine fighting herd was brought up by hand on a baby's bottle.

The calf then runs with others of its age until the branding (*herradero*), some time shortly before its first birthday. There is no need to describe this operation, which differs from that on a beef ranch only in that the animals, of both sexes, are marked with a numeral as well as the rancher's brand, and are given individual names; these, together with those of both parents, are noted down in the ranch stock books. In addition to the brand, most breeders cut their own distinctive notch or slit on one or both ears. After this, the calf goes back to the open pasture and has no more adventures until it is two years old. Then comes the event that decides its future destiny: the bravery test (*tienta* or *tentadero*).

Today, this differs fundamentally for bull-calves and cow-calves. As the former are intended for the ring, they must on no account be 'torried', that is, played with a lure, or have any other avoidable experience similar to that of the fighting in the ring, for the whole *lidia* is built up on the assumption—guaranteed by the breeder—that they come to the *plaza* quite virginal in that respect. This does not apply to the females, which are accordingly tested rigorously in a small bullring attached to the ranch, where they undergo something very similar to an actual bullfight, omitting only the *banderillas* and of course the kill.

As was said in Chapter 1, the indispensable gauge of bravery and caste is the pic, which nothing can replace. This is accordingly used, even on males, but in their case under very different conditions from those of the ring. Formerly this too was done in the small ring, but it was found that the disadvantages exceeded the advantages, and today a strict testing of all cows, and of stud bulls that will never be fought, is good enough, when added to the test in open country for male calves.*

This test is made by the process—a genuine sport in itself—called *acoso y derribo* ('pursuit and knocking over'). The tester himself, that is, the picador, is assisted by one or more pairs (*colleras*) of horsemen, armed with poles (*garrochas*). The latter ride to the bunch of calves, and cut one out. It promptly makes off at top speed; they ride it down, and when it begins to slow up, one horseman hems it in while the other leans forward and sideways in the saddle and gives it a poke on the hindquarters with his pole, which throws it off balance and knocks it down. It gets up at once and probably starts off again. This process is repeated until the calf turns at bay.

The picador, who has been keeping up with the proceedings, now plants himself in front of the defiant calf, which charges him and receives a pic thrust; the pic point is naturally much smaller than that used in the ring. Very careful note is kept of the animal's entire performance from start to finish: how many bumps it needed before turning to fight, how it charged, how bravely it took the pic, whether it came back eagerly for more, and so on. Not more than three or four pics are given, but to a skilled eye that is quite enough to make the decision whether the calf is fit to be raised as a fighting bull. If he has complied, but not really to the rancher's satisfaction, he may be set aside as a *desecho de tienta* or throw-out, to be sold off at three years as a *novillo* for a junior fight. If he has failed to show enough bravery for this, he is either sent to the slaughterhouse for veal, or is castrated and placed among the trained steers to learn a longer-lived but less glorious profession.

The cow-calves are given a much sterner testing in the closed ring, first with the pic, as often as they will come back

* Even this open-country test has today largely been dropped.

for more, and then with cape and *muleta*. Here even more detailed notes are kept: not only the number of pics and recharges, but the animal's attitude, style, speed, smoothness, nervousness or calmness, nobility and mode of going for the cloth lures. The result goes down in the stud book in the form of a letter (the initial letter of the Spanish word for Bad, Moderate, Good, or Excellent), with three subsidiary markings expressed by one or more dots after the letter. Whether the rancher is content to breed from cows that rate a straight G or perhaps G-plus, depends on the standard he sets. Some breeders will not touch anything below a straight E, and aim always at E with two or three dots (*superiorisima*).

The same test is given to future stud bulls, which are normally re-tested at the age of three or four before starting their duties. Here the fight may sometimes reach epic proportions. A *semental*, recently re-tested on a famous Andalusian ranch, took seventeen pics recharging hard, and when at last the breeders called a halt it still wanted more, and charged furiously at the cattlemen's horses so that they had to ride for their lives. I rather think that this animal has just been sold to South America for 250,000 pesetas. However, even one of the two-year-old cow-calves is quite capable of overthrowing the horse if the picador misses, and there are always professional toreros standing behind *burladeros* ready to do a *quite* if required.

Apart from its primordial purpose, the *tienta* is a great training-school for future toreros. After the more serious part of the work is over, they and amateur friends of the breeder are given a chance to try their hand with cape or *muleta*, and many a triumphal career started with a string of *verónicas* given at the breeder's invitation by some unknown lad in the home-made ring on the ranch.

If our bull-calf has passed his bravery test, there now lie before him two clear years of placid life on the pastures without further interference from man. The only episodes will be his fights with other bulls. These are more in the nature of fencing-matches than real battles: the bulls meet head on and struggle, horn to horn, until one prevails and the other slinks off hanging his head in defeat. Serious injuries are rare, and this is where the bull learns how to use his horns. It is only in closed corrals that bulls will sometimes fight to the death.

At last the time comes for the full-grown bull to leave the ranch, as one of a string, normally six, that have been bought by a bullring impresario. The latter will generally have visited the ranch to see the animals some time before, and the rancher will have booked six particular individuals for him.

A suitable number of days before the fight, the *mayoral* and his men cut out the six bulls from the herd, with the aid of the trained steers, which obey words of command as cleverly as sheepdogs. When the bunch of six have been isolated, the steers surround them, the cattlemen ride before and behind, and the party moves off towards the ranch-house. This is the *encierro* or round-up. At the ranch, there is a walled corral waiting, with a smaller one opening off it. Two fences, first wide apart and then narrowing down like a funnel, steer the bulls to the corral gate, and as the riders get within this stockade they urge the animals to full gallop, so as to get them all corralled before they realise they are caught. The gate is then shut and the bulls are captive. It now remains to get them into their travelling-boxes.

The main corral has a door, operated by ropes from above, giving access to a smaller corral. The latter has also a doorway leading into the open; but on this occasion it leads into what looks like a long, very narrow passage.

This passage is actually composed of six travelling-boxes placed end to end. Each is just large enough to contain a bull, and both its end panels can be slid upwards by a man on the roof. At the moment all twelve panels are up, and you can see right through from the corral to the field outside.

The door between the corrals is opened and one bull comes through. The door slams behind him and he is alone. But he can see what looks like a passage leading out into the field. He enters it, but cannot turn in it. Just as he reaches the last box, the front panel falls before his face, and a second later the other panel falls behind his tail, and there he is, boxed. This box is now detached, and the same process is repeated with each remaining bull. Finally, the boxes are sent off to the *plaza*, as described in Chapter 3.

In provincial *ferias*,* the unboxing of the bulls, three or four days before the first fight, is an event worth seeing. It takes place in the bullring, where the boxes will have been deposited in a semicircle, ranch by ranch. The end panel of the first box is raised, and the bull comes out and the public can have a good look at him. Each of his brothers is then released in turn, and then the steers come out, round up all six bulls and lead them off to the corrals. This is repeated for each string separately, until all the bulls are corralled, and the public expresses its opinion of the various strings by applause or the reverse. On no account must bulls of different herds be allowed loose together.

The unboxing is a moment of great anxiety for the *mayoral*, for the bulls are dejected and uncertain-tempered, with swollen feet and possibly feverish after their journey, maybe of hundreds of miles, and their eyes are dazzled as they come out of the boxes. As the panel slides up, a bull may dash furiously out into freedom and may injure its foot, or may in its half-dazed condition attack another bull. For these reasons, the Miura ranch always has its boxes placed back-to-front, and the Miura bulls always emerge hindquarters first from the box. This prevents any sudden rush or stumble, and gives the bull a couple of seconds to get its eyes accom-

---

* Annual fairs, generally lasting a week, with three or more fights in an important town.

modated, while it turns round. It is accordingly less likely to charge another bull.

It is a mistake to think that a bull is necessarily brave because it behaves aggressively or defiantly at the unboxing. In actual fact, a bull that blusters and throws its weight about then is more likely to be a coward that is bluffing (*bravucón*). The really brave bull is confident in its own strength, and behaves with quiet dignity.

In Seville and Madrid, before the big weeks in April and May, the above unboxing does not take place. Instead, the bulls are on public view for several days in open-air corrals, at the Venta de Antequera and the Venta de Batán respectively, on the outskirts of the city. In both places there are cafés and restaurants, and a visit to the bulls is quite a fashionable event, as well as being of exceptional interest. It may also help you to make up your mind which fights you want to see. But when assessing bulls, it is well to remember that black bulls always look smaller than they are, and piebalds or skewbalds (*berrendos*), reds (*colorados*) and light-coloured bulls look larger.

CHAPTER FIVE

Theory and Organisation of the Fighting, in Three Acts

I

At this point, it would be useful to define what is meant by 'fighting' the bull. It must be clearly realised that 'fighting' does not mean 'trying to wound or kill'. The only time the matador attempts to inflict any wound on the bull is the moment at the end when he kills it with a sword-thrust— one thrust only, if possible. Otherwise, he never uses a weapon at all. He 'fights' the bull in the same way as a fisherman fights a tarpon or a tunny on a line: the creature is far stronger than he is, so he has to make it fight itself until it is worn down enough to be finished off. The only difference —a big one—is that this final moment is when the bull is more dangerous than ever before; also, unless the man cheats visibly, he must then deliver himself fully into the range of the horn and give the bull its big chance to kill *him*.

It is true that the bull does receive some wounds from the picadors: normally three in minor fights and four in major ones. But it is the bull that attacks the picadors, not the reverse; and these wounds are given, not in an attempt to kill the bull, but for quite another reason, as will be seen. There are also the *banderillas*, but these do not cause a real wound or inflict any appreciable injury. In a modern fight, the pics and the *banderillas* together amount to only a very small proportion of the so-called fighting; ninety per cent of the work is done by either the matador or his foot assistants, with a silk cape or a piece of red flannel on a stick, and there is no question of harrying the bull with weapons at all. Further, apart from a few special moments, never more than one man at a time is engaged with the bull.

2

Bullfighting is both an art and a science at once. It is commonly compared with sculpture, but really the parallel with architecture is closer. The reason is that the object of sculpture (I mean modern European sculpture, not Romanesque or Oriental) is single, namely to arouse a given æsthetic emotion in the beholder, but the object of architecture is twofold. Beauty of form alone will not do; there is also, and chiefly, the functional purpose, namely to produce a suitable building.

Now, bullfighting is primarily functional, the object being to kill the bull from in front, with a sword. The doing of this calls for various kinds of rhythmic movements, not only at the moment of the sword-thrust, but in the necessary preparation —which starts with the first cape-pass. If these movements are executed with the maximum efficiency in each individual case, they produce plastic beauty automatically. No doubt some bullfighters have more natural grace than others, but the true origin of the artistic beauty is the correct performance of the different acts.

The fundamental beauty of a Gothic church is its perfect efficiency, economy, and adaptation of the style to the end sought; the carved pinnacles and other decorations are not essential but only something added afterwards. But when architecture gets degenerate, ornamentation for its own sake becomes the chief aim, and the result is Baroque. In the same way with bullfighting, it degenerates when efficient bull-control is sacrificed to a lot of filigree work that has no special purpose except to look pretty. The risk of serious degeneration in this sense hardly existed until about twenty-five years ago, because with a five-year-old bull, as fought until then, the man has to be relatively efficient all the time, if he wants to stay out of hospital. But with the four-year-old bull of today, bred specially for honesty, weighing more than 200 lb. less, and with horns of only medium size, much of the work you see, though very 'artistic', has no fundamental purpose, and may justly be labelled Baroque too. However, to analyse or judge a craft, one cannot do so by its more or less temporary decadences and aberrations, but only by its basic purpose and the operations that this calls for. So that is what I shall do in the following dialogue, in which you, Reader, are rather improbably supposed to be visiting the Natural History Museum with a torero. As the curtain rises, you and he are contemplating a stuffed buffalo.

READER. I wish you'd show me how a bull is killed.

TORERO. Why don't you try yourself, in pantomime, with this fellow? There's no one looking. You've got a stick. Let's see what you make of it yourself.

READER. I suppose I run him through the chest, like this . . .

TORERO. Oh dear no, you'd get a fearful *bronca* from the crowd for that. That's a *golletazo*, most dishonourable: it gives the bull no chance to get *you*. Your blade would go straight into the lungs, there'd be pools of blood, a foul death for the bull. You might be arrested, and you wouldn't get a second booking in a hurry.

READER. All right then, I'll go for the heart. By the way, where *is* it? My knowledge of bull-anatomy is not too good.

TORERO. Behind the chest, in here, about so-deep.

READER. But I'd have to thrust downwards, from above, and my stick won't reach that far. Is a sword-blade longer?

TORERO. No, just the same, three feet.

READER. Then how can I reach the heart?

TORERO. You can't. The bull's heart is out of reach.

READER. Well, what *do* I aim at?

TORERO. There's only one vital spot, the big blood-vessel called the rear aorta. If you can cut that, the bull falls dead at once. To reach it, you've got to drive the sword downwards at forty-five degrees, from *this* point.

READER. But that's the buffalo's hump.

TORERO. Yes, this is a buffalo, of course. The fighting bull doesn't have a hump as big as this, but a large muscle about half the size. Now, just ignore the hump, and put yourself in position.

READER. All right. How's this?

TORERO. No good. Look at your sword, it's nearly horizontal. You won't strike the aorta like that in a month of Sundays. . . . No, still no good . . .

READER. Well, if I were seven feet high I could do it, but I have to reach up over the right horn, and then I've no power left to drive downwards.

TORERO. Exactly. As it stands there in its normal position, with its head high, you just can't do it—not even to a stuffed bull.

READER. All right, you win. Now you tell me how it's done. And while you're at it, show me how I prevent that right horn from letting daylight into my stomach when I do the trick.

TORERO. Just pass along to the next exhibit, please, and tell me what you see.

READER. A fine specimen of a Tibetan yak. Now, this fellow's a different proposition. Let me have a go. Look, how's that?

TORERO. Yes, not bad, you got it about right that time. The yak hangs his head low, and you managed fine, except for that business of getting your stomach past the horn. That's another question and we'll deal with it another time. But you've got the main idea. Except by a fluke or a foul, it's almost impossible to kill the fighting bull with the sword when he first comes out. He holds his head up high, almost like a horse. It's held up by the biggest muscle in his body, which gives him that humped look at the shoulders. Before you can kill him, you've got to tire that huge muscle until his head hangs low like a yak. To do that, you have to use his own strength against him. First catch your fish,

Plaza of Seville, showing the parade before the fight

Plaza of Madrid, showing layout of seats, *callejón*, etc., and a torero beside a *burladero*

then play him. Catching him means that you must stop him from charging madly at anything and everything. You must get him concentrated on one target, namely a moving lure. It's only a bit of bright-coloured cloth, but it looks solid to him, because he's never seen such a thing before. You must make him charge when and where *you* want, not as *he* wants. You must make him charge at the cloth, not at your body. You must make him think each time that he's got it, and then he'll toss furiously—against nothing. In that way, you'll gradually wear him down, and his great head will begin to hang lower.

READER. And if I keep on doing that long enough, will it do the trick?

TORERO. It might, if the bull were a complete fool and you had the strength of Hercules. But in fact you can't keep the bull charging indefinitely at the same target. He gets wised up, and starts to go for your body instead. So a fresh target must be introduced. In minor fights in small rings, with little animals of two-and-a-half to three years, that's all that need be done. But with even a big three-year-old, to say nothing of a proper grown bull of four to five years, some quicker way of weakening him and slowing him up is necessary as well as change of target. Otherwise, maybe night would fall, with the bull still in the ring, knowing all the answers, and the men in hospital—or worse.

READER. And what is that quicker means?

TORERO. The pic act, which incidentally is the only way in which the bull's bravery, or lack of it, can be proved. In the pic act, the bull is given a real solid target, namely the horse's padded body, if he can get through to it. He gets tired and slowed down by the effort he expends on that, and also by the loss of a certain amount of blood from the pic wounds.

READER. And how many wounds does he get?

TORERO. The regulations say four proper pics for a full bull, and three with a smaller pic for a *novillo*. That's the minimum, but the discretion lies with the President.

3

As bullfighting is not a sport, there are no 'sides' and no 'scoring', and of course no 'referee'. But there must be someone in charge, not only of the fighting, but of the audience, the attendants, and every other person in the building. This is the President, normally a high official designated by the Chief of Police in Madrid and by the Civil Governor in the provinces. He makes all the general decisions. His routine orders are given by showing a hand-kerchief from his box, whereupon a trumpet is blown; any special orders are telephoned down to his agents below, who include the *alguaciles*. As regards details of the fighting, each matador directs the work of his own team, subject to the overriding right (or duty) of the senior matador to super-vise the fighting as a whole and to correct or advise the others.

The normal number of matadors is three, and of bulls, six. Each matador kills two bulls: the senior man kills Nos. 1 and 4, the second man 2 and 5, the junior man 3 and 6.*
A full-scale fight with picadors should last a little over two hours, on an average; two-and-a-half is very slow. So the fighting of each bull takes about twenty minutes. It may sound plenty, but when you realise how much has to happen, you will appreciate that things happen fairly fast.

Each matador's team consists of five assistants: two picadors, mounted, and three peones or capemen on foot—also called *banderilleros* because they plant the sticks called *banderillas*. Thus, when the show starts with the ceremonial parade (*paseíllo*), there are a large number of men to be seen, in this order: three matadors, nine peones, eight picadors (including two reserves), and also the ring servants

* Except when there is an *alternativa* ceremony. See Index-Glossary. Then the order is: junior, senior, second; senior, second, junior.

and mule teams; total, eighteen fighters excluding reserve picadors. However, only a fraction of these are in the ring at any one time. The assistants work only in those bulls which their own matador is to kill, and the picadors only in the first part of that. The matador whose turn it is stays on the job all the time in that bull, either personally or giving orders to his men. The other two matadors are also on duty actively in the pic act, and thereafter standing by in case of need. In the last part, the matador whose turn it is frequently clears the ring and fights the bull alone. But in no event can there be more than six foot-fighters in the ring: the three matadors, and the peones of one of them. Now let us get to the three acts of the fighting.

The bull has to be 'fixed' (meaning, its attention has to be concentrated on the cape), slowed down and dominated, and its head made to hang low, before a decent kill is at all likely; and to achieve this, as was said, he must be played like a game fish on a line. But it is necessary to change the lure, and this is done three times. As the lure is changed, the method of fighting is varied also. These three changes correspond to the beginning of each of the three acts; they also correspond to three different physical, and psychological, states of the bull, called *levantado* or 'elevated', *parado* or 'halted', and *aplomado*, meaning roughly 'weary but wiser'. Each state implies a psychological change, which the matador must naturally take into account.

When the parade is over, and all except the senior man's team have retired into the *callejón*, the President shows a white handkerchief and the first bull is let out. It comes out *levantado*, elevated, with its head as high as possible and the huge neck muscle bunched into a hump. It is full of confidence, and will charge furiously, but not very accurately, at anything in sight that moves. It is now the job of the peones to 'run' it, *correr al toro*. That means, to wave capes at it, get it to charge the capes, and give it long-distance passes. These are called *largas*, the big cape being held by one tip and sent flying out at full length. Indeed, 'casts' would be a better name than 'passes'. As the bull charges through, the matador, standing in one of the small screened gaps in the barrier, called *burladeros*, watches very closely, to see what kind of charge the bull gives, how it turns, and which horn, if either, it prefers, and whether it hooks either way. After this testing, a matter of one minute or so, the President has the trumpet blown again and Act I begins. The bull is still *levantado*, full of bluster. So far, it has charged at nothing but capes. Now the picadors come out: first change of target. The new target is a solid one, namely the horse, in addition to the capes. All three matadors are now in the ring, plus the two picadors and the senior matador's three peones.

In Act I, the bull is kept charging at the horses until a minimum of four normal pic thrusts have been administered to it, after which the President again signs for the trumpet and a change of Act. The number of pics is not rigid: more than four may be given if they were very light ones or if the bull clearly needs more, less if they were very heavy or the bull recharged hard under the iron, for with the *peto* the contact may last some time, and not be broken at once as in the pre-*peto* days. I have seen a bull of T. and I. Vázquez recharge eleven times in three pics, but that is an exceptional breed. Three hard pics, with steady shoving by the bull, may well equal eight or nine fairly light ones of the old-fashioned type.

Of course, the picador and his horse may be overthrown, and that is where the matadors come into the picture. As the picador falls on the sand, the first matador rushes in with his cape, to distract the bull from goring the fallen man. This rescue job is called making a *quite* (two syllables, *ki-té*, from *quitar*, to take away), and is usually followed by some formal passes by the matador. The second time, matador No. 2 does the job, and so on in turn. These *quites*, at least the artistic part, are generally performed even if no picador falls, so each matador gets a turn to do capework in each bull.

When this Act is finished, the bull is no longer 'elevated'. He is now *parado*, halted. His head is carried in roughly the same straight line as his back. He may still feel master of the ring as the picadors ride out, but he does not charge wildly any more. He is now aiming more deliberately, and may well be suspicious of the cape by this time, if the *lidia* or general strategy has been faulty, and the *brega* or tactical capework clumsy or excessive. From now on the cape should be used very sparingly.

The second Act is very brief (about two minutes), unless the matador himself elects to do the job. If not, the peones do it, but they must now be called *banderilleros*, for they carry a *banderilla* in each hand and no cape. Acting by pairs in turn, they run in a wide curve, the bull charges them, constantly altering direction, and as its head goes down to toss, they plant the pair of sticks on top of the withers behind the neck muscle; all done at the run. One of the spare matadors stands in the centre to control the bull if necessary, the other near the barrier to do a *quite* to the *banderillero* if he is pursued by the bull. The *banderilla* act is a 'decorative' *suerte* rather than one of 'punishment'. It is supposed to give the bull a breather after what the pic act has taken out of it. The *banderillas*, which sting rather than wound, often spur the bull into giving a better charge for the last Act, hence they used to be called *alegradores* or 'enliveners'. The matador should watch the *banderilla* work with care, for this is the precise moment when he can best appraise the condition of the bull and plan his solo work in the last Act.

When the trumpet blows for this, the bull is in the state technically known as *aplomado*, though not excessively so if he has caste and the *lidia* has been sound. He should not be exhausted by any means, if well bred and not over-pic'd, nor carrying excess fat through overfeeding so as to draw the correct weight when too young. He is slower in his charge, but more knowing and more dangerous. Unless exceptionally strong or brave, he will now charge only when he really thinks he will catch the man. Again the lure is changed; it is now the smaller red cloth called the *muleta*. The matador, acting alone now, holds this cloth as well as the sword. His job is to use the cloth to dominate the bull by efficient and artistic passes, until it stands with its four feet square and its head hung low. Then, at last, he can crown all his other work by the supreme hazard of the kill.

And that, in bald outline, is the theory of the three Acts. We must now examine how all these things are actually done in detail.

CHAPTER SIX

The Death of the Bull: Act I

I

In the Middle Ages and Renaissance times, all bullfighting was done from horseback, by nobles and gentlemen only. There were two styles: with the *rejón* and with the lance. The *rejón* style still exists and will be described later. The lance method was more common: in this, a knight on horseback awaited the charge of the bull, and tried to kill it by transfixing it with the lance. This style disappeared long ago, but the vestige of it remains in the picador with his long, steel-pointed wooden pole. The old lance-fighters sometimes used assistants on foot; these were lackeys of their own, who waved cloaks at the bull to divert its attention when required. Finally, if the horseman failed to kill the bull outright, it was finished off by a more or less professional killer with a sword, who put it to death as best he could, without any artistic pretensions. Thus the horseman was everything. He was a cavalier, and the rest were just servants to help him or clear up after him. When the lance act disappeared, foot fighting came to the fore (though for a period the picador was the chief fighter, in the early eighteenth century), largely owing to the invention of the *muleta* by Francisco Romero, grandfather of the immortal Pedro Romero. Thus the matador became the chief fighter, and the servants with cloaks evolved into the present-day peones

55

with capes, for the bullfighting cape is in fact a Spanish cloak, and you can even see it being worn at times, if rain falls, by fighters off duty who are awaiting their turn in the *callejón*. It is nowadays made of two thicknesses of heavy silk, the outside being blotting-paper pink and the inside generally yellow. It is very strong, but even so it is not infrequently ripped or even slit in half by the bull's horns. When this occurs, there is often some laughter from the audience, or part of it, but the matador is not amused at all, for he has to buy the capes for his entire team, and at present they cost 1,400 pesetas each.

The cape is the fundamental instrument of bullfighting, and is used by the peones all through the fight, by all three matadors in Act I, and sometimes by two of them in Act II. It is held in two ways.

If the maximum extension is required, it is held by one corner of the skirt and is flung out at full length in the cast called a *larga*, as in the 'running' of the new bull, already described. The peones also use it at times during the routine capework (*brega*), for shifting the bull about, and with no artistic aims, whereas the *largas* in the running of the bull can be highly artistic if the work is done in the best possible way, as it generally is, for example, with the grand peón and *banderillero* Migueláñez. This short, tubby figure, forty-five years old, will run the brand-new bull with three or four beautiful coloured arabesques sculptured in the air, which delight the audience while at the same time extracting from the bull all the information the watching matador wants to obtain. In the hands of a matador, the 'artistic' *larga* is today chiefly used in two modalities: the *larga cambiada* or *afarolada*, generally given kneeling, and the *serpentina* or *revolera*.

The former is just an isolated, spectacular pass, chiefly for display, given to the bull when still *levantado*, and above all, in its first rush out of the bullpen into the ring. When the trumpet blows for the new bull, the matador walks across the ring and kneels down some ten yards from the bullpen door. It opens, and the bull charges straight at the kneeling figure. He has the cape bunched in his right hand, and at the critical moment he raises his arm sharply and flings the cape out over his head, opening like a giant fan on his left side. If all goes well, the bull swerves, takes the big lure, and charges through at a reasonable distance. This hazard is more spectacular than effective, but serious accidents can easily happen if the timing is not perfect. When well done, it always gets a big ovation, and warms the crowd up from the very start of the fighting. If the cape is sent streaming upwards rather than to the opposite side, and is accompanied by a pivot of the man, the pass is called *afarolada* from its resemblance to the *farol*; the word *cambiada* or *cambio* always implies that the bull's trajectory has been made to swerve by means of a lure. The *serpentina* and *revolera* are used only to round off a series of two-handed passes, and we shall come to them later.

In two-handed passes, the cape is held on either side of the collar. The fundamental pass is the *verónica*, and with one exception all the regular passes are variants or developments of it. The short, brusque two-handed passes given in the *brega* are really elementary or truncated *verónicas*, bearing the same relation to them as the common wild flower bears to the cultivated garden variety. The name *verónica* is derived from the attitude of the man holding the cape out in his two hands, which resembles that in which St. Veronica is depicted holding out the towel to Our Lord on the way to Calvary. No irreverence is intended in this; in traditionally Catholic countries, where everybody, including illiterates, is familiar with religious pictures and images from childhood, such metaphors are common and natural. In the same way, a sword-thrust delivered very badly and so crooked that it goes through the bull sideways is known as a *dolorosa*, from the swords shown transfixing the Blessed Virgin in statues of her as Our Lady of Dolours.*

When the *verónica* is properly done, the man should stand facing at about forty-five degrees to the bull, holding the cape forward at a height just clearing the ground. It is thus between his body and the bull. If we assume the bull to be to his right, then he will have his left foot advanced (with legs well apart); and vice versa. The bull charges, and as it is about to crash into him he swings the cape through to his left and outwards, with a smooth, powerful arm movement, thus deflecting the line of the bull's charge and indicating the direction of its exit from the encounter. This action of turning on the power, as it were, is called *cargando la suerte* and is of the first importance. The man should not stand bolt upright, but slightly bowed over the cape, and should sway in unison with the arm movement. Everything should be smooth, rhythmical and plastic, with nothing stiff or jerky, and above all, with free play of the arms. Keeping them close to the ribs (*codilleo*) is a fatal defect. The bull will have finished up beyond the man, on his left and a little forward of him. He can now advance his right foot and repeat the pass in the opposite direction, and so on as often as he cares to repeat it, though more than four or five *verónicas* are uncommon at one time. It will be noted that strict control is exercised over the bull, whose trajectory is dictated and modified by the action of the man, who also gains one pace of terrain on the bull after each pass. For this reason the

---

* In such countries, even today, the tradition is still so all-pervasive that even its professed enemies are still apt to think and talk like believers. There is a well-known case of one 'free-thinker' who proudly proclaimed: "Thanks be to God and His most blessed Mother, I am an atheist," and in the Civil War, when a Protestant clergyman in Madrid was trying to convert some Communist militiamen, one of them replied: "But why should we believe in your religion, when we don't believe in the true one?"

verónica is the most beautiful and functional of all passes, and never palls when properly done.

A vitiated form of the *verónica*, not *cargando la suerte* but simply standing with feet together and letting the bull pass to and fro, is unhappily more common, and, which is worse, more applauded by the ignorant section of the audience. No pass of any kind given with the feet together can exercise effective bull-control; in this pseudo-*verónica* the man not only gains no ground but often has to step back to give the next pass, and in any case he stands edgeways on to the bull, so that its original trajectory is not aimed at his body and therefore requires no deflecting. The only merit, much over-valued by those who applaud so heartily, lies in how near to the presumed trajectory he can stand without flinching.

Needless to say, the whole virtue of the *verónica* in either form is lost if the man takes a step backwards when the bull arrives. But a matador should not be judged harshly on the first two or three passes he gives to the new, 'unfixed' bull. He may legitimately use a lot of foot movement while he is still trying to 'collect' the hitherto erratic bull and teach it to concentrate on the cape. He may thus give two or three ragged *verónicas* first, and then, when the bull has been caught, as it were, on a string, he may proceed to give a formal series of passes *parando, templando* and *mandando*.

These last three terms express the three classical rules of Pedro Romero, and mean: stand fast; swing smooth at the exact speed so that the horns are always just about to reach the cloth but never quite do so; and control the bull. To these three, said Domingo Ortega in the never-to-be-sufficiently-recommended lecture already mentioned, we should add (though implicitly contained in the word *mandando*) a fourth, namely *cargando la suerte*, which I have described above. This holds good for all passes in which bull-control and not mere decoration is the object.

I have expended a good deal of space on the *verónica*,

because it is the pass of passes, and what is true of it applies *mutatis mutandis* to all others, including those given with the *muleta* or red cloth. In the hands of a master, the rhythmic power and beauty of this pass, by which a piece of silk can control a half-ton of death travelling at twenty miles an hour, produces a deep and noble emotion, comparable only with some thrilling chord of a great symphony.

When the series of *verónicas* is completed, the usual practice is to finish it off with the so-called *media-verónica*. In this, the man starts one more *verónica*, but in the middle of the hazard he does not *cargar*, but gives a sharp pull on the cape with the leading hand and a slight pivot on the balls of his feet. The cape swirls round rapidly and disappears from the bull's eye like the shutting of a fan; the animal, in trying to turn in less than its own length, is brought up sharp to a halt, and the man can safely turn his back and walk away, for the twist to the bull's anatomy in making so sharp a turn prevents it from charging again for a few seconds.

For this reason precisely, the half-*verónica* (which falls under the heading of *recortes* or 'cutting-short') can be much abused. To break down a *bronco* bull of excessive power, it is most effective; but with a smooth, noble bull it can ruin the animal's charge and even rick its back if given to excess or violently. Accordingly, at times, good matadors prefer to finish off their series of passes in a gentler way with a *larga*, either curling round their legs in the spiral form called a *serpentina*, which gives a very graceful effect similar to that of a dancer's full skirt in a rapid pirouette, or else in the form of the *revolera* in which the cape swirls above the man's head. These ornamental *largas* will bring the bull round to a stop gently, without punishing it, and are extremely beautiful to watch. The term *revolera* is often loosely used for *serpentina* and *vice versa*.

Developments from the *verónica* are the *farol*, the *navarra* and the *chicuelina*. All begin as for a *verónica*, but in each case the man pivots sharply in the middle of the hazard, in the direction contrary to the bull's charge. In the *navarra* (long obsolete but recently revived), he keeps his hands level, and the cape flies out horizontally, disappearing from under the bull's nose; in the *chicuelina*, he raises one hand and drops the other, and the cape winds round his rotating body; in the *farol*, he flings both arms upwards and the cape swirls up above his head, with the bull sometimes rearing up spectacularly in an effort to reach it.

The *farol*, though an admirable pass, is dangerous, and very hard to do gracefully, so a complete set of *faroles* is not very common. More often one *farol*, or rather a half-*farol*, is used as the prelude to a series of *gaoneras*. This latter pass, less correctly called *de frente por detrás*, was invented in 1909 by the great Mexican matador Gaona. After the half-*farol*, the cape falls into position behind the man's back. Now, showing the yellow side to the bull, he extends one arm and pivots slowly as the bull passes; then he drops that arm, extends the other, and brings the bull back in the opposite direction, repeating as often as desired, and generally finishing off with one of the ornamental *largas*.

Derived from the *gaonera*, and perhaps describable as a sort of alternating-current version of it, in which the bull never actually passes, is the *mariposa* or 'butterfly', which is described in *Corrida* 1 of Chapter 15, though it is hardly ever seen today. It will be noted that in both the *gaonera* and the *mariposa* the man's body is fully exposed in front of the bull's face, and not occulted by the cloth lure. There are a few other passes or variants occasionally seen, but in the space available it is impossible to deal with them here.

2

After the preliminary 'running' by the capemen, the matador is normally expected to take the bull over and give it a set of formal passes, which are almost always *verónicas*. Meanwhile, the picadors enter the ring and ride round the barrier, anticlockwise, to their stations. The one who is to give the first pic (or rather, who is to give all the pics, barring accidents, to this bull) will normally proceed to a point well in the shade area, while the other stays about one-third of the circle further back. The horses are supposed to have their right eyes bandaged over, so that they can see properly to be ridden round the ring but cannot see the bull as it charges them. In practice this regulation is a dead letter, and both eyes are always covered, which seems to give better results, for a panic-stricken horse is a rarity nowadays; I can remember seeing about two cases in the last six years.

There is a circle, called the *tercio* line, marked on the sand, one-third of the way from the barrier to the centre of the ring (ten yards out, in Madrid). This line may not be crossed by a picador's horse when challenging the bull.*
After the picador is in position near the barrier at the desired spot, the matador or a peón draws the bull across, by capetrailing or a series of short zigzagging half-passes, to the corresponding point on the *tercio* line or thereabouts. The picador will have swivelled his horse round so that it now has the bull on its starboard bow. He ought to hold the pic pole about the midpoint, and also gripped higher up under his

---

* The object of the line is not to protect the picador by setting a limit beyond which he need not advance, but to prevent a cowardly bull from being made to attack against its will by being practically ridden down by the picador, thus obtaining undeserved credit for its breeder. This idea corresponds to a viewpoint a good way removed from that of today; but the tide already shows signs of turning.

arm. The horse-servants (*monosabios*) must keep well to the rear of the horse (a rule often broken), and all the foot toreros must stand to the near side of the horse, not further forward than the stirrup, leaving the off side perfectly clear. That at least is the regulation, and in Madrid it is fairly well observed; I have even seen an *alguacil* 'move on' a peón who was loitering on the off side. In provincial fights outside the big cities, anything goes.

The object of this rule is to give the bull free exit from the pic-thrust. The real name for the pic is *vara de detener*, literally 'pole for holding-off', and in theory what happens is as follows. The picador rides slowly forward towards the bull, it charges, and just as it arrives he jabs the pic down on top of its shoulders behind the neck muscle. He is now supposed to hold the bull off from the horse, by leaning hard on the pole, while swivelling the horse's hindquarters to the left, and pushing the bull off towards the right. In other words, the action is similar to that of a man with a boat-hook who uses it powerfully to avoid contact with another boat which is about to ram his starboard bow. The bull is thus supposed to exit from the encounter on the off side of the horse. And I *had* seen the hazard so executed, notably by the grand picador Farnesio, who recently retired after thirty-seven years in the ring. It was beautiful to watch. But, one feared, it was doomed to vanish for ever, until, to everyone's surprise—that of the old *aficionados* who despaired of ever seeing pic work done decently again, and that of the younger generation who had read about it but hardly ever seen it, like myself—it was revived in all its majesty by two young Mexicans. The first was Chano, working in the team of the Kansas-born Mexican matador Jesús Córdoba, in 1952; the second, who seems even better, is Sixto Vázquez, who appeared in Madrid on 31st July, 1955, working as second picador in the team of the junior matador Jaime Bravo. His work in the fourth bull (the first was pic'd by Bravo's other picador) so amazed and delighted the audience that he was awarded a round of the ring, and I cannot resist quoting what was written about him in the leading bullfighting weekly:

After seeing so many calamities in the first act, did you suspect that the pic'ing of a wild bull could be something artistic? Yes, my friends, artistic. There is Sixto Vázquez to prove it. Sixto Vázquez deserves what Guerrita achieved, in his days as an assistant fighter, namely to have his name printed on the posters in the same size type as those of the matadors. . . .

Any picador who seeks to resemble Sixto Vázquez in this art must place himself in front of the bull, and then, without the aid of *monosabios* or anyone else, get the horse to advance straight forward towards the enemy. If he thinks the bull will be slow to charge, he will incite it by lifting up the pole, parallel to the ground, for the bull to see, or even standing up several times in the stirrups to make the bull respond to an apparent provocation. But if all that fails, then the bull must be made to charge by torrying it on horseback, in a gallant interplay of advancing and retreating, not at the horseman's caprice, but exactly measured to produce the desired charge. This being achieved, it is not allowable, or at least should not be, to wait till the bull has its horns well into the *peto*, and then to jab in the pic with impunity. Sixto Vázquez does it very differently: he thrusts in the point before the horns reach the *peto*, and halts the attack as far as possible. Then, without altering position or closing up the bull's exit, he puts the power of his arm to the test against the brute force of his enemy, and concludes the hazard by swinging the horse to the left with the reins, while shoving the bull off to the right with the pic. That is how it was done, all three times, by this magnificent horseman and grand picador.

Three pics, three ovations; two salutes hat in hand; another ovation when he rode out, with a large part of the audience standing up in their places; and after the death of the bull, a round of the ring. Who says that the pic act is of no interest now? When it is an art, it arouses interest, emotion and enthusiasm.

This mode of pic work, however, was often more theoretical than actual, even before the horse-protector was worn. A very large number of bulls always did get through and wounded or killed the horse. But in those days, if the picador deliberately let the bull get through, he did so, well knowing that he would probably get the horse killed under him, and suffer a crashing fall himself, with the chance of a goring as well. Today, with the oversize *peto*, the horse is hardly ever wounded, and it is three or four to one that it will not be bowled over. So in most cases the picador lets the bull arrive, and while it is whacking away at the mattress, he uses the pic as an instrument of punishment rather than as a *vara de detener*. In any event, the normal exit of the bull from the encounter is no longer on the off side of the horse; it may be in any direction, but even with respectable pic work it is often on the near side, after passing across the bows of the horse which has received the charge nearly broadside on.

On account of the many abuses (such as *barrenar* or screwing, and the *carioca* or '*suerte* of Atienza'—see Index-Glossary) which the oversize *peto* has made easy to practise, some people are apt to regard the pic act as a necessary evil. I do not agree: the sight of a brave, powerful bull being pic'd honourably by an Aldeano, a Boltañés, a Hiena II or a Curro de la Viuda, to say nothing of a Chano or a Sixto Vázquez, is a fine one, and with a discerning audience such as that of Madrid, apart from one or two fashionable fights which are 'social occasions', both man and bull will get a round of applause. The restoration of the full-sized bull has done something already to adjust the balance; the senior matador now on the active list, Antonio Bienvenida, who is a master of the *lidia*, never permits such abuses by his subordinate fighters, thereby setting a valuable example; and it seems likely that the authorities will shortly modify the out-of-date pic point, and reduce the *peto* to its proper dimensions, which would go far towards rehabilitating the pic act.

Certainly that is the desire of the good *aficionado*, in whose eyes this hazard represents for the bull the same as that of the sword represents for the man, namely 'the hour of the truth', the moment when it becomes plain to all what stuff he is made of. In *Death in the Afternoon*, Hemingway makes his raffish old lady say she enjoyed the pic act because "it seemed so homey when the bull hit the horses". Some of the sayings of that memorable old lady were no doubt intended merely to shock the bourgeois, but I do not think that one was, though not everybody would put it in quite that way. Intelligent spectators always have plenty of sympathy (not 'pity') for the bull, when it is brave, and while assuredly not desiring any injury to the honourable picador, they derive a deep and noble dramatic emotion from the sight of the brave bull exultant in his fearlessness and power. His victory is the first act of the tragic drama.

3

If the horse goes over or the picador falls, danger may arise and a *quite* must be done, as was explained in Chapter 5. The matador who is to kill this bull makes the *quite* after the first pic, and afterwards the others in order of seniority. In the *quite* proper, any sort of cape flap or cast will do; the sole object is to get the bull away from the fallen man. When you read that Fulano "did a *quite* by *verónicas*" (or by *gaoneras*, or *faroles*, etc.), what is meant is: "After Fulano had done the business *quite* with any sort of a cape flap, and got the bull well away, he then performed a set of *verónicas*" (or whatever pass was named).

In case of imminent danger the turn does not matter, the thing is to save the picador from a goring, quick, and everyone piles in. As a rule, the matador on duty gets in first, because he will have been standing nearer. But if the man fell in a different way, and a companion of the matador was first in with the cape, he would hand the bull over to the man on duty once he had got it clear. In theory, a matador may not do capework to another matador's bull except with the latter's consent, but this consent is taken for granted in routine *quites*.

A *quite* does not necessarily imply danger. When the pic thrust is completed, the matador may and should use his cape to draw the bull away from the horse. He may then choose to do some artistic passes, or he may be content simply to lead the bull smoothly back and place it in *suerte* again before the horse. Such an omission to please the audience with artistic work need not be due to apathy or cowardice; it may be the result of nice judgment of the most appropriate *lidia* for the bull in question, or, on windy days, to the virtual impossibility of doing decent capework.

As has been stated, the regulation minimum number of four pics (three in *novilladas*) is intended to mean 'single thrusts'. Now, a bull without overmuch courage may keep on attacking, but may break loose at once each time without shoving against the iron, and so the pics it receives may be very light ones, perhaps barely puncturing the skin at times. Such a bull may well be given six or seven pics and still not become properly *parado*. On the other hand, a brave bull which is noble but not too powerful may recharge two or three times, without overturning the horse, in each of two heavy thrusts; in such a case the President will have the trumpet blown at once, even though theoretically only two pics have been given, for two such pics will be equivalent to four or five of the kind intended by the regulations.

The bull that is plain cowardly, and will not charge the horses at all, or never again after the first touch of the pic, sets a problem that has never been, and can never be, satisfactorily solved. The danger of such a bull is evidently considerable: on the one hand, its cowardice will probably prevent it from giving a frank charge, and may even make it go on the pure defensive, the worst thing of all from the matador's standpoint; and on the other hand, it retains the whole of its original power. Clearly some partial substitute for the missing pics must be applied, and this will be described in the next chapter.

CHAPTER SEVEN

The Death of the Bull: Act II

Ordinarily, nowadays, the *banderilla* act is little more than a routine formality and lasts two minutes or less. The matador's orders are to get through with the job quickly: efficiently if possible, but quickly. What the public has primarily come to see is Act III, and the second Act is only a minor interlude.

This was not always so. At the end of the nineteenth century, matadors still 'rose from the ranks', and served as capemen-*banderilleros* to established matadors until they were themselves admitted to the *alternativa*. The second Act was highly appreciated, and the great Guerrita, before he took the *alternativa*, was a bigger draw on the programme, as a *banderillero*, than the matador for whom he worked. Today it is the other way round: quite a number of peones are failed matadors who have 'reverted' to the ranks through which they never passed on the way up.

Newcomers always enjoy the second Act, because it is so easy to follow what is occurring; but the regular public pays very little attention to the *banderillas*, unless the matador himself places them.

The routine way of executing this *suerte* needs no more description than has been already given in Chapter 5. It is the method always used by the peones,* and is called *al cuarteo*, an expression really meaning 'on the zigzag', as in

*Though I have occasionally seen the excellent peón Migueláñez use the *poder a poder* method. For description of *banderillas*, see Index-Glossary.

driving a horse up a steep hill. In this case, however, it means running in an arc so that the bull's speed is cut down by the frequent alterations it has to make in the straight line of its charge. The geometry of this can be seen very clearly from a front-row seat in the *andanada*.

After peón No. 1 has placed a pair of sticks, No. 2 does the same, then No. 1 again, after which the trumpet is normally blown. In the same matador's other bull, peón No. 2 will alternate with No. 3, and No. 1 will act as capeman in the ring. The sticks stand up straight for a few moments if well placed, then droop over and hang horizontal. They should be placed as near as possible together, on top of the shoulders. They should not be poked horizontally into the bull, but planted smartly downwards, after raising the arms well up. If a *banderillero* makes three successive false runs, he loses his turn.

When the matador himself performs the *suerte*, an event more common in Mexico than in Spain, it regains its ancient glory, and in provincial rings the band plays throughout. The matador acts alone, with no one else in the ring, and frequently makes a showy preparation, sometimes giving deliberate false runs and dodging the bull by nimble footwork (*recortes a cuerpo limpio*).

For the placing of the sticks, he may use the *al cuarteo* method also, but it will be done in a much more spectacular way: either by making a much longer run, so that when he meets the bull he is going absolutely all out; or by running in an arc that will merge into the curve of the barrier, so that he plants the sticks at the moment when the bull seems just about to crush him against the planks; or *de dentro a fuera* (from inside outwards), starting from the barrier or even from its *estribo* or ledge and running outwards into the bull's territory, to finish up in the middle.

A method more spectacular in itself, without adventitious enhancement, is that which is known as either *de frente* (from in front) or *poder a poder* ('power to power'). Some people seem to regard these as two separate methods, but I propose to lump them together and regard the latter as simply the limiting case of the former. When the *suerte* is done like this, there is indeed a *cuarteo* or arc, but only at the last moment. The man challenges the bull face-on from a distance, marching slowly towards it. When the bull breaks into a run, so does he; when this becomes a charge, the man breaks into a very small semicircular run, at absolutely top speed to avoid the bull's change of direction, and smacks in the sticks as he clears the horns. If a true *poder a poder* is done, the man holds to his straight course so long that the final arc to miss the horns is almost a rapid sidestep in his forward course.

Finally, there is the method *al quiebro* which is the most brilliant of all. It bears the same relation to the *poder a poder* as the kill *recibiendo* bears to the kill at the *volapié*. In this, the man again challenges from a distance, but stands stock still and allows the bull to charge straight at him. When it is within a yard or two, he makes a rapid feint in one direction with his arms and trunk, but not (in pure theory) moving his feet. This sudden movement of the target causes a bend (*quiebro*) in the bull's trajectory, not a large deviation, but enough to make it miss the man as he sways back quickly into his original position. As he does so he drives in the sticks, the bull's body grazes him as it hurtles past, and the *suerte* is complete with the man standing where he was at the start. After that he can walk or run back to the barrier.

The total immobility of the feet is in practice just about impossible, but if the *suerte* is properly done there should not be anything amounting to a sidestep. The foot may move a few inches as the man throws his whole weight on it when making the feint, and as he sways back it returns to its normal position.

In addition to the ordinary *banderillas*, there are the explosive kind, called *banderillas de fuego*. These are used only on bulls which have proved cowardly in the first Act and refused to charge the horses; "four proper pics or be fired" is the wording of the regulation. When all attempts to get the bull into the horses have failed, the President changes the Act by signalling with a red handkerchief instead of a white one, and the *banderilleros* are then issued with these special sticks instead of the ordinary ones.

Their length of shaft and point is identical, but they are more bulky, like tightly furled umbrellas, because they carry three detonators inside. These go off successively after the point is driven in. There is a lot of smoke, a fizzing blue flame for a moment, and then the three very loud bangs. The things are designed to explode upwards, and the firework nearest the point is three inches above it; consequently there is no actual charring of the animal's skin.*

To say that these contraptions replace the missing pics would be a vast exaggeration, but in the great majority of cases they do manifestly do something more, even a good deal more, than the ordinary *banderillas*. Perhaps they have little effect on a bull that is vicious and cunning, but they often have plenty on one that is merely sluggish and without aggressiveness. Such bulls often pay little attention to the ordinary *banderillas*, and even when the special ones are planted they have little effect for the first few seconds while the smoke and flame come out; but when the bangs go off, this startles the sluggard and makes it jump about, toss furiously, and in many cases decide to give a respectable charge in the third Act. At worst, they are still *banderillas* and have the same effect as ordinary ones, besides acting as a public sign of disgrace to the breeder of the cowardly bull, and a notable vent for the indignation of the audience.

These *banderillas* are more difficult to place, first because their bulk makes them clumsier, and secondly because by

* Originally they really did burn the bull, but the clause about exploding upwards was added in 1930 to avoid this cruelty.

hypothesis the bull is cowardly and will not charge properly. So it is rare for matadors themselves to do the 'firing', though I have seen it done brilliantly at times, if the bull will charge men but not horses. The best exhibition I have ever seen was that of Pepe Dominguín with a very fast red Miura at Saragossa in 1948; he did it like a wing three-quarter racing down the line, with the bull 'corner-flagging' across to cut him off, and he smacked in the 'rockets' when he and the bull were both going absolutely all out.

Since 1951, in Spain the 'firing' of *manso* bulls has been symbolical only; the red handkerchief is still shown, but the sticks have no fireworks. The position is rather curious. As no one had ever pretended that the 'rockets' were a real equivalent for the missing pics, it was suggested—by the Catalan matador-poet-actor Cabré, I think—that a different device would give better results. This was to be in appearance an ordinary *banderilla*, but was to have a six-inch leaf-shaped blade like the *rejones* of the horseback fighters, which do have about the effect of a pic thrust. The element of disgrace was to be supplied by decorating the sticks with black paper instead of bright colours. In practice, the things have proved a total failure. It is my own belief that the longer blade was never used at all; it would be extremely difficult for a foot-fighter to drive in such a thing, two at a time moreover, downwards through the thick hide. The 'mourning *banderillas*' now in use are simply common ones except for having a double barb instead of a single one, and of course the colour; and unfortunately nobody has yet bred a bull on which the colour black will have the same enlivening effect as three giant squibs. But the innovation was never embodied in the regulations, and as it is now condemned as *contraproducente* or worse than useless, by toreros, bull-breeders, critics and the general public with complete unanimity, it will probably be abolished before long and the normal practice (never dropped in Peru) resumed in Spain.

CHAPTER EIGHT

The Death of the Bull: Act III, Scene I

I

In earlier times, what the audience primarily went to see was the bull's battle against the picadors, and the large variety of artistic capework which accompanied the many *quites*. By the end of Act I the bull was generally about spent, and *banderillas* were then placed, mainly to stimulate it into giving a few more charges so that the swordsman could kill it by the receiving method. Thus Act III consisted of the kill, preceded only by just so much work with the red cloth as was strictly necessary—seldom more than half a dozen passes.

However, the artistic possibilities of the red cloth (*muleta*) were developed more and more, while selective breeding produced braver and nobler bulls, and from 1900 to 1920 the two major Acts were about balanced. The contemporary period began with the introduction of the *peto*, immediately followed by a substantial reduction in the minimum legal age and weight of the bull.

Consequently, the emphasis has today shifted entirely to the third Act. In one respect, the decadence of the first two is regrettable, because it unbalances the fight as a whole, exalts into an end in itself the preparation which is rightly only a means, and diminishes the need for scientific all-round *lidia*. In another, the expansion of the third Act makes the spectacle less violent, and gives the audience a chance to see plenty of brilliant solo work.

2

Once the trumpet has blown 'for the death', as it is still called, the matador alone is responsible* for the rest of the fighting until his bull is dead. This is called his *faena* or 'job', and the maximum time allowed is fifteen minutes, reckoned from the moment of the first pass. This is far more than is required; if the matador cannot kill his bull within ten minutes, it means that either he has fallen down on his job, or the bull presents quite abnormal difficulties. Normally, with a reasonable bull, a *faena* which aims at artistic merit and not mere lining-up (*aliño*) should last from four to seven minutes, not counting the kill.

If the bull is still alive after ten minutes, the President shows a white handkerchief and a trumpet warning (*aviso*) is blown. This is commonly regarded as a disgrace, though it need not imply any; hence Presidents tend to be lenient if the man is doing well and strict if he is not. That is an error: the warning is only a warning; the regulation should be applied automatically in all cases; the audience can judge well enough whether the man deserves applause or the reverse. If the bull is still alive after thirteen minutes, a second *aviso* is given; and after fifteen, the signal for the third is given with a green handkerchief. This colour is at the same time the signal for the trained steers to come out and lead off the live bull to the corral. At the third *aviso*, the matador must at once leave off trying to kill the bull, and retire to the barrier. By the second warning, or the first if given late as it usually is, there will certainly be a heavy barrage of whistling and

---

* With a good bull, he will often do all the work alone in the ring, which is the most meritorious. But he is entitled to have his capemen present to help him, and on a windy day or with a difficult bull he is wise to use them. Excessive intervention by them however robs a *faena* of most of its merit, and is rightly resented by the audience.

75

booing in progress, which will thereafter grow into the full-scale roaring row, peppered with hoots and catcalls, known expressively as a *bronca*; and indeed the sight implied by the three *avisos* is nearly always a repugnant one. In major fights such an event seldom occurs more than once in two or three years; in Madrid, the last time on record was in spring 1947. It was a lamentable sight: a gipsy, with his nerve gone, and quite out of training, was pricking and stabbing away uselessly at a brave bull, while El Andaluz, the best killer in the world, had to stand idly by. In another bull, No. 3 of the day, Antonio Bienvenida tried to get the fight back on to an even keel, and in giving a dangerous left-hand pass in a high wind he received a serious wound which kept him out of the ring for a long time. So the gipsy had to kill *his* bull too, and he got another warning in that one. Only Andaluz, the second swordsman, saved the day by grand *lidia* and superb killing in his own bulls.

3

During the *banderilla* interlude, the matador has selected a *muleta* from his stock. This is a piece of red flannel about a yard square, with one corner rounded off. One edge has, attached to it by a spike and a thumbscrew, a wooden handle which does not project beyond the cloth; it thus amounts to a large* red flag with the staff snapped off. There are two thicknesses of scarlet flannel, sometimes with a central lining for more weight. On days of wind—the bull-

---

* There is no fixed size, and the matador's stock may include *muletas* of different sizes. But the use of an outsize one is a suspicious sign, indicating that there is likely to be some faking in the *faena*, and especially in the kill. Sincere, classical work in a pure style cannot be done with a huge cloth. In English writings, I have constantly seen the *muleta* described as 'heart-shaped'. This is not so now, if it ever was.

fighter's worst enemy—the cloth is often damped and scuffed in the sand to increase the weight still more, but there is a limit to what the wrist can manage, especially in right-hand passes.

Whichever hand is used for the *muleta*, the sword must always be held in the right. So the only way to hold both tools in the right is to have the sword-point poked into the remote corner of the cloth and to use the combination as a single unit. Thus the weight wielded by the right wrist is considerable, for the sword may weigh a pound and a half, and the *muleta* about the same if it is wetted, and a very strong wrist is required to handle the two with ease. On the other hand, the sword-point spreads the cloth, making the lure larger, so that the bull passes less close and the danger is less. On this account, right-hand passes of the kind called *natural* (Spanish word, accent on the last syllable), the basic passes of the *faena*, are regarded as less meritorious than those given with the left, other things being equal. But if there is much wind, the use of the left hand is seldom very effective or worth the risk; again, if the bull is not buoyant and noble in its charge, but inclined to be *bronco* (irregular and violent), then a more or less extensive use of the right hand will be needed to get it dominated, at least at the start of the *faena*.

At the sound of the trumpet, the matador selects a sword from the leather case—rather like a golf-bag—held by his *mozo de estoques* or sword-handler, and, holding both it and the *muleta* in his left (for the nonce) in the form of a cross, and his cap (*montera*) in his right, he steps out into the ring and walks across to beneath the President's box. (I assume this to be his first bull of the day.) Here he makes the *brindis* or dedication. Raising his *montera* aloft, he dedicates the death of the bull to the President. This is a regulation order, and the toast is purely formal. He then throws his *montera* to the *alguacil*, who retains it till the bull is dead, whereupon the matador returns, bows to the President, and takes it back again. In his second bull, he need not make any *brindis*, but he often does dedicate the bull, either to some notability who is present, or to a personal friend, or to the audience as a whole. In the first two cases, he goes to the point of the barrier nearest to the spectator's seat, makes a little informal speech of dedication, or perhaps only a few words, then throws up the *montera* to the 'brindee' to hold during the *faena*, returning to collect it afterwards. In the case of the entire audience,* he advances to the ten-yard line, holds up the *montera*, and gyrates slowly so as to embrace the whole audience in the silent *brindis*, then drops the hat on the sand, where it remains throughout the *faena*.

Notabilities to whom the matador dedicates a bull, but who are not his personal friends, are expected to respond to the honour by giving him a present. The *montera* is returned with a visiting card in it, and next day the *mozo de estoques* calls to present the matador's compliments—and receive the present. Sometimes these presents are very valuable: two or three years ago, the young Kabaka of Buganda toured Spain and became very keen on bullfighting and, when the three matadors in a certain big fight dedicated bulls to him, he presented them with handsome gold watches.

After this, the matador addresses himself to the bull, which his capemen have kept hemmed in or have transferred to the part of the ring where he wants to start work. The scene shown in a certain American film, in which a matador is killed by the bull when his back is turned to make the dedication, is an impossibility; however, I do remember one occasion in 1948 when Manolo Andaluz was trying to dedicate a bull in Madrid—to the Argentine ambassador Dr. Radío, I think—and he had a lot of difficulty. The bull

---

* A matador new to the *plaza* frequently does this in his first bull, after previously saluting the President; the same applies to royalties and persons of exceptional rank.

was a *toro de bandera*, the bravest of the brave, named Tejero, of Pablo Romero, and it knew its enemy and was 'rarin' to fight'. It took little notice of the capes of the peones; Manolo alone interested it, and it got so impatient at the delay that he actually had to make his little speech from the cover of a *burladero*, while watching Tejero out of the tail of his eye. Tejero charged like a racehorse as soon as he got a chance at Manolo, who fought and killed him magnificently and cut the ear by acclamation. The bull also got a great ovation.

An experienced matador will already have made up his mind what kind of *lidia* the bull requires. His primary object is to get it dominated and fully under control. After that, he can work on it by the artistic and fundamental *natural* passes; finally, he can add such decorative work as he thinks fit, and then line the bull up and kill it.

If the bull is a tough customer or a bad hat, the dominating process may constitute the whole *faena*, no spectacular work being possible. Much the same applies to a bull that is of poor caste and has run out of gas after the pic act, or is a *manso* or coward and will not give an honest charge. If the bull is noble and buoyant (as in the case of Tejero), the matador need hardly bother about the first part, but can start artistic work forthwith. But in such a case he should not go on and on indefinitely, however much the audience may cheer. There comes a moment in every *faena* when the bull is absolutely ripe for killing: it seems to line itself up automatically as if asking for the sword-thrust. If the man lets that moment go by, the bull's condition goes off the boil, and so may the enthusiasm of the audience, and the result may be only a moderate or even a clumsy finish to a *faena* that was all set for a triumph.

4

Muleta passes can be divided into two kinds: effective ones, and pure decorations (*pases de adorno*). A photograph and a brief definition will do for the latter, but something must be said of the former, as regards both their mechanism and their main purpose. In a rough and ready way, they can be instantly distinguished by eye into three classes, namely high, low, and circular; that is, over the top of the horns, at ground level, and in a horizontal arc of a circle, respectively. Again, broadly speaking, the high ones (*por alto*) are showy but exercise little bull-control, the low ones (*por bajo*) are not spectacular but have the greatest dominating effect, and the circular ones (*en redondo*) are given in series and are both artistic and effective in wearing the bull down.

A stricter, scientific classification, which covers all possible *muleta* passes, is the division into *natural, cambiado,* and *ayudado* passes. A *natural* pass is one from which the bull exits on the same side as the hand that holds the cloth: in a left-hand pass, the bull finishes to the left of the man, and in a right-hander, to his right. A *cambiado* pass is the reverse: in a left-hand one, the bull starts from his left and finishes on his right, and *vice versa*. An *ayudado* pass is one in which both arms work together, sword in right hand and cloth in left, but as one single unit. Fair English equivalents for these three terms would be 'forehander', 'backhander' and 'two-hander'.

As any of these passes can theoretically be finished off *por alto* (high), *por bajo* (low), or *en redondo* (in an arc of a circle), there are nine possible combinations, and the forehanders and backhanders can be given with either hand; total, fifteen, excluding variants. But in fact only a certain number require special mention or are regularly employed. The

Bulls fencing on a ranch. This is how they learn to use their horns.

Fine bull of Vistahermosa caste in corral. In the background are travelling crates.

Two *toros de bandera*. 'Caribello' of Arranz, fought September 1948 in Madrid, made Mario Cabré sweat the big drop; 'Zamarrito', of Andrea Escudero, is seen in his tenth charge at the horses.

chief of these are: the *ayudado por alto* or two-hander over the top; the right-hand pass *por bajo* (whether forehand or back-hand is immaterial), and its reinforced version, the *ayudado por bajo* or two-hander at ground level; the *natural en redondo* or circular pass, with either hand; and the *cambiado por alto* or backhander over the top, always known as the *pase de pecho* or breast pass. These really boil down into only three modes: the high spectacular curtain-raisers, the low dominating 'benders', and the main dish or *natural* passes with the breast pass as their normal complement.

5

The first thing to realise (and unfortunately only too many matadors do not) is that to give passes to a bull is not the same as to 'torry' it (*torear*). *Torear* means to exercise control over the bull at all times, and to work on it as desired. What is desired will vary from bull to bull. If it is still too powerful, it must be softened up; if its head is too high, it must be made to lower it, and if too low, to raise it. If it is hooking either way—but above all, to the right—that defect must be corrected if possible. The man must try to get its attention fixed on the red cloth so that it can think of nothing else. If it is charging too fast, it must be slowed down; if it is sluggish, it must be enlivened; and if slow to accept the lure, encouraged. This is the time when many bulls have reached the stage of *aplomado*: what they have lost in physical faculties they have gained in knowingness, hence they often will not give a charge unless they feel pretty sure that they are going to connect this time. That illusion must be preserved by every means. All this goes under the heading of *lidia*, and this is where the experienced matador, even of the second class, will always score over the more brilliant but less seasoned newcomer, who will sometimes fail to get the best out of his good bulls, and will do worse than he need with the inferior ones.

One favourite way to start a *faena* is with the pass *ayudado por alto*, the two-hander over the top, which can be given in two ways: either with the feet slightly apart and with a follow-through of the arms so as to *cargar la suerte* to some extent, or else standing bolt upright with feet together, and simply raising the cloth like a curtain as the bull passes beneath at full gallop. This type, formerly called *pase de la muerte* (pass of death) and today *pase estatuario* (statuesque), is commoner; it is less graceful and exercises no bull-control, but is perhaps more spectacular. If the bull is noble, it will charge through, turn, and recharge of its own accord, with practically no movement by the man. If you see an experienced matador start his *faena* with this pass, in either form, it means that this bull requires no softening up. The pass looks good, and after the bull has been to and fro a few times, the man has only to drop his left hand and remove his right, and he can go straight into a series of left-hand *naturales*, an opening which will warm the crowd up thoroughly.

But in the majority of cases the man will start with a right-hand pass *por bajo*, low down. If he is going to give a series of these, they will be alternately forehand and backhand (*cambiado*). Both work the same way. He stands with feet wide apart and holds the cloth well forward from his body. As the bull reaches the centre of the pass, he sharply withdraws the cloth sideways under its nose, by pulling in his extended arm. The bull twists round, trying to turn in less than its own length, and the man, moving freely on his feet, thrusts the cloth forward again, in a lunge which brings one knee almost to the ground. This increases the strain on the bull's anatomy as it twists still further round. When given smartly, in-out, with the arm moving like a piston-rod and the whole body co-operating, this pass exerts a most powerful softening-up effect, and after two or three of them, most medium bulls will be well in hand. A powerful bull, however, if *bronco* or insufficiently pic'd, may take six or even eight and still not be dominated. The piston-rod movement is essential; merely withdrawing the cloth and letting the bull slip past has little or no effect.

If this pass is given as a two-hander (*ayudado por bajo*), the effect is greater still, for the use of the sword can considerably increase the travel of the cloth and hence the arcing of the bull's spine. In either form, this pass is graphically known as a 'bender' (*doblón*) or *pase de castigo* (punishment pass). Given in isolation, at the end of the *faena*, it acts just like a *recorte* with the cape, and is thus most valuable when the man wants to get the bull fixed and standing square on for the kill.

After the first stage of the *faena*, when the bull is now following the cloth smoothly and obediently, the matador may proceed to the central part, which normally consists of passes *en redondo*, that is *natural* passes with either hand. These are not normally given in isolation but in series of three, four or more. The distance from which the bull is challenged will vary according to how *aplomado* or how buoyant it is, but the procedure is the same. The man should stand facing the bull at an angle, not edgeways, and with feet somewhat apart. A *natural* pass given with feet together is unnatural-looking and worthless as regards bull control. If the bull does not charge at once, he can move nearer, or advance the cloth in the bull's direction. When it charges, he stands firm and swings the cloth round in an arc; to his left if it is a left-hand pass, to his right if a right-hander. The bull's trajectory is accordingly also bent in an arc, hence the *natural* pass performs useful work on the bull. The bull is not now being violently whip-lashed as in the 'benders', but is being smoothly worn down. Any pass that changes the bull's natural straight line into a curve has this effect, and the smaller the radius of the arc the greater the effect. Hence the left-hand *natural*, other things being equal, is more effective than the right-hander, because the lure is smaller and so is the arc;* but, of course, the danger is greater because the bull passes closer.

In the left-hand *natural* the sword should be held parallel to the man's right leg, or behind his back. It should never be in front of his legs, pointing into the cloth or touching it; this robs the pass of its beauty, and also of its efficiency by increasing the distance, and in fact it turns the true *natural* into a clumsy sort of *ayudado en redondo*. Only in a strong wind is it justifiable to use the sword in this way.

As the bull goes through in its curved trajectory, the man gyrates on the balls of his feet, following through well with the hand that holds the cloth. Thus at the end of the pass he is in the same position relative to the bull as when he started, and can repeat the pass without further movement. After about three such passes he has described a full circle, in the ordinary way, though some matadors can prolong the *natural* into about a semicircle, even with the left hand, and one man, L. M. Dominguín, regularly gives a right-hand *natural* of a complete circle in a single pass—an astonishing and most beautiful sight.

To produce its full artistic effect, a series of left-hand *naturales* should be finished off with a *pase de pecho* (breast pass), that is, the *cambiado por alto* or backhander over the top. This ought to be spontaneous, as if forced on the man by the bull (*forzado de pecho*); if it is given 'deliberately' by the man to an unwilling bull (*preparado de pecho*), it looks laborious and artificial. When done correctly it occurs thus:

The man may have decided to end the series of *naturales*, in which case he will not swivel round in the last one; or else the bull may have turned very quickly and caught him,

* The other great advantage of the left-hander is that it teaches the bull to hook to the left rather than to the right, a most valuable tendency at the moment of the kill, when a hook to the right may be fatal.

apparently, on the wrong foot. In either case, he has the bull far round to his left, nearly behind him. As it recharges, he 'takes' the charge on the reverse side of the cloth, and guides the bull through, past his chest from left to right, then out and away from him, moving his left arm—at fuller and fuller stretch horizontally—so as to keep the cloth dangling in front of the horns. At last he can stretch no further; his left foot is on tiptoe, and his body is nearly in the attitude of a left-handed golfer at the conclusion of an iron shot. At this point the horns come level with the cloth, which is then lifted over the top, while the whole length of the bull's body passes under it. The bull finds that the lure has vanished, and whips round to find it, and the man walks calmly away.

The series has been finished off with the pass that is perhaps the most plastically beautiful of all. It gives satisfaction of an almost intellectual kind: the bull is returned to its original position in one brilliant, smooth motion in reverse, balancing or 'discharging' the tension that has been piled up by the succession of *naturales*. It is like a musical movement that finally returns to rest on the original major chord. This language is not a fanciful exaggeration, but answers to a deep desire for harmony, balance, compensation, which everybody feels at some time or other. A string of *naturales*, however well done, is simply not the same without the logical conclusion of the breast pass to round it off; one feels there is something missing, something lopsided or incomplete, which leaves a feeling of dissatisfaction. Yet if a torero does a breast pass out of the blue, it is nothing; it may even look awkward and pointless by itself. And, of course, with the right-hand *natural* the presence of the sword robs it of most of its beauty, so that the right-hand *pase de pecho* is seldom used—another thing that robs the right-hand *natural* of emotion and balance.

After this, not much remains to be said. There are one-handed *pases por alto*, which are simply *natural* passes finished off by lifting the cloth over the horns instead of swivelling round as in the *en redondo* type. Sometimes, however, in the right-hand variety, the man does pivot completely round, in the *opposite* direction to the bull's charge, so as to end up facing it and ready for another right-hander over the top. This pass is called the *lasernina*, from the matador La Serna who invented it. Later, Domingo Ortega introduced a variant in which the man also passes his left arm behind his back and grips the lower edge of the cloth with his left hand. This was called the *orteguina* but is now generally called *manoletina* owing to its having been popularised by the late Manolete. It is easy to do, showy, looks dangerous but is pretty safe, and is the least risky of all passes in the wind. It has been so overdone in recent years that it has become thoroughly discredited in serious *plazas*. It is a pure *adorno* and has no effective action on the bull.

Passes of *adorno* are numerous, and each new 'phenomenon' that appears seems to think it necessary to invent one. Two that are of respectable antiquity and are both elegant and difficult to do gracefully are the *molinete* and the pass *afarolado*; both are recognised forms of finishing off a series of right-hand *naturales*. In each case the man pivots fast in the direction contrary to the bull's charge; in the *molinete*, the cloth winds round his rotating body, in the *afarolado* he raises his arms and it swirls up above his head. They are thus *muleta* versions of the *chicuelina** and the *farol* respectively. In addition to passes of *adorno*, the man may indulge in other pieces of business for emotional effect, once the bull is well dominated. These may be of the swashbuckling or the humorous type, including the touching or stroking of the bull's horn or even head; or perhaps a hat thrown into the ring by an enthusiastic spectator may play a part. *Desplantes* means acts of bravado or defiance, such as

* Its real origin is the *navarra*, the *chicuelina* being a quite recent invention.

86

kneeling down with one's back to the bull a yard away, and looking up at the audience as if to say "What about that, eh?" A little of this stuff goes a long way, but an occasional touch of the picturesque is very acceptable.

When the man has decided that the bull is ripe to be killed, he has one more task. He must get it standing in front of him with its feet squared; that is, each pair of feet side by side and close together. The forefeet are more important than the hindfeet, but it is best to square (*cuadrar* or *igualar*) all four. The reason is that if one forefoot is advanced, the opening between the shoulder-blades, through which the sword must enter, will close up; further, the bull that is 'squared' will be slower in starting to charge as the man comes in on it. Whether he wants it to charge at all, or to remain motionless, depends on the manner in which he proposes to execute the final and supreme *suerte*.

CHAPTER NINE

The Death of the Bull: Finale

I

The killing of the bull is well described in Spanish by two
expressions: *la suerte suprema*, the supreme hazard, and *la
hora de la verdad*, the hour of the truth. It is the supreme
action, because if you omit the kill (as they do in Portugal,
but only to butcher the bull profanely and ungallantly in a
private shambles outside), then all the rest of the *suertes*
become pointless, like those rather silly *objets d'art* which
serve no purpose: vases that will not hold flowers, miniature
pieces of inlaid furniture, and the like. They are only
intended to be stuck on a shelf or in a glass case and to look
pretty. But a true piece of art by a silversmith or a potter or a
cabinet-maker is a thing not only artistically made but also as
suitable as possible for its proper purpose. Such things are
not just pretty but truly beautiful—for instance, a Tibetan
teapot, a Persian carpet, or one of those superb saddles
turned out by Myres of Texas or Porter of Arizona. However, this is not a treatise on art in general but on that of bullfighting in particular; let us return to 'the hour of the truth'.

This name is also an excellent one, because it is the one
hazard in which any faking is instantly apparent. It is very
sad to see an apparently beautiful and brave *faena* 'crowned'
by a miserable performance with the sword. It is also sometimes a revelation to see what happens at the moment of the
truth. Most of us who go to bullfights are far from experts,

Larga cambiada to the new bull (L. M. Dominguin)

Running the new bull by one-handed *largas* (Boni)

Two *verónicas* by Andaluz: *above*, to 'fix' bull as picadors ride out; *below*, at the moment of *cargar la suerte*

and we may well have been mistaken. When we see the kill we may realise, from the way the man does it, that what we had taken for lack of good will or of courage in his *faena* was nothing of the kind, but that the bull was in fact much more difficult than we had supposed. Conversely, we may discover that the marvellous-looking *faena* must have been largely due to the extreme docility of the 'bull running on rails' that he had been lucky enough to draw. We can tell that clearly if, after a *faena* punctuated with shouts of *Olé!* and ovations, he shamelessly throws himself outwards, beyond horn range, when the hour of the truth arrives.

2

The Spanish for the sword is *la espada* (feminine), but there is also the expression *el espada* (masculine), meaning the swordsman. In this way one speaks of the senior matador as *primer espada*, first sword, the second as *segundo espada* and so on, the man being identified as it were with the implement typical of his craft. The implicit lesson in this is neglected by too many matadors, who seem to think that ability with the *muleta* is the be-all and end-all of their profession; if it were, then they would not be called *espadas* or Swords, a word evidently implying a sort of traditional caste, but *muleteros*, which also means muleteers.

A set of bullfighting swords consists of three or four ordinary ones for thrusting, plus the special *descabello* instrument which we shall come to later. The ordinary ones usually have two or three channels cut in the blade, to admit air into the wound and thus accelerate death. In a book which an authentic matador published in English in 1952, the price of a set of swords (a very special one, admittedly) is given as $1,500. I can only state that the normal price to matadors (who are automatically overcharged for everything) in a shop today, with prices much higher than then, is from 4,500 to 5,000 pesetas ($100 to $125), and if the matador cares to go to the swordsmith himself he can get them for 400 to 500 pesetas each. I have this on the authority of a Toledo swordsmith who is a friend of mine, and I mention this cheapness because it is unexpected, since these swords require a special temper, the reverse of that of a fencing foil. The foil must be very flexible but stiff enough for thrusting and parrying, and it has no cutting edge; the matador's sword, on the contrary, needs a cutting edge and is essentially a stiff sword, yet with enough spring not to break —or to break the man's wrist—if it strikes bone. Some of these swords, not many, are still made at Toledo, but the great majority come from Valencia nowadays. The blade is generally thirty-three or -four inches long; of this, the eleven inches at the point are ground to a fine edge on both sides, and this part, which is called *la muerte* (the death) is slightly curved so as to facilitate its entry at a downward angle. The hilt is of iron with a crosspiece and a small semicircular finger-guard, for only two or three fingers are inserted there to guide it; the blade is driven home with the heel of the hand, pressing on the pommel. The latter, formerly of iron too, is now made of rubber or cork to ease the jar if the sword strikes bone. Even so, injuries to the wrist are not infrequent.

3

In these days of dreary standardisation, many young toreros seek to manufacture a 'personality' for themselves by inventing stunt passes or freak *adornos*, which first thrill, then rapidly bore, the public. If the young matador would cultivate the sword, instead of these ephemeral mannerisms, he would have a solid basis for future fame. In the confusion at the end of the Civil War, it was consummate swordsmanship that brought Manolete instantly to the top, not the eccentricities he later permitted himself. And I can think of nothing that would galvanise the public so much as a real revival of the old-time method of killing by the 'receiving' method—the *estocada recibiendo*.*

This classic thrust was the normal way to kill bulls for a hundred years. It has grown rarer and rarer since the 'eighties: the great Guerrita practised it freely in the 'nineties, Bienvenida around 1910, and Joselito till his death in 1920, but hardly any others. It is still performed regularly and correctly, perhaps once in a hundred fights, not to mention attempts in which the sword does not go home. I myself have seen the hazard consummated about four times in ten years: by Mario Cabré fairly well in 1948, by L. M. Dominguín brilliantly in 1949, by Antonio Bienvenida also brilliantly in 1955, and a borderline case by Rafael Ortega in 1951. Of many other cases reported in newspapers, I cannot be certain, for many kills so reported are in fact not *recibiendo* but *aguantando*, which will be explained later.

The receiving method is not suitable for all bulls (hence the invention of the attacking method by Costillares in the eighteenth century), for the essential thing is that the bull shall still have enough gas for a good strong charge. There-fore the *muleta*-work must be abbreviated—itself no bad thing, for many *faenas* today are prolonged to the point of boredom: in bullfighting, as in everything else, we are living in the Reign of Quantity. For the receiving hazard, the bull need not be played to a standstill, but merely dominated enough to be sure it is following the cloth faithfully. Its head need not be held as low as for the ordinary method.

---

* After these lines were written, Antonio Bienvenida, formerly a weak killer, started using the *recibiendo* method regularly in the last months of 1955, and was bringing off the hazard about every other fight he appeared in, like his father forty-five years before. It was the one thing wanting to make him the supreme figure of the present generation.

Nor need the bull be standing with its feet exactly squared, for the essence of the hazard is that it charges the man. He stands a few yards away, edgewise on, left side to the bull, with sword raised to shoulder level. With his left, he holds out the cloth and waves it, and he may also stamp and withdraw his left foot, to provoke the charge. The bull comes at him, he performs the first tempo of the breast pass to steer the bull past his chest, and in the centre of the *suerte*, as its head goes down for the toss, he thrusts home the sword on top of the withers. The bull's own impetus will drive the blade home unless it strikes bone. For a moment, the man and bull form one mass; then the bull comes out and the group breaks up, with the man standing still, and the bull, if the thrust has been a sure one, carried forward a dozen yards by his momentum before falling dead on the sand. The gallantry and sculptural beauty of this hazard are indescribable when it is executed to perfection, and I can witness that for once the newspapers are not exaggerating when they describe the effect on the audience as one of sheer delirium.

One reason given for the decline of this method is its extra danger, since it is said that a wound received when performing it is more likely to be in the chest or belly than the usual place which is the thigh. However that may be, one thing certain is that it is far harder to do well than the ordinary thrust. The first reason is that the man is thrusting at a fast-moving target. The second is that the chances of striking bone are much greater, for even if the mathematically correct target is hit, the vital opening between the shoulder-blades may be momentarily closed; and the third is that the right horn cannot be made to deviate so much as in the ordinary thrust, so that the chances of the sword's going in *atravesada*, crosswise, are much greater. Even the great Montes, Pedro Romero's best disciple, who wrote a treatise on bullfighting, failed in this way more often than not.

4

In the ordinary mode of killing, the man runs in on the more or less stationary bull. Hitherto, apart from *banderillas*, the bull has always been attacking the man; now the man attacks and the bull defends itself. The sudden change-over is most dramatic; also it clearly increases the danger, for formerly he could deflect the charge with a wave of the cloth, or sidestep out of the way, but now he has to go right in on to the waiting horn. The bull sees him coming, and unless he cheats completely—a thing instantly obvious to the spectator —he is bound to deliver himself, for a moment, into the range of the horn. What puzzles the newcomer at first is how he gets his body past that horn, which, if you are sitting in the line of bull and man, you can see sticking out in his way. It is there at the start, and again at the finish, but in the middle it mysteriously seems to vanish.

The secret lies in what is called the *cruce* or cross-over. They say of a good swordsman that he "kills the bull with the left hand". What happens, in slow motion, is this. The man profiles to kill, left shoulder forwards. He sights along the sword at the spot on top of the bull's shoulders. His left hand holds the cloth low down, with its tip touching the sand, a little forward of him and to his right. The bull's gaze must be fixed on that cloth, or the man will probably go up in the air. Now he starts his short run in, and as he is approaching the horn, he swings his left arm out across his chest to his right. The bull sees the cloth move sideways and turns its head to its left to follow it. The right horn momentarily ceases to stick out, and in that moment the man's body, with belly drawn well in, passes, and he plunges in the sword. The essence of the whole thing is timing: two quite different movements, both difficult, must be exactly synchronised. That is why there are so few good killers.

5

Now, discounting the kill *recibiendo*, let us assume that the man intends to use the method just described; that is, the *volapié* method, invented by Costillares to deal with bulls that would no longer charge. The same word is commonly, but generally wrongly, used today for the standard kill. The true *volapié* is rare; all that the reporters mean is the attacking method.

When the man goes in on the bull, there are in fact four possibilities. First, the bull itself charges unexpectedly as he is just starting or about to start. He can then sidestep or give the bull a pass, and then line it up again: no disgrace in this. But also, if he feels equal to it, he can make a virtue of necessity, stand firm, and deliver the thrust as if *recibiendo*. This method is called *aguantando* and amounts to an unprepared version of *recibiendo*. It is not very uncommon and is very meritorious when done well, but as it is by definition never aimed at, no more need be said of it.

Second possibility: man and bull both start together and meet in the middle, both at full speed. This time, there is no getting out of it; the man must chance his arm. This kind of kill, even more than the last, is accidental, and is far the hardest to do right. It is called *a un tiempo* (sometimes *al encuentro*) and it takes a real master of the sword to emerge triumphant from this unsought encounter, for the man has to improvise like lightning in the middle of the hazard. No more need be said about this spectacular but chancy method, which again is never sought deliberately.

Third possibility: the man runs in, but before he has fully arrived the bull is also in forward motion. This is called *arrancando*, which means 'starting off'. This is how ninety-nine out of a hundred bulls are actually killed today. I will not deny that it is the elegant way. The man is quite

94

prepared for the bull to start, in fact he wants it, for a reporter will often excuse a matador's inefficient kill by saying that the bull "did nothing for him", that is, did not start off. Having got the bull's feet properly squared, the man enters as described, at an easy run, not too fast. He wants the bull to come forward at him just as the sword goes in, so that its own impetus will drive the blade home, while he makes a nice easy exit along the right flank. If all goes well the whole thing looks effortless. A whole thrust or a half can be given according to convenience. Nobody can offer the slightest criticism of a perfectly placed thrust given that way and after entering straight.

Yet there still remains the fourth possibility, that is, the pure *volapié*, done in the way that Costillares conceived it, but done far better. The old-timers did it against their will as a last resource; but the modern *volapié* is deliberately sought and executed with majesty and power. It is very difficult: it calls for great speed, great courage, a sure eye and a strong arm. But the effect is tremendous: nothing 'clever' or 'effortless' about it, no help from the bull or anything like that, and the audience has to watch closely to see it happen. But when it comes off, it stands a much greater chance of toppling the bull over dead on the spot, for the target is, by definition, stationary. Again, with a bull that carries its head too high (a perpetual difficulty with the Pablo Romeros, in addition to their great size and power), or one that is uncertain in following the cloth, it may be the only way, when nothing but sheer speed can get the man past the horn.

For the pure *volapié*, the bull must be lined up with quite exceptional care. Both pairs of feet must be perfectly squared: this is essential, because the object is to drive the sword home before the bull has moved at all. If it takes a step forward, once the man is launched into a genuine *volapié*, his chances of getting the sword in properly are very small. Next, the man must enter from very close: El Andaluz, the most classic exponent of the *volapié*, seldom entered from more than about six or seven feet from the bull's nose; Rafael Ortega, his successor, from about eight feet, and his failures are generally due to entering from too far away. Thirdly, he should advance the cloth carefully and slowly, and lay out the pointed tip of the flannel (the corner not rounded off) half-furled on the sand, as near the bull's left eye as he can reach. When the cross-over comes, it is going to be sharp and sudden, allowing him only a fraction of a second to get through. Then he raises the sword and takes very careful aim at the exact spot he intends to strike. All this preparation has a dramatic effect on the audience. It proclaims: "This is the real thing"; and you can almost see the spring being wound up, as it were. He rises on the balls of his feet like a sprinter about to take off; then suddenly he is in on the bull as hard as he can go, *volapié*, 'feet flying'. A sharp flip of the wrist, out goes the cloth, round goes the bull's head, in goes the sword-blade; but it takes about four seconds to say those words, whereas the action is all over in less than two. If the bull is cunning or uncertain, the man may leave a piece of his frilled shirt-front on the horn tip as he drives home the sword with all his power, but he is through and out. The impact is violent and thrilling, but the *volapié* is immensely sure. By sheer speed and timing, the man has kept the target stationary. The master of the *volapié* seldom needs a second thrust.

6

Even a perfectly delivered thrust is not necessarily mortal at once, whereas a defective one (too far forward or too low down) may at times kill almost instantaneously. A thrust that produces a vomit of blood is nearly always defective, through piercing a lung. If the man has given a satisfactory thrust but the bull still seems fairly lively, he should take a fresh sword and go in again; it will probably pay him in the end. However, that is up to him, for after one thrust he is legally entitled to use the *descabello*. This is a quick stab on the nape of the neck, which severs the spinal cord at the top vertebræ and kills instantaneously. A special shorter sword is used, having a solid 'dead' shaft, not sharpened, a cross-piece six inches from the point, and then the real blade; in other words it is really a dagger on a long handle. He must get the bull's head right down to ground level, which is done by dangling the *muleta* before it, with or without a cape or two fanned out on the sand by peones as well. Then he stabs down with the special sword, and if he gets it right the bull simply collapses. This job is harder than it looks, and if the bull lays back its head while stretching out its neck, it will close the vertebræ up and make the *descabello* almost impossible. There is also considerable danger if the stab does not connect, for the bull will surge forward and may easily catch the man.

If the bull goes down after the thrust, but is not dead, it passes out of the matador's jurisdiction, and is stabbed dead in similar fashion, but with a hand dagger (*puntilla*) by a ring servant called the *puntillero* who is dressed as a torero. If he misses and the bull gets up again, it returns into the matador's jurisdiction, to his natural disgust. It is no discredit to have to use the *descabello* (unless several jabs are required), or to have the *coup de grâce* administered by the *puntillero*; but naturally the thrust that kills the bull outright is the best, and is what provokes most enthusiasm. This, if moderate, is expressed in applause, amounting to an ovation if unanimous. If it is really strong, when a grand *faena* has been crowned by a good kill, the spectators wave handkerchiefs in an appeal to the President to allow the bull's ear to be cut off, as a trophy for the matador, before the mule-team drags out the carcass. This ear was once a token, denoting the gift of the whole bull to the matador to dispose of for his own profit; today it is merely a sign of triumph. When the work has been super-excellent, the appeal continues and a second ear may be cut if the President gives the signal. With the ear in his hand, the matador will then make a round of the ring, receiving a tribute of applause from each block in turn, and afterwards saluting from the *tercio* line or even the centre. If the petition is not granted, he will also generally make such a round, or even without any petition, if encouraged to do so by the public applause. If the applause is less, he will come out and bow in acknowledgement from the *tercio* line or from a *burladero*.

If the audience wants to show satisfaction with the bravery of the bull, it applauds during the drag-out; in exceptional cases, the bull itself is dragged slowly round the ring by the mules, and the breeder or his *mayoral* will acknowledge this tribute of posthumous honour to the brave animal from their herd.

CHAPTER TEN

Cavalier in the Bullring

Of the two ancient styles of horseback fighting, the lance act survives only vestigially, in the picador. But the other style, the *rejón* act, remains substantially the same as it was hundreds of years ago. It is more popular in Portugal, but is also quite common in Spain. It is interesting to see once in a way, but to watch a whole string of bulls fought in that way would be intolerably boring; accordingly a *rejón* act is today generally put on as a prelude to an ordinary *corrida* on foot.

The chief attraction is really the horses, which are of the finest Spanish breed, mostly of Arab origin, and their magnificent appearance and flashing speed is equalled by their intelligence and absolute trust in their riders. Their training is elaborate, for the act of riding straight at the bull runs counter to the horse's natural instinct to flee. So perfectly are they trained, and so great is their riders' skill, that they hardly ever get injured, even slightly—for of course these horses wear no protectors. Nevertheless, the risk is taken by the horse and not by the man (barring some extraordinary accident), and that, for me, robs the act of most of its interest; moreover, honesty compels me to add, the bull has really no chance at all after the first few minutes, whereas the man often changes horses three times. Furthermore, not only has a large dose of the circus been introduced by riders who make their horses waltz and cavort to the sound of the band, and perform *haute-école* evolutions which have nothing to do with bullfighting, but the horns of the bull are always heavily blunted, and outside Madrid they are generally sawn off square. A much more acceptable way of avoiding danger to the horses would be that used in Portugal, where the horns of the bull are previously sheathed in leather gaiters ending in round balls. Such *embolado* bulls used to be provided in the old days by the Madrid management for amateurs in the audience to torry, if they liked, after the main show was over (which is how the great Vicente Pastor first became known).

The *rejoneadores* who perform in this act are technically deemed amateurs and have 'Don' put before their name. Sometimes they really are amateurs; a recent successful *rejoneador* was the Duke of Pinohermoso, who used to give away his fees to charity. The greatest exponent of this kind of fighting today is Angel Peralta, who has raised it to a point of perfection which it would be hard to imagine being surpassed. An interesting feature of this work is that it is the only bullfighting in which women are allowed to appear in Spain. A few years ago, Señorita Conchita Cintrón, Peruvian by birth with a mother from the United States, was a champion performer equal to the best men; she retired on marriage to a Portuguese grandee.

Spanish-style *rejoneadores* of both sexes wear Andalusian country dress: waist-length jacket, trousers tucked into short boots, stiff broad-brimmed Cordova hat, and leather chaps. In the Portuguese style, the riders wear a knee-length coloured riding-coat, richly trimmed with braid or brocade and with frilled cuffs and lace *jabot* at the throat, top boots, and a three-cornered hat with plumes—the outfit of the old-time *cavalheiro.*

The weapon called the *rejón* is a stick five feet long, with a leaf-shaped steel blade six inches long by two inches wide. It is held by the top end. There are theoretically three Acts in this fighting too, but as the same action is repeated in all three, the division is not very sharp, and in fact the regulations are very slackly applied all round. The *rejoneador* does all the real work himself, but he is allowed to have two peones with capes, to run the bull at the start and to do a *quite* in case of emergency. The best riders use these capemen as little as possible. The good horseman, who is already in the ring when the bull comes out, will generally prance his horse about until the bull goes for it, and then will fling the horse into full gallop and give the bull the slip by sheer speed or a clever swerve. A little of this warms the bull up and 'runs' him much better than capework. All this time, the man is controlling his horse with his left hand and holding the *rejón* in his right. The *rejónes* in the first act are supposed to have a flat washer above the blade so that they cannot sink into the bull's body, the idea being to tire the bull and slow it down like the pic act in foot fighting.

After a while, as horseman and bull manœuvre for position, the man will see a favourable opportunity and will send the horse forward towards the bull on its off side. As the bull charges, the horse breaks into a swerving gallop past the horns, and the man leans out in the saddle and plants the *rejón* on top of the shoulders—the same place as the picador aims at. As the point goes in, the shaft, which is drilled through, snaps off and a little flag breaks out at the top end. If the *rejón* was well and vertically placed, the man gets a round of applause and rides across to the barrier for another. This process is repeated not more than three times (in theory), then the trumpet blows (again in theory), for Act II, and the man usually rides out and changes horses.

In Act II, a similar-looking weapon of Portuguese origin called a *farpa*, which is really only a long *banderilla*, may be used; but most Spanish fighters prefer to place *banderillas*.

These are the same as in foot fighting, but tied together and placed in, two at a time with one hand. As they are much shorter than the *rejón*, this act is more spectacular, since the man leans out much further in the saddle. The highwater-mark of good riding, practised today by Peralta and Landete, is when the man places *banderillas* like a *banderillero*, one in each hand, using nothing but his knees to guide the horse. After two or three pairs of *banderillas*, there is another change of Act and probably another change of horse.

In the final Act, *rejones* are again used, and the idea is to kill the bull with them, for which reason the regulation says that the washer is omitted from the socket so that the blade can sink in as the bull runs, and produce the same effect as a sword-thrust. In actual practice, I have seldom seen a washer in Act I, and the thing used in Act III has a blade about the same as that of a Roman legionary's sword. Angel Peralta often kills his bull outright with *rejones*, but not many others, for it demands exceptional accuracy plus a good deal of luck.

The time allowed for killing the bull in this way (again in theory, for the regulation is never enforced) is five minutes, after which a trumpet warning is supposed to be blown and the rider must retire (though not in any disgrace), and leave the bull to be formally put to death by a supernumerary matador attached to his team. However, many *rejoneadores* place only one or two *rejones* of the killing kind, and then if the bull has not fallen they dismount and kill it themselves with sword and *muleta* like an ordinary matador. This, however, is not officially part of the *rejón* fight, and what the *rejoneador*, quite unconsciously, is really doing is performing the job of his own hired servant. In the seventeenth century, it is recorded, a certain lady refused the homage of her knight—a *rejoneador*—because he had dismounted to kill his bull, thereby 'losing caste', and degrading himself from the rank of *caballero* or cavalier to that of a peón or footman.

But today the distinctions of caste are mostly lost, and all that remains is the *rejoneador's* right to have 'Don' prefixed to his name on the posters, and to be described, not as a mere torero, but as *Caballero en Plaza*—a Cavalier in the Bullring.

Brave bull charges from far. L. M. Domínguín, on right, stands by for *quite* if required.

Pablo Suarez 'Aldeano' gets the pic home on top centre (but the horse's position is bad).

A *quite* saves picador Atienza from a goring.

Mariposa by El Estudiante during his last triumphant campaign in South America

PART TWO

Then and Now

CHAPTER ELEVEN

The Homeric Age

1   Pedro Romero

In 1954 a bullfighting bi-centenary was commemorated at the little Andalusian town of Ronda. The chief event in the celebrations was naturally a bullfight, and the toreros appeared in Ronda's eighteenth-century ring wearing eighteenth-century dress, though fortunately for them and the audience the bulls were of twentieth-century type.

The bi-centenary was that of Pedro Romero, who was born at Ronda in 1754 and often fought in this ring. But it might as well have been called that of modern foot bull-fighting, for before him it was a very haphazard and crude affair.

Pedro Romero is the Homer of bullfighting: first in time and still unchallenged in supremacy. Grave, hieratic, with the air of a judge and the face of an aristocrat as Goya depicts him, he made it into a science and an art, and laid down the classical, imperishable norms of how to dominate a wild bull with a piece of cloth. No one has ever departed from those norms except to his own physical cost and to the detriment of the art; and after the aberration has run its course (as is occurring now), the art has always reverted into its classic channels—differing from age to age in points of detail, but always based on the principles of Pedro Romero.

He fought his first bulls in 1771 as apprentice to his father Juan, a matador of no great note, but himself the son of

Francisco Romero, the inventor of the *muleta* or red cloth on a stick, which Pedro made into the fundamental instrument for the domination and artistic killing of bulls. Pedro took the *alternativa* in 1776 and continued on the active list till 1799. Between 1771 and his retirement he dispatched over 200 bulls each season, mostly by the receiving method, which is today almost obsolete on account of its difficulty and danger. But he was also a master of the *volapié* or attacking method, then recently invented by the matador Costillares as a resource to deal with bulls which would no longer give the charge required for the receiving hazard.

He was no less famous with the cape, above all in his *quites* to fallen picadors or other fighters in danger. Several of these *quites* have been recorded by himself or by eye-witnesses, and are classic anecdotes of the bullring. Of them, and of his unerring thrusts, a ballad of the day said:

> *que en su capa está la vida,*
> *y en su espada está la muerte*
(for in his cape is life, and in his sword is death).

Writing about 1800, don Juan de Tixera, who had certainly seen Romero in the ring, calls him "a fighter of gigantic courage and power, both in his handling of sword and cape, and in the *quites* that he assiduously made to all the fighters on horseback or on foot, delivering them from the most decided and visible perils".

As for his *muleta*, we have another contemporary tribute in a letter published in a Madrid newspaper of 1795: "The rudder of this ship is the *muleta*, with which Romero is inimitable, now moving it horizontally at the speed of the bull's charge, now drawing it along as if sweeping the ground where the bull is to fall, or is to pass willy-nilly; that *muleta* which ever flees yet never departs from before the eyes of the bull" (in other words, *templar*), "which obeys it, at times, as a horse obeys the bit" (in other words, *mandar*). "On this *muleta*, Romero stakes his life; with it, we have twice this year seen his escape from the horns of the bull when it had him caught and pinned against the barrier."

That is how they spoke of him in the eighteenth century. And this is how he is spoken of today, by the greatest matador since Belmonte, Domingo Ortega. In his famous lecture before the Madrid Athenaeum, on 'The Art of Bullfighting', Ortega said:

"History is telling us: there are no forms but the classical ones given by Romero. . . . There is the Titan of bullfighting. Can you imagine it, to kill nearly 6,000 bulls and never have one of them lift you off your feet? We have discussed the complex reactions of the bulls of *today*; but just think of the bulls of those times, when there was little or no selective breeding" (Ortega is a bull-breeder himself). "Already in the bullfighting treatise of Montes (Romero's pupil) one sees very clearly the amount of viciousness and cunning the bulls of that period had. Many of their vices, of course, were acquired in the ring, owing to their age when fought, but others were due to the anarchic state of most ranches. And with those elderly, cunning bulls, Romero has left a record still unsurpassed, because he was a master of every single department of the art."

When the Royal School of Bullfighting was founded at Seville in 1830, Pedro Romero was living in poverty, thirty years after retirement. However, he wrote to the King and asked for the post of Director, saying that he was not yet too old, if occasion should arise, to dedicate a bull in the ring to Their Gracious Majesties. He was given the post, at the age of seventy-six; the school did not last very long, and he survived it. Later still, when in Madrid on private business, he was 'discovered' by the *aficionados* of the capital, only a few of the oldest of whom had ever seen him fight. For the ordinary spectator, he represented an *ancien régime* which had passed into history with the French Revolution and the Napoleonic Wars. The old man allowed himself to be persuaded into appearing in the ring for the last time, at the age of about eighty. Of his performance we read: "He killed the bulls that fell to his lot, and although without elements now, at so advanced an age, he was seen to perform this task in accordance with the same principles that he so much recommended."

Hale and hearty to the end, Pedro Romero died at the age of eighty-four, and when his body was laid out for burial, not the slightest scar was to be found upon it.

So much for the bare outline of his life. But mere dates and facts are of small moment compared with the rich feast provided by contemporary correspondence, including Romero's own which is distinctly salty at times, for he was a man of some education and wit, apart from his reputation for scrupulous honour, dignity and sobriety, which gained him friendships among all classes.

If anyone thought that Romero's appointment as Director of the Bullfighting School was just a sinecure for an old man unable to earn his bread, they were quite mistaken. A letter from a gentleman of Seville, who attended the opening of the school, states: "Three very brave steers were let out, and after don Pedro Romero had saved one of the pupils from a goring by a timely *quite*, the steer turned and went for the said Romero, who stood fast, with the cape in his right hand, and gave the steer three passes, and then sent it out and away from him; this was loudly applauded by all present."

Actually, in this brief report, we can see an illustration of Romero's three classic principles of *parar*, *templar* and *mandar*, meaning 'stand firm, swing smoothly at the right speed, and control the bull by *cargando la suerte*', which I have discussed in detail elsewhere. However, those three canons refer only to the execution of passes. Pedro Romero had other precepts as well, some technical and some psychological, and he caused eight maxims to be painted up in large letters on the wall of the school for all to see and learn by heart:

1 A coward is no man; and for bullfighting, men are required.

2 More tosses come from fear than from bulls.

3 A matador's honour lies in not fleeing from the bull, and in never running when in its presence, if he has the sword and *muleta* in his hands.

4 Once the swordsman has gone out to meet the bull, he should never jump the barrier, for that is in itself a disgrace.

5 Get in close, and calmly await the toss of the horns; the bull charges blindly*, and nothing can be done to avoid the horn-stroke.

6 The torero should rely on his hands, not his feet; and in the face of the bull he should kill or be killed, rather than shrink away or degrade himself.

7 Stand fast as if to let yourself be caught: that is the way to make the bull give in and lay himself wide open for the sword-thrust.

8 In the bullring, you can do more with a bushel of courage and a pint of intelligence than with a bushel of intelligence and a pint of courage.

Some of these maxims may seem a little like the 'glory or the oil-cloth' type of torrying. Yet there was the old man, who had proved himself right six thousand times without a scratch.

As an institution, the School was a failure, and most of the pupils forgot the instruction Pedro Romero had given there. I say 'most', for its greatest pupil was Francisco Montes, one of the greatest toreros of all time. Montes indeed adopted many of the romantic elegancies and baroque stunts frowned on by the classical Romero but practised brilliantly by his

* This does not mean that the bull shuts its eyes to charge, which is a fable.

rival Pepe-Illo. But Montes knew the rules which he allowed himself to break—sometimes to his physical cost—and in the treatise he wrote on the art, the first ever written personally by a champion torero, the principles of his immortal master are implicit on every page.

The rivalry between Pedro Romero the classical master, and Pepe-Illo the daring and flowery innovator, was the first of the great rivalries which have always marked high spots in bullfighting history (Chiclanero-Cúchares, Lagartijo-Frascuelo, Bombita-Machaquito, Joselito-Belmonte). Such rivalry need not prevent the two opponents from being good friends personally, as was the case with Joselito and Belmonte at the time of the First World War. The same was true of Romero and Pepe-Illo at the start, as the former relates in a letter about their first meeting, unfortunately too long to quote in full. It was at Cádiz where Pepe-Illo had a strong local following and Romero was unknown. Out of courtesy he ceded Pepe-Illo the first bull, and then:

"He went to the bull, gave it one pass with the *muleta*, and then took off his beaver hat, and using that instead of the *muleta*, he killed the bull with a single thrust. As he had many local supporters there, and I was unknown, I leave your Honour to imagine what a riot that raised in the plaza."

However, the hierophant from Ronda was quite capable of putting on a stunt himself when he thought fit, and in the next bull, with the audience agog to see what he would do,

"as soon as I'd got the bull's attention, but before it made a move, I threw the red cloth to one side, took off my hair-snood, threw that away too, and pulled out a little comb, a thing about two fingers wide, which was used to fasten the snood on, and I took three or four steps towards the bull. Seeing me so close, it charged, I got the sword home right on top, and sent the bull

Media verónica (A. Bienvenida)

Farol (P. Dominguín)

Gaonera (P. M. Vázquez)

Chicuelina (Andaluz, about to pivot to his right)

rolling over; I leave it to your Honour to imagine what a riot *that* raised in the plaza."

After that the President had them up and told them not to throw the *muleta* away again. "We finished the fight," says Romero, "both using the *muleta* to kill with, and he became a good friend of mine. The most he ever used to say behind my back (and people told me of it later) was: 'That man never knuckles under!' "

Next year (1779), however, Pepe-Illo's friendly feelings started to cool off, partly owing to a dispute as to who held the seniority, but no doubt chiefly after the Royal Festivities in Madrid to celebrate the birth of Prince Charles. Here the fights were held in the Plaza Mayor, or Main Square, which remains practically unchanged today. The trouble was that the two other chief swordsmen both objected to the Castilian bulls, the formidable old *toros de la tierra* of Old Colmenar, which were notoriously coarser, tougher and craftier than the more 'noble' bulls of Andalusia. These two swordsmen were Pepe-Illo and the celebrated Costillares (inventor of the *verónica* and the *volapié*, no less!). Even in those days, one observes, certain stars tried to put the veto on what they did not fancy tackling in the way of cattle. Here again we have Pedro Romero's own account:

"Señor Armona, the Corregidor of Madrid, sent for us to see who was to be senior swordsman, and the post fell to me. Then he said: 'Now, Señor Romero, as you are to be first sword, do you undertake to kill the bulls from Castile?' My answer: 'If they are bulls such as eat grass in fields, then I do, indeed; but Your Lordship will please tell me why I am asked that question.' He turned away and opened a desk and took out a paper, and said: 'This is why I ask.' It was a memorandum put in by don Joaquín Rodríguez 'Costillares' and don Joseph Delgado 'Pepe-Illo', and it was read out in the presence of us all. It requested that the bulls of Castile be banned, and hence the question I had been asked. If I had been in their shoes at that moment, I'd have fallen down dead on the spot.

"The time for the fight arrived, and I proceeded to kill all the Castilian bulls, as I had undertaken to do, except for one of them, which was let out for Pepe-Illo by mistake, though I reckon it was done on purpose by old Gallón who sorted the bulls into their pens. At the trumpet for the kill, the bull went over into the corner by the Royal Weights and Measures Office. Pepe-Illo made straight for the bull, and as I saw what a spot he was in, I said: 'Let be, comrade, we'll get him out of there.' He turned and stared at me without saying a word. At that, I stood back a little and let him go on. The result was that he was caught and got a bad wound. We picked him up and carried him up to the balcony of Her Grace the Duchess of Osuna. I was there about a quarter of an hour, and when I got back to the ring I found that the bull was still in the same spot. As soon as the other swordsmen saw me, they all started assembling their *muletas* to go and kill the bull. I said: 'Gentlemen! So after all this time no one has killed the bull, and now you *all* want to go and kill it! Please retire.' I got out the *muleta*, went straight to the bull, profiled at a fair distance and challenged, and at one of my challenges he charged, I took him in the receiving hazard, and killed him with a thrust."

One of Pedro Romero's most remarkable feats with the sword was when he found himself in the nasty though fortunately rare predicament of facing two bulls at once. In the early 1780's he was fighting his first bull of the day, and had given the *faena* of a few passes and his usual thrust *recibiendo*, which did not, however, kill outright. He then goes on: "The bull took some little time to die, and when it was getting dizzy, and I had my back to the bullpen, I heard a noise and a shout of 'Run! Run!' I turned my head and saw another bull coming at me" (apparently let out by mistake) "and instantly decided to receive it on the sword for a kill. The sword went home so well that it died quicker than the other bull behind me, and I remember that the mule-team hooked up both bulls and dragged them out together."

Pedro Romero's quiet, matter-of-fact style, like that of Julius Cæsar, just says what occurred, without explanation or comment. It all sounds quite easy. Only afterwards do we realise the difficulty and the skill involved. Those huge old bulls normally needed a dozen pic-thrusts to get their heads lowered; this one was completely fresh, and Romero was staking his life on his ability to make it follow the small red cloth perfectly the first time it ever saw such a thing.

In later years, if asked how he managed the feat, Romero would probably have pointed to the eight maxims on the wall of the School and indicated numbers 3, 6 and 7.

2   El Chiclanero, who had vergüenza

Of all the old-time toreros—I mean the real old-timers of the heroic days—the one I personally feel most affection for is El Chiclanero. He was the typical bullfighter of the age: uneducated, swaggering, boastful, generous, extravagant, a tremendous fellow for the dames and the firewater, loud, quarrelsome—but simple as a child, without a pinch of malice, brave as a lion and a model of professional honour.

He came from Chiclana in Andalusia, the home town of Francisco Montes, the greatest disciple of Pedro Romero and now first swordsman of Spain. Montes protected him and took him into his fighting team, where the lad learnt the bullfighting art from A to Z. That was the way in those days; over a period of four or five years he served his apprenticeship with cape, *banderillas*, *muleta* and sword in turn, until he knew as much as Montes himself. He became the best *banderillero* ever seen hitherto, his cape was excellent, he was better with the *muleta* than anyone except Montes himself, and when Montes conferred the matador's *alternativa* on him at the age of twenty-four, in 1842, he was a better killer than his master. At the receiving hazard he was outstanding, without the tendency to put in the sword *atravesada* or cross-wise which Montes suffered from; he was also a past master of the *volapié*, and at the emergency thrusts which were often needed for the old, tough and unreliable bulls then fought.

His actual name was José Redondo. *Redondo*, literally 'round', also means 'all-round' or 'complete', and he used to boast: "I'm *re'ondo*, like my surname." The word likewise means foursquare or honest, and blunt or plain-spoken, and he was all those, too. His public career was one long rivalry —the second of the classic rivalries in bullfighting history— with the celebrated Cúchares. Cúchares was also a supreme master of the art, though he could never quite get the better of Chiclanero; on the other hand, he was crafty and malicious and full of bitter hatred for his rival, despite his own superior physique. Cúchares knew all the tricks and fakes, and used to go in for every kind of baroque effect and eye-filling stunt; he never received a horn-wound in his life, whereas Chiclanero's professional honour sometimes compelled him to 'stand up and take it'.

This sense of honour—what the old Greeks called *aidôs* and bullfighters call *pundonor*** or *vergüenza*—has immortalised Chiclanero in the following story, which ought to be better known to some of the star matadors today. In 1846, Chiclanero was booked for a fight at Seville. He came up the river by boat from Chiclana, and went straight to the corrals at Tablada to see the animals he was to fight next day— another practice that has fallen into disuse now. After taking a good look at them, he drove to the café frequented by the fight promoters. He was received with open arms and shouts

* In this sense, the dictionary gives the two words as synonyms, but I should say that *pundonor* normally dictates what a man shall do, from 'honour', while *vergüenza* is what forbids him to do something, for 'shame'.

of delight, and drinks and cigars were pressed on him. Amid the general uproar and jubilation, he bluntly declared: "Gents, the fight tomorrow 's off."

"What d'you mean? Starting your jokes already?" asked one of the promoters.

"No, señor Berro," said Redondo; "I've just seen the cattle at *Tabla'a*, and I've come straight here to say I'm taking the first boat back to Chiclana. José Re'ondo ain't no apprentice mata'or."

"But, man alive, what are you talking about?"

"Just this: those bugs are only four years old, and the man to kill 'em ain't me, 'cause I got too much *vergüenza*." With that, he turned and marched out. There was no fight next day.

In those times, no animál which had not completed five years was reckoned a full-grown bull; four-year-olds were fought by *novilleros* or apprentices. Today, the official age at which an animal may be fought as a full 'bull' is four years completed, and in fact, until the clean-up at the beginning of 1953, many star matadors of 'bulls' were freely fighting three-year-olds outside the capital. A lot of water has flowed down the river to Chiclana since the days of José 'Re'ondo'.

The furious partisans of Cúchares in Seville, both *aficionados* and newspaper critics, started by belittling Chiclanero and belauding Cúchares on all occasions, but by half-way through the first season of the rivalry they had to yield to the evidence. Only one rabid Cúchares fan still held out, and continued to depreciate Redondo's capework, and even his work with the *banderillas* and sword. This man was a celebrated carpenter, who was known as 'The Patriarch of San Bernardo', this being the bullfighting quarter of Seville. Redondo, who was going from strength to strength with every fight, encouraged by his friends, told the Patriarch one afternoon, before the show began: "Today I'm going to give you a basinful of torrying, and I'm going to kill my bulls *a gorpe cantao.*" This expression, which is Andalusian dialect for *a golpe cantado*, roughly means 'nominating my strokes in advance', as if a golfer told his opponent: "I'll place my drive ten yards short of the bunker on the left, I'll chip up on to the green with a Number Six, and I'll sink the putt for a birdie three."

The first bull came out, and no sooner was it in the ring than Chiclanero shouted: "I'm going to kill this one with two passes and one thrust, *recibiendo.*" When his second came out, he declared to kill it with one thrust at the *volapié*. The third was *manso*, a cowardly bull, and he turned to the 'Patriarch' with dry, arrogant sarcasm and said: "Well, me lad, there ain't no material here, so I'm giving it no passes at all, and I'll kill it with a *golletazo* that'll make the blood fairly squirt out of its tail!" (The *golletazo*, it should be said, is a low thrust, generally messy, normally dishonourable though practically instantaneous, but legitimate in certain circumstances. Chiclanero, having declared to kill the first two bulls by the noblest and most difficult methods, was showing his contempt for the cowardly bull—and for the 'Patriarch'—in the third.) Sure enough, he did everything exactly as he had predicted, and he heard the most thunderous applause of his life, in which his former enemies joined heartily. When the final *golletazo* was delivered, the 'Patriarch' hauled down his flag, and shouted down to Redondo in the ring: "*Andá*, you're wiser than Solomon, and from now on I'll never hoot at you again, you popinjay!"

Chiclanero was a sure-fire killer, and knew it. He always approached the bull for the supreme hazard with a cheery grin on his face. If the sword-thrust went home, as it usually did, and the bull fell dead, he was delighted with himself and guffawed loudly with joy; but when it occasionally failed, he went all serious and crestfallen, and his opponents used to call out to him: "Not laughing now, are you?"

But the days of Chiclanero's glory were short. He was

little over thirty, but drink and the dames had undermined his constitution, and he caught the great 'occupational disease' of the old-time torero: consumption. For two years he burnt up what remained of his vitality like a torch, in the bitter struggle with Cúchares, who with his sound health and incredible cleverness could still not match Chiclanero with cape and sword. His good looks were gone now, but not his courage or professional pride. At last, in February 1852, he had to decline a booking in a royal *corrida* to celebrate the birth of the Princess Isabel (the famous 'La Chata' beloved of Madrid, who died only quite recently), because he was physically incapable of appearing. He suffered catarrhs in the winter which prostrated him completely. The time drew near to sign contracts for the Madrid season, and one of the Cúchares family brutally remarked: "There's a horn-wound that's got lost in Madrid, and we're going to see which of us can find it." Chiclanero staggered out of his bed, and that season he sent up his ultimate remaining energies in a colossal bonfire. He did such *quites* with the cape as never before, and dealt out such fulminating sword-thrusts that he seemed once more a youth in the first flush of health and vigour. The wily Cúchares tried every trick he knew to break Chiclanero, but the dying man beat him to it every time. Friends of the two rivals brought about a public reconciliation, but there was not much sincerity in it. Before going south to Chiclana at the end of the season, he once again signed up for the next year in Madrid, and in March he arrived back in the capital; but the very sight of him convinced the promoters that the long, long journey from the south had been in vain. Nevertheless, he was billed as First Swordsman.

On the day of the opening fight, Chiclanero, weak as a newborn kitten, lay in bed. When he heard the noise of the carriages in the street, and the toreros being cheered by the crowds on their way to the *plaza*, he staggered to his balcony, raging in impotence and praying to God for just the strength to put on his fighting clothes and go out to the *plaza* for one last round of applause. But time passed and passed, and he could not make it. He was to have been senior swordsman; by now, the first bull, *his* bull, would be coming out into the ring. . . . He let his head fall back on the cushion. A friend helped him back into bed, where he lay face downwards. Half an hour later, one of his capemen called him to give him a cup of broth. There was no reply. The man bent over him, saw the waxy face and the stain of blood on the pillow, and knew that José Redondo, El Chiclanero, had finished his mortal *faena*.

CHAPTER TWELVE

In the Days of our Fathers

1   *The Case of don Luis Mazzantini*

The career of don Luis Mazzantini is in the strictest sense unique. He stands alone; he had no predecessor, and he can have no successor; his world no longer exists.

In character and appearance he was anything but a Spanish bullfighter. His father was an Italian railway engineer and his mother a Basque. He came into the world at Elgóibar, the ironworking town in Guipúzcoa, in 1856, but spent his childhood in Italy, whence he returned at the age of fourteen as a page in the suite of Amadeo of Savoy, when that prince accepted the offer of the Spanish throne. After finishing his education, Mazzantini became a railway telegraphist, and was promoted to stationmaster at a small Toledo town. But this life would not do for him. He had big ideas. He spoke three languages fluently, and aspired to burst into Spanish high society. As he himself observed: "In this prosaic land of chickpea-eaters, there are only two things a man can be: a tenor at the Royal Opera House, or a matador of bulls." He tried the opera-singing line, but failed; and so, without having any special enthusiasm for bulls, he set about becoming a bullfighter, with all the tirelessness of the Italian and the immense will-power of the Basque. He was already twenty-three, which is far too old to start on such a profession.

He began by knocking around the village cape-fights. His

chief on the railway repeatedly reprimanded him and eventually fired him. Then he got a couple of bookings in *mojigangas*: this form of show, now extinct, was a sort of mixture of pantomime and comic bullfight. He was an already mature man, with a tendency to put on weight. People called him *El señorito loco*, the crazy young gentleman. At first he did pretty badly, for he knew next to nothing of the art of torrying—indeed to the end of his life he was never more than competent with the cape and the red cloth and was very moderate with the *banderillas*, though in his later years his ringcraft and *lidia* were masterly. But what he did learn in those obscure early fights was the great secret of the successful matador—matador in its literal sense of 'killer'. He discovered the knack of the *cruce*, the compound cross-over movement of the left arm holding the cloth and the right arm holding the sword, so that the right arm strikes at the mathematical moment when the left arm with the cloth diverts the bull's head. If this is perfectly executed—as it rarely is—the matador can go in dead straight to a bull with the widest horns and drive the sword home as unerringly as if there were no right horn at all. But it needs the 'eye' of a Babe Ruth. This extraordinary eye, in fact, was what Luis Mazzantini had inherited from his Basque mother. The Basques have turned out few good toreros, and those have been noted more as killers than anything else. Notable cases were Castor Jauriguebeitia Ibarra ('Cocherito de Bilbao') and Diego Mazquiarán Torróntegui ('Fortuna'); if you see a man on the programme with a weird and apparently unpronounceable name, you have a fair guarantee that whatever his work is like with the cloth lures, he is not likely to fail at the hour of the truth.

So, the *señorito loco* burst upon Madrid, Seville and Barcelona as something quite new and extraordinary. He was tall, corpulent, distinguished-looking, no longer a boy. His work with the cape and *muleta* was fairly ordinary, though always brave, and superbly opportune at the *quites* to rescue a fallen companion; but when it came to the sword, ah, that was the thing! In those days of the 'eighties and 'nineties, the sword-thrust was esteemed above all other hazards put together, and the greatest killer of the century hitherto, Frascuelo, was at the decline of his long career. He was succeeded by Guerrita, probably the best killer ever, since Pedro Romero. This was the comparison that young Mazzantini had to face. He himself, in later days, said: "Nobody has ever killed as well as Frascuelo." But Guerrita, who was even better than Frascuelo, and who could dominate any bull, whereas Mazzantini never really learnt to dominate them at all, said of him: "Mazzantini is the best killer of bulls that has ever existed, for two reasons: first, because no one has killed as he does, and secondly, because he kills them *green*, whereas *I* kill them *ripe*."

Once the public of the great cities had seen the new phenomenon, there was no holding him. People put up with his rather clumsy work in the first two Acts. The real Mazzantini came when he took out the sword. The tall, rather heavy man went in to kill from what looked an excessive distance, executed his marvellous piece of geo-metrical timing, and the biggest bulls rolled over dead as if struck by lightning. His fame rose like oil stock after the strike of a gusher. Before long all the Madrid shops were selling 'Mazzantini handkerchiefs', 'Mazzantini walking-sticks', 'Mazzantini cigar-holders'. He wore a frock-coat and top hat by day and full evening dress by night, and was received into aristocratic mansions as an honoured guest, a thing unheard-of for any bullfighter before. His con-versation—in rather florid style, typical of a nineteenth-century Italian diplomat or *littérateur*—was highly esteemed. Everyone called him 'Don Luis', a title never accorded to a bullfighter on the active list before or since. He became rich, but he lived extravagantly, for he was a connoisseur of good pictures and books. In a few words, his career lasted no less than twenty-five years, and his fame in Spain was equalled by his fame in Mexico, Cuba, Uruguay and other parts of Spanish America.

Needless to say, there are hundreds of stories about him. Some deal with the ring, in which he had a stainless reputation for honour. On one occasion, the ranch of Martínez (the famous red Jijona bulls of Old Colmenar near Madrid, then crossed with the Vázquez caste) sent a string to Madrid for a fight in which Mazzantini was engaged to appear. Frascuelo had also been booked but was injured and unable to appear. One of the bulls was seven years old and had horns as big as an elk. Mazzantini, contrary to custom, turned up at the *plaza* to see the bulls on the morning before the fight, and chatted to the cattle-steward while he looked the animals over. The steward guessed what was coming when he asked the obligatory question: "What do you think of them?"

"Well, I don't know what to say. . . . Five of the six are fine-looking and nothing out of the way in size or horn—just the type of bulls that are being fought in all the rings. But I can't understand why you've sent along that huge, elderly, ugly creature with horns so long and wide apart that if you put a canary on the tip of each horn they couldn't hear each other singing. That mastodon should have stayed behind at Colmenar, to be put with two or three other 'cathedrals' and fought in some village show."

"Well," said the steward, "that bull has always been the odd man out, because he clashes with all the rest. He had to go *somewhere*, because we didn't feel like eating him."

"I should think not. That 'birdie' would give anyone indigestion. But I maintain that he shouldn't have come in this string, because he makes the others look small and spoils the ensemble. A breeder's reputation for care depends on how evenly he presents his strings of bulls."

"Agreed; but sometimes there's a reason which isn't obvious."

"Would you tell me what it is?"

"Certainly. Frascuelo was booked for this fight, and as he is a friend of ours, don Vicente Martínez ordered this bull to be sent, precisely for Frascuelo to kill. But there you are, 'Man proposes and God disposes' . . . Frascuelo is injured . . . and now I'll have to carry the can back. I don't know what we'll have to do with that old chap."

Mazzantini looked searchingly at the old steward, and realised he was telling the truth, for he knew him, and he knew Frascuelo too. After a while he asked: "Who's deputising for Frascuelo tomorrow?"

"Well . . . er, I'm told *you* are."

"In that case there's no more to be said. That bull is for me, and I will not for anything allow it to be allotted to another torero. Is that clear?"

"Thank you very much, don Luis, in my own name and that of my master."

The cattle-steward was hoping, naturally, that the monster would at least prove brave and give Mazzantini a success. But it turned out a real bad hat, and don Luis had to sweat the big drop to put paid to it. However, the news of the interview had got around, and the audience applauded his gesture of *pundonor*.

His wit and mastery of rhetoric were celebrated, but occasionally he came off second best. One day an old picador called on him in the morning to ask for a job. Mazzantini, emerging from his bath, received him in a snow-white dressing-gown edged with red silk ribbon, and was greatly offended because the man smelt violently of cheap liquor. "Angel," he said, "you've been drinking."

"*Sí, señó*," said Ángel; "I shoved in a couple of jolts on the way here."

Mazzantini gave him a dressing down. Who had ever seen

a morning call paid by a person in such a state? The picador waited till he had finished, and then said tartly: "Listen, don Luí, maybe you ain't never seen this what I done; but *I* ain't never in my life seen a mata'or of bulls wrapped up in a piano-cover."

By 1904, Mazzantini was forty-eight. A big, fat, slow, heavy man now, he was obviously in decline, yet he still sometimes pulled off the fulminating sword-thrusts which sent the big bulls rolling over like ninepins. He took his wife over to Mexico with him, and proved that he was not quite finished yet. Indeed, he was so successful that an invitation came from Guatemala, and he crossed the border and fought there too. But while he was away from Mexico City his wife died suddenly. He dropped everything and returned post-haste to Mexico. And there, standing in tears over his wife's dead body, he took a pair of scissors, cut off his pigtail—the caste-mark of the torero, which he had always worn despite his top hats and frock-coats—and tied it round her wrist to take with her to the grave. It was a theatrical gesture, yet not insincere, and not unworthy of the man. Thus Mazzantini retired from the ring.

After his retirement, he had a successful career in politics and administration. He was a notable member of the Madrid Provincial Council, and was highly respected as Civil Governor of Avila and Guadalajara, and shortly before his death in 1926 he had been chief commissioner of police in Valencia and Barcelona.

As is well known, King Alfonso XIII married an English princess. She had heard of this remarkable man, and on seeing him one day at an official opening, she asked a Minister to present him to her, adding that he would have to interpret, because her Spanish was not yet good enough for a conversation. The Minister assured her that this would not be necessary, since don Luis spoke perfect French. This increased her curiosity. After chatting with him for a while, she asked him how many bulls he had killed in his long career. He said he could not be quite sure without referring to his papers, but roughly 3,500. "And which life have you found more difficult," she asked in conclusion; "bull-fighting or politics?"

"Madam," replied don Luis, "I find it harder to get along with my forty-nine fellow-councillors than it was to torry and kill those 3,500 bulls."

This was true, at least to some extent. Mazzantini's ardent monarchism and florid but telling oratory often involved him in political disputes. On one occasion a fellow-councillor insulted him so gravely, in his view, that he publicly challenged him to a duel. The other man, however, refused to fight. When his friends asked him why he avoided an affair of honour, he excused himself thus: "No, I'm not going to fight Mazzantini. You see, if I win, people will say that Mazzantini has received his last *cornada*; and if I lose, they'll say that Mazzantini has delivered his last sword-thrust. But whichever it is, *I* play the part of the *bull*, and I'm not wearing horns just to please don Luis." This piece of very Spanish wit so delighted Mazzantini that the two men shook hands and were publicly reconciled.

He was not always ostentatious. Once, during the un-happy war with the United States in 1898, Mazzantini's train drew into a station where there was another train full of repatriated sick and wounded men from Cuba. He went to the station buffet, changed a big bank-note for all the silver they had in the till, and ordered that a ration of food, a drink of wine and a silver coin should be given to every soldier on the train. Someone recognised him and called out *"Viva Mazzantini!"* but he just said: "No, son, you're mistaken. I look a bit like him, that's all."

2   *The First Ear ever cut in Madrid*

When a matador has done very well, he is rewarded with the ear of the dead bull as a trophy. This is said to be a vestige of the ancient custom of giving him the whole carcass to dispose of for his own benefit.

Now the symbolic ear, as a token of triumph, is all very well. Applause for sound work; an ovation for good; a round of the ring for brilliant; and the supreme reward of the ear for superlative. That is how things were at the beginning of the century. One ear, and one only, was granted in provincial rings for a performance that was regarded as sheer perfection. But in Seville the ear was hardly ever awarded; and in Madrid, never. Such dissections were thought unworthy of the world's chief *plaza*.

But today we are living in what has been called the Reign of Quantity. "When everybody's somebody, then nobody's anybody," to quote the words of Gilbert. Today, nearly every Englishman is officially addressed as 'Esquire' and nearly every Spaniard as 'Don', though these used to be titles of rank. If a king were to award knighthoods for the most trifling services, lords would rapidly become chicken-feed and very soon nothing short of a Duke would mean anything. That is what has happened with ears in most bull-rings. They started giving the ear for less and less; then they had to give the two ears to mean 'really good'. Finally, they started cutting off the tail as well, and even sometimes the foot. In smaller provincial rings today, the ears mean 'competent', the tail 'very good', and the foot signifies what one ear used to be given for.

In Seville and Madrid, things are not as bad as that, but Seville has been known to award the tail, which automatically robs the first ear of any meaning; and even Madrid often grants two ears, though the bulls may be a year younger, and may weigh 200 lb. less, than in the pre-ear days. Of course, all this of ears and other trophies is a matter of public taste; what matters is the actual fighting. But a little explanation had to be given, before coming to the story of the first ear ever cut in a serious fight in Madrid.

It was granted in October 1909, but the recollection is still fresh in the memory of a number of older *aficionados* who were present, and the great torero who won it is still very much alive; he celebrated his seventy-sixth birthday in 1955, and still walks very straight and sees perfectly without glasses; he acted as technical assessor to the President in the same year, at the best bullfight I have ever seen, and his intervention was lynx-eyed and unerring. His name is Vicente Pastor, and no braver, more upright and more honourable man ever walked. A Madrilenian born and bred, he had the dry, dominating, Castilian style in the ring, and he was one of the great swordsmen of this century.

Now, I cannot pretend to have seen that epoch-making event of the first ear. But I recently listened to an account by an old-timer who did, and this is how he described it:

Look at this ancient yellow photograph (he began). It's the old Madrid *plaza*. You can't see the audience, only what looks like a snowstorm. Those 'snowflakes' are eleven thousand handkerchiefs waving in wild enthusiasm. I know you see the same every day now, whenever some lad does a few pretty passes to a three-year-old calf. But the old Madrid *plaza* was a very serious place. They just applauded, they didn't go *loco* like this—until that day in October 1909.

The bull was something formidable even for those days. It weighed a good thirty *arrobas* (nearly 1,300 lb. on the hoof) against your modern minimum of 1,030 lb. Its horns were enormous and it was just on six years old. Such bulls—'cathedrals', we used to call them—needed all the softening-up the picadors could give them. But as soon as this one came out, it put its head between its forelegs and started scraping and pawing.

No one could get it to charge the horses. It seemed a copper-bottomed bad 'un, old, crafty and as strong as a rhinoceros. It wouldn't take the pics at all.

The President showed the red handkerchief and the peones tried to put in the firework *banderillas*. I tell you, they sweated ink. The bull wouldn't give a charge, it just stood and waited to catch them on the horn. After a dozen false runs and hair-breadth escapes, they managed to plant two *banderillas* each, and I say 'two', not 'a pair', because those *banderillas* were planted in the same way as they are made—one at a time. When the trumpet blew again, the bull was *encampanado*: lord and master of the ring, standing defiant, out in the middle, with his 600 kg. of power completely intact, and a mean look in his eye.

That is the sort of situation where the world's best matadors have seen the fifteen minutes slip by, the three trumpet-warnings blown, and their bull led off alive to the corral.

Now, you know that nobody ever starts a *faena* out in the centre, where the bull 'weighs' heaviest and charges least. Vicente Pastor had told his capemen to bring it over near the barrier. But they just couldn't budge it; it refused to follow their capes. After a while they stopped trying, and it was useless to persist in ordering the impossible.

Then a dead hush fell on the audience. Slowly, step by step, with set face, Pastor advanced towards the centre alone. The bull stood scraping and eyeing him murderously. He got nearer and nearer. Still no sign of a charge. He halted two yards from it and unfurled the red cloth in his left hand. The bull made as if to charge—and then returned to its scraping. Pastor took one step nearer. He was one yard from the horns. Our hearts were in our mouths. Up went the bull's tail and it hurled itself on him, wildly, uncontrolledly. He stood fast, and emptied out that avalanche of destruction in a long, sweeping *natural* pass. The bull turned in fury and came back at him again. This time he gave it a tremendous 'punishment pass', the two-hander low down, in and out like a piston, which arc'd the bull's long body like a bent bow. You could almost hear the bones creak, so violent was the twist on the spinal vertebræ. And another, and another, and another, with all his power, almost touching the bull's ribs with his own. Pastor with a yard of cloth had to break it down, he had to do all the work that the picador's lances should have done. The suspense was fearful—the battle for life or death between the two figures alone in the wide ring. There was dead silence except for the flap of the cloth and the thud of the bull's hoofs on the sand. And now the monster surrendered, and was following the cloth smoothly and bravely as the master's left hand guided it. Pastor had known how to extract the latent bravery in that bull, by the sheer courage of his heart and the strength of his wrist and his will.

Amid the cheers of the crowd, the bull came out of a pass with its feet squared. Pastor didn't waste an instant: he raised the sword, sighted, and went in like an arrow, with his characteristic little jump over the horn tip, to bury the blade up to the hilt on top of the enormous shoulders. The bull whipped round and surged at him one last time, but as the head went down to toss, its knees collapsed. It knelt before him, as if in homage, for two seconds, then rolled over, feet upwards, dead.

There was a moment of stupefied silence in the *plaza*; then a storm of cheers and eleven thousand handkerchiefs waving, as you see there in the picture. The President, forgetting his top-hatted dignity, was standing and cheering too. Maybe without realising what he was doing, he too pulled out his handkerchief and waved it like all the rest. And that was the sign—perhaps intentional, perhaps not—for the first ear to be cut in the bullring of Madrid, for Vicente Pastor, the lion-hearted torero with the honour of a paladin and the simple, lovable nature of a child, who was seventy-six the other day.

3   *The Great Rivalry*

If you mention bullfighting to someone who knows little or nothing about it, he will probably tell you that all he knows is the name of one man—Belmonte. Belmonte, without a doubt, is the most world-famous of all bullfighters, which does not necessarily mean the best. But before his day, bullfighting was a closed book to anyone but Spaniards, Portuguese and Latin-Americans; since Belmonte, nearly everyone at least knows that one name. It is an easy name to pronounce and remember, and it has a sort of epic ring about it. It is one of those names, like Steve Donoghue, Babe Ruth or Pavlova, which have come to be synonyms for the performers' actual professions.

For an account of his career, I can cordially recommend the book *Belmonte, Killer of Bulls*, by Chaves Nogales, who wrote down all that Belmonte told him in dozens of conversations, and edited the lot into an autobiography. The English version* also has a useful introduction on bullfighting (as it was, twenty years ago) by the translator, who is no less than Leslie Charteris. I read the book myself before I had ever seen a fight; I found it most exciting and perfectly understandable, and it helped me considerably when I saw my first fights later.

Belmonte was born at Seville in 1892. His father owned a small ironmongery business, which did all right for a while. The boy went to school from the age of six to twelve; all the rest of his education he got for himself, for he always loved reading. The business declined and he was sent to his uncle's at Huelva, but he soon returned, and this was when he started his midnight escapades. He and a group of daredevil lads used to sneak on to the fighting-bull ranches by night, cut out an animal, and play it with a cape, by moonlight or with an acetylene lamp. Chaves Nogales speaks as if these animals were always bulls, but Belmonte himself now says they were cows. That makes no difference as regards danger, and the difficulty is even greater because the cow is wirier and turns quicker; but it is much to Belmonte's credit if correct, because fighting bulls are very expensive, and if

* Published by Heinemann, 1937. Not to be confused with *Belmonte the Matador* by Baerlein (Butterworth, 1934), in which Belmonte, like a true Sevilian, has told Mr. Baerlein some very tall stories indeed.

once torried they are useless for the ring, but in the case of cows it does not matter. At all events the lads had plenty of adventures dodging the rangers, and that was how Belmonte learnt to torry, the hard way.

He also knocked around in village fights, against elderly and defective animals which 'knew Latin'. He got plenty of tosses, and often enough no pay. In one or two better-class fights, he did brilliantly; but then he had a disaster at Seville itself, with both his bulls returned alive to the corral because he failed to kill them. Things looked desperate then. Life was irregular, food was very scarce, and only the blind faith of the old *banderillero* Calderón, and the occasional backing of one or two impresarios, pulled him through. It is a fascinating story to read.

The result of all this was the appearance of what I would describe as 'the first Belmonte' in about 1912. How the first Belmonte changed into the second Belmonte—the world master—we shall see in a moment. But what burst upon an astonished public about the time of the First World War was this: a thin young man with a haggard face and a suggestion of tragedy; physique, feeble; slow and clumsy on his feet; a poor killer; repertoire of passes, very limited; grace and arrogance of bearing, non-existent. People's hearts melted with compassion to see him. It looked sheer suicide. And the opponent he was put up to rival was Joselito—Joselito, perhaps the greatest master of all time, gay, gallant, agile, with superb faculties, who dominated every bull and could perform every pass and other *suerte* to perfection, who seemed a sort of invulnerable Achilles. Yet the rivalry between the two produced what is called the Golden Age of modern bull-fighting.

The first Belmonte, he of the 1914–18 period, 'had no legs'. His rival, Joselito, was essentially what the Spaniards call a torero 'with plenty of legs'. The meaning of these rather odd expressions is this: In fighting a bull in the correct or classical manner, strong and agile legs are a necessity. Not, of course, to run away from the bull with, though in placing *banderillas* (a thing Belmonte never attempted) and at certain other moments, it is most legitimate and desirable to be able to move quickly; but what is really meant is the footwork that is all-important, as in tennis or boxing. Joselito's faculties and reflexes were prodigious, he was never caught on the wrong foot, he could improvise like lightning in the middle of a pass, and, like most gipsies, he was as graceful as a cat. And his health was perfect. Belmonte was always torpid on his legs; he could not run at all, and he was always on the point of physical collapse. But he did have two things: first, unbounded courage and will-power; secondly, enormously long arms.

For him to compete with Joselito according to the sound classical rules was out of the question. What he attempted was to do the whole thing in quite a different way. His style of bullfighting was completely revolutionary, and the revolution he started has barely spent itself yet. As he had no legs, he torried with his arms. Here, he could do things (when the right bull came out) that were beyond even Joselito. His *verónica* and his left-hand *natural* pass with the *muleta* were long-drawn-out symphonies that went on and on, and sent the spectators crazy. If anything went wrong, well, it was just too bad. He had no faculties for an elegant adjustment or a swift change of position. He could not even run for the barrier, and if he had got there he could not have jumped it. He just had to stand and take what was coming.

The appeal of Joselito—incomparably the better torero at that time—was to the intelligence and the æsthetic sense: his work was a marvel of science, ringcraft, and effortless art and grace. But the appeal of Belmonte was to the raw emotions. The danger inherent in the bullfight ceased to lurk in the background: it came out openly, instant and agonising. The gaudy-coloured puppet that couldn't run stepped forward into the forbidden territory which by all the rules belongs to the bull; and every time those long arms swept the bull grazing past, you could see death staring him in the face.

The retired master, Guerrita, said of Belmonte: "Anyone that wants to see him had better hurry up." Belmonte's friend, the then romantic novelist Valle-Inclán, used to tell him: "All you need now is to die in the ring." Another writer, while placing him above Joselito, says: "Joselito is a fighter who takes the risks all right, but if he is booked for ninety fights a year, he fights all ninety. Belmonte, either through the perilous nature of his superb art, or from sheer fatality, fulfils less than half his bookings."

'Sheer fatality' is of course nonsense. If you break all the rules, as Belmonte did because it was the only way for him, then you take the consequences. Pedro Romero, who created—or rather, discovered—the rules, killed 5,600 bulls and never got a scratch. Joselito, who kept the rules, got four serious wounds in his life, and the fifth one killed him. Belmonte broke the rules, all the time; how many wounds he has had, he probably could not even tell you himself. He was tossed regularly at least twice every afternoon, and even after two or three years as a full matador he was missing about thirty bookings a season through being in hospital. Yet an amazing fortune watched over him, and a guardian angel always intervened between him and sheer destruction. The public passion he aroused was incredible; and though he often failed badly if the bulls were difficult, he had a sort of mysterious aura about him, as the man who couldn't live yet never died. But this could not go on for ever: flesh and blood would not stand it. And gradually, the queerest 'trans-fusion' or 'osmosis' started to take place: a little of Belmonte began to communicate itself to Joselito, and a lot of Joselito to Belmonte.

Joselito himself said that he was taking something from his rival, whose sheer lawlessness and defiance of all the canons forced Joselito to fight nearer and nearer to the bulls. Belmonte was the whetstone that put the final edge on Joselito's tempered steel.

But Belmonte too was changing. At first, all he sought were those spectacular effects of tragic emotion: the semi-cripple defying death, a sort of magnificent anarchism. As for the *lidia*, the general ringcraft, he admits he knew nothing of it and cared less. But as from about 1917, after hundreds of tosses and many wounds, his first ardour began to wane. He no longer went out each afternoon resolved on either triumph or the operating-table. He began to pick up the secrets of defensive fighting. He no longer needed a very special bull in order to do well. He began to kill respectably, and to fight in a way that called for less of the footwork that he was unable to do; in short, he started to dominate the bulls. By 1919 the bulls were hardly catching him at all, and he appeared that year in the record number of 109 fights. He himself says: "I had gradually been acquiring a professional skill and a sureness of which I should never have believed myself capable a few years ago."

Then came the tragedy of 16th May, 1920, at Talavera. Joselito, the invulnerable Achilles, was killed by a freak bull. It was small and scraggy (for those days), with poor horns, and it would have been rejected for insignificance in a first-class ring such as Madrid (Talavera is third-class). But it was five years old, *bronco*, powerful, very fast, and deadly accurate with its horns (it killed three horses with as many strokes)—and it was long-sighted. Close up, it could not see the red cloth. Joselito, thinking he had it momentarily dominated, withdrew a little distance from it to let it get its breath, and proceeded to arrange his *muleta*, but in retiring he had come into the bull's range of vision again, and it charged like lightning. Joselito gave it an ordinary pass to deflect its charge, but the bull ignored the cloth which it could not see, tossed him in the air, and killed him with the second stroke as he fell. To be sure, Joselito was well aware of the bull's special danger, for he had ordered his brother Fernando (acting as extra peón) out of the ring as being devoid of faculties. Why he allowed himself to be caught by a danger he had already foreseen is one of the unexplained mysteries of bullfighting, like the thoroughly comparable lapse, or oblivion of the most elementary principles of ring-craft by a veteran fighter, which caused the death of Manolete in 1947.

The public had found it hard to believe that Belmonte could live, but they found it harder to believe that Joselito could die. The whole of Spain was shaken to the core. Belmonte, who was Joselito's personal friend as well as his rival, locked himself in his room and refused to see anyone. Two days later, he had to go out and fight without Joselito in the Madrid ring where they had appeared side by side the week before. The toreros paraded with bare heads, and with black armbands. And while the train bore Joselito's body southwards to Seville, Belmonte in Madrid scored one of the greatest triumphs of his life. The responsibility of the *fiesta* was all his now.

From then on, it was as if the spirit of the vanished master had been added to that of his former opponent. The survivor was not just Belmonte, the brave man with the short repertoire; he was Belmonte *plus* Joselito, the short and the long, the classical and the romantic: the total torero. The great rivalry was over: the two streams of art had mingled into one.

CHAPTER THIRTEEN

With the Long Pole

1 *The Grand Old Man of the Mounties*

There are many picturesque slang terms for the picadors in Spanish. They range from simple expressions such as *Los varilargueros* ('the long-pole men') or *Los del castoreño* ('the beaver-hatted ones') to the quaint and vivid *Los de aúpa* ('the oopsadaisy boys', from the frequency with which the picador in the ring needs a helping hand to remount; *aúpa* is the nursery word that children use when they want to be lifted up). But I think the one that appeals to me most is *Las plazas montadas*, the mounted troops, or the cavalry, among whom the bull is said to cause *bajas*, which means at the same time 'descents' and 'casualties'. With the modern outsize horse-protector, indeed, these 'descents' are far less frequent than they were, and some unkind reporters have gone so far as to replace the expression *Las plazas montadas* by *La división acorazada*, or the armoured division, in view of the unfair way this horse-protector is exploited by certain picadors.

Such criticism, however, is never applied to the man whom I would call the Grand Old Man of the *plazas montadas*, namely Emilio Ramón, nicknamed El Boltañés, from the little town of Boltaña where he was born, in the foothills of the Pyrenees. I have included him in this gallery of old-timers because he in fact is one, though he is still pic'ing bulls fairly and squarely at near seventy years of age and is one of the two or three best picadors in the Spanish ring.

You will never see him screw with the pole or give the *carioca*, or do any of the other unpleasant things that earn many picadors a *bronca* from the audience and a fine from an occasional President who is keen on his job. Boltañés has been pic'ing bulls for well over forty years and has never been fined yet. He used to boast, also, that he had never been injured by a bull; but that ceased to be true in 1954 when he received a wound of some consequence.

The matador of today is not the romantic figure of yesterday with his swagger and the special, attractive clothes of his caste. He has gained plenty in social status and education since the times of Belmonte—the first torero ever to wear a bowler hat, ichabod!—but he has lost his picturesqueness and personality. Also, his career is much shorter than it was, in most cases. He makes his pile in a few years and retires, or else he fails and fades out. No, if you want an adventurous, Bohemian story, you must go to the picadors; in any case, a number of these are old-timers who have been at the game for twenty or thirty years.

To see Boltañés at work, wearing his beaver hat, you would just see a notably good picador. You would never guess that he was sixty-seven, or suspect that he had been in turns a civil guard, a bull-breeder in America, a cook, a city mayor, a building contractor, a bullring manager and a few other things.

In 1889, when he was born, his father was the local chief of the Civil Guard; Emilio enlisted too, when he was only fourteen, and served in the corps till he was twenty. One day he was on duty as guard to a mail train, and he started chatting to a matador's team that was travelling on it. "What does it take to be a torero?" he asked the *banderillero* Pinturas, an Aragonese like himself and a man of few words. "Courage," said Pinturas. "Well," said Emilio, "if that's all, then I'll be a torero by the next time we meet."

So he resigned from the Civil Guard, went to the Saragossa horse-contractor whom he knew, got a letter of introduction to the contractor at the Valencia bullring, and asked for a job as a picador. His offer was accepted immediately—on condition that he would stand guarantee for any horses that might be killed under him! This would have been an Irishman's rise, even in those days when they used worn-out horses from the U.S.A. at five dollars a head. Emilio declined with thanks.

After a while he got to know a junior matador who consented to give him a try-out as reserve picador at a small-town fight, in 1908. At the sorting-out in the morning, one of the bulls attacked a trained steer (a most unusual occurrence) and gored it to death, a grisly sight. The new picador, as he rode out of the horse-yard that afternoon, could still see those terrible horns at work. On the way into the ring, *to pic the same bull*, he saw another picador—the man for whom he was substituting—lying covered with blood and apparently dead. Actually, it was concussion from a fall, and the blood was off the bull, but Emilio did not know that; he just remembered the one-word answer that Pinturas had given him in the train. At the bull's first charge, he shut his eyes and thrust hard with the pole. Nothing dreadful occurred, he opened them again, and found the crowd applauding a fine pic, right on the top. At the second charge, it was not so good; everything went from under him, and there was one dead horse. He quickly mounted a fresh one, and the third time he got the pic home on top again. The new picador rode out of the ring amid an ovation.

After that he rose rapidly to the first class. In 1912 he caused a sensation in Madrid by pic'ing all six bulls of the day, and taking their first charge at the actual gate of the bull-pen. In 1913 he was even granted the ear of a bull, a thing which had never happened before and has never happened since.

But he wanted something new; so he turned *rejoneador*, and

competed for years with the best of the gentlemen horseback fighters. One day he was sent for in a hurry, to substitute for the champion *rejoneador* don Antonio Cañero. He managed to reach the *plaza* in time, but there was no chance to bring his horses (the *rejoneador's* horses are splendid thorough-breds and elaborately trained). When he rode out to do the *rejón* act on an ancient crowbait borrowed from the picadors' stable, the audience laughed, but the laughter soon turned to cheers, and the handkerchiefs all waved when he floored the bull with a finely placed *rejón*. Were this feat of horseman-ship not vouched for by numerous eyewitnesses, I should regard it as incredible.

After this, he fought for a while in both styles, with the pic and the *rejón*. He had made a lot of money, and invested it in the Valencia ring and became an impresario. In the intervals of activity at that, he joined the bullfighting teams that went to Rome and Budapest, and acted as *rejoneador* with success in both. His last *rejón* fight was in 1927; meanwhile, he had gone into partnership in the building trade, and put up the houses for a new suburb of Cordova. The people liked the houses so much that they elected him district mayor.

He may have lost money on these commercial ventures, for in the same year, 1927, he packed up and went to Peru, where he had once worked as a picador in 1920. He managed the Lima ring for three years with success, then turned bull-breeder. The matador Belmonte, now also ranching in Spain, had presented two stud bulls to the President of Peru; with these, and with forty cows of Vistahermosa caste, Boltañés founded the fighting ranch of La Viña, which is nowadays about the best-known in Peru, though in the last few years the quality of the bulls has gone off somewhat and the blood needs refreshing at the time when I write. It may be that one of the magnificent stud bulls, recently sold to South American ranches by don Tulio and don Isaias Vázquez, has gone to La Viña. Being of the same Vistahermosa caste, this would be a true 'refresher' and not a crossing, and would undoubtedly put La Viña back in its right place.

From Peru, Boltañés went north to Colombia and ran the fighting ranch of Fernando Vélez. All this time, he was making big money, but he always reinvested it in the bulls, and he ended up broke. So he returned to Spain, this time as manager to a famous matador, who let him down. Once again back to Peru; but this time with a debt of 50,000 *soles* hanging over him. So on arrival he advertised in the papers: "Spanish chef, just arrived, seeks job." Next morning he got two offers: one from the Callao railway company, the other from an important hotel. He chose the hotel, and suggested introducing Spanish home cookery. What he did not know about cooking would have filled a library; but each evening his wife taught him how to make the dishes for next day, and he is one of those people who can turn their hands to anything. The Spanish home cookery proved a great success, he squared his debts, and came back to Spain in 1938, aged just on fifty. In Spain, he pic'd for three well-known matadors, then went back to America, did some more ranching, discovered some promising young toreros whom he launched, and once more returned home— to continue with his permanent profession, one might even call it vocation, of picador.

I have seen him pic many a bull, and never anything but well. His performance at Valdepeñas, with the 'terrorific bulls of Tulio and Isaias Vázquez', which I have mentioned elsewhere, was masterly. His mate, who pic'd bull No. 1, received a well-earned *bronca* for the abuses he committed in the last pic, which discomposed the bull and left it in quite the wrong condition for the matador. Boltañés only gave one pic-thrust in that bull; but in No. 4 he gave all the pics, which numbered either three or fourteen, whichever you like, for the bull recharged eleven times under the iron; he pic'd magnificently, on top every time, to a bull of tremendous power, and he left it in such condition that the matador was able to cut the only ear of the day, while the brave bull was given the round of the ring. Earlier in the same year, pic'ing for Llorente in Madrid, I saw him give eight pics to a cowardly but silly bull, which never refused to charge the horses, but fled at the first feel of the iron. The *lidia* was laborious but well done; the act took no less than thirteen minutes, but every one of the eight pics (very light ones of course, for the bull never shoved at all) was mathematically on the top centre. The audience was not a very intelligent one, and few applauded Boltañés that time, but I was glad to be one of them.

Perhaps his best performance of recent years was at Barcelona, in a junior fight in 1952, working for Dámaso Gómez shortly before he took the *alternativa*. Though it was called a *novillada*, the bulls were large, tough, powerful, and the last three were five years old, one of them (the last) being furthermore blind in one eye and long-sighted in the other, so that it could not see the red cloth at close quarters. This was probably the most testing afternoon that Dámaso Gómez will ever experience. Each man got through his first bull all right, but in No. 4 both the other matadors were put out of action, leaving Dámaso with the three five-year-olds, including the prize packet at the end, to kill all by himself. He said at the time that he would never have got through the test, but for the magnificent pic work of old Boltañés, to whom he dedicated one of the bulls, and made a triumphant round of the ring after killing it, in company with the picador.

Boltañés is the only picador I have seen, apart from old Farnesio, now retired, who sometimes pics the bull in the old-fashioned, correct, and really beautiful way, holding the bull off as he swings the horse round to the left, and giving the bull its natural exit from the encounter on the off side of the horse. There are two young Mexicans who do it too, I understand; but I have not seen them myself.*

Today, Emilio's son is an engineer and his eldest daughter a successful actress. But after half a dozen different careers, and, with his round clean-shaven face and bald head, looking more like a priest than a bullfighter, Emilio is still planting the pic on top of the withers. He is sixty-seven years young and he still loves the game; but in November 1955 he announced his 'temporary withdrawal from the active list' to act as *apoderado* or managing agent for a promising young apprentice matador. The lad is certainly in good hands.

2 *Nine Lives for a Hyena?*

If a cat has nine lives, how many has a hyena? There seem to be no statistics on the point, but I know one who has had over half the cat's ration so far, and looks like exceeding it comfortably.

His name is José Martín Alonso, and his bullfighting nickname is 'Hiena II', or 'Hyena the Second', and it is certainly an odd one to choose ('Hiena I' was an obscure apprentice matador in 1928). At any rate, apart from a massive jaw, there is nothing hyena-like about the second of that ilk. He is a picador; a spruce, well-built man of forty-odd, with a fair, fresh complexion and thick black hair, and looks distinguished even on foot. I had never seen him close up, until one day a couple of years ago when I was in the horse-yard of the Madrid Plaza. It was a glorious day, and as I had arrived early, I went round back to see the toreros come in.

Matadors come by car, with their foot teams, but the picadors still keep up the old custom and come in a horse-

* See Chapter Six.

Banderillas de frente (P. Dominguín)

Pepe Dominguín gives the bull all the advantages in a spectacular pair on the boards.

Veteran Pepe Bienvenida in a superb pair *poder a poder;* note left horn tip

drawn buggy. They drove right into the yard and got out, smiling and not at all nervous. A few minutes later Hiena was astride a very fine grey horse, much superior to the usual bullring jade. Except for his broad beaver hat he looked like a Life Guardsman. We got talking, and when he saw I knew his story he showed me the famous scar, which has healed so well that you hardly see it at three yards, especially when he is mounted.

"It starts here," he said, pointing to his cheek. You could see the operation scar running up to the outside of the eye, through the end of the eyebrow and up to the temple. Then he took off his beaver hat, parted his thick black hair with his fingers, and there it was again, running straight back and then bending outwards, like an inverted L, across to the side of the head. We talked a little more, I checked a few points I was in doubt about, ther I wished him luck and said good-bye. He pic'd well that day, as always when I have seen him. He was working for Rafael Ortega that season. Here is his story.

Hiena was born at Seville in 1912. His father was in the horse-contracting business and sometimes acted as a *monosabio* in the ring. The young cub had his first 'life' at the age of twelve. He was working with his father in a northern *plaza*, and one night he was dressing an injured horse, not in the stables but in the yard outside the butchery department, because there was a convenient trough and hose-pipe there. As he worked, he saw some dark shadows approaching. He turned, and found himself facing a complete string of six fighting bulls which had got loose from the adjoining corral. The boy's nerve held, and he kept off the bulls with the hose-pipe until his shouts brought his father and brother to the rescue.

Life No. 2 was when he was just under sixteen. The fight was at Béziers in France, and as José Martín, senior, could not go, he put young Hiena in charge of the horse arrangements. He started by firing the two *alguaciles*, who were a couple of grasping and quarrelsome gipsies. They instantly decided on revenge, and poured some strong disinfectant into his dinner-time bottle of wine. Hiena managed to swallow an antidote or an emetic in time, and was able to appear in the ring as a *monosabio*, with his head going round in circles. This was bad enough, but when a picador fell and was in danger, Hiena did an emergency *quite* by pulling the bull's tail; the bull lashed out with its hindfoot and smashed his collarbone. However, as he humorously observed when he told the story, the pain in his neck from the kick made him forget the pain in his stomach from the poison.

The first time he appeared as a picador, he had another escape. On being thrown from his horse in front of the bull, he forgot the picador's first rule, which is: Lie still until the *quite* is over. Instead, he suicidally started to get up. Luckily his father, acting as a *monosabio*, was beside him with a stick, and reduced him to immobility with a tremendous whack in the kidneys. When he could move again, the bull had gone.

But all these brief interviews with death were long-distance snapshots compared to the good protracted close-up he had in 1947. That year was a tragic one in the bull-fighting world. Four toreros, three of them matadors, were killed: Manolete in Spain, Carnicerito de México in Portugal, and the Spanish *novillero* Joselillo in Mexico, were the matadors; the other man was the *banderillero* Cerrajillas, who got a fearful wound in saving his own matador Parrita by a *quite*. Apparently Hiena was booked for No. 5: he certainly made the trip, but he had a return ticket. Here is his own account, as given in one interview in hospital soon after Manolete's death, and in another later one, which I have put together with what he told me in the Madrid *patio de caballos*:

"I was working for Paco Muñoz that season. We went off

for the *feria* fight at Calatayud* on 9th September. The other two matadors were Luis Miguel and Luis Mata. The first got wounded the day before, and was replaced at the last moment by Antonio Bienvenida. But he hadn't had time to bring his own team, so our lot had to help him in the first bull.

"The bull was a cast-iron *manso*, and stopped by the gate, preventing the other picador from coming out, so I decided to go ahead. The way my *cogida* happened hasn't been correctly explained. Some have said that the injuries were caused by the hoof, but that isn't so. At the first thrust, the pic pole broke, and as I swayed forward the bull hooked me out of the saddle, and then knocked the horse over. I thought it would go for the horse, but it didn't, it turned back to where I was lying. When I saw the horn coming at my face, I quickly turned my head aside so as not to get my face smashed. The horn went into my right cheek, and penetrated right up as far as the parietal bone."

The journalist in the hospital told him that was the kind of wound which the medicos regard as 'necessarily fatal'.

"Yes," said Hiena, "one medico did. They had drawn the bull away, and they took me to the infirmary. Once there, my misfortunes continued. When they laid me on a bench—after all the efforts they'd made to carry me there, because they couldn't manage me properly among four of them—the bench broke, and I fell to the ground again. At last they got me on to a stretcher. Then the doctor who was examining my wound gave some preliminary whistles, and fell down in a faint. Another doctor had to come in. He had more nerve and gave me the first treatment. A friend of Bienvenida's rushed me to Madrid in his car; at least, we started out, but as we passed through Alhama de Aragón, with another 120 miles to go, I had a collapse. Everyone, including myself, thought my last hour had come. The priest there gave me

* The ancient Roman *Bilbilis*, birthplace of the poet Martial.

147

the Last Sacraments, and as I recovered a bit, the journey was resumed with all precautions. Dr. Jiménez Guinea (the Madrid horn-wound specialist) had been telephoned to, and was waiting at the Toreros' Sanatorium with his assistants. After the complicated operation, the doctors were very pessimistic. A rumour got around in the street that I was dead. My family had given me up. The report reached Barcelona, and a week later Cagancho, Llorente and Robredo, and their teams, made the *paseíllo* in the ring there with black armbands on."

Anyone might think that, after that, Hiena spent the rest of the season, if not the next, in convalescing. But he didn't; there is something about a picador that is tough, tough, tough. This is what he says, and I remember the fight— though I didn't see it—because the bull (of Benítez Cubero) was the biggest seen for many years, and was fought as late as 30th November.

"A month and a half later, thanks to the Blessed Virgin, Dr. Guinea, and my own strength, I was back in the saddle, to pic the last fight of the year in Barcelona. Actually, it was a half-fight, with three bulls only, and Llorente as sole matador. The final bull was the biggest seen for years, it weighed 1,450 lb. on the hoof.* It was *manso* and came away loose from the pics, so that I had to ride out to the ten-yard line and pic it in the open, facing the wrong way round. I gave it five pics that way" (it took ten, after a fashion) "and was loudly applauded."

And that, really, should be about all. But it is not quite. In one of the fights described in this book (Chapter 15, *Corrida* 8), when Antonio Bienvenida was tackling six bulls solo in Madrid, Hiena got the toughest assignment of the lot, and I have described how he was unhorsed again and again by the powerful *manso* of Galache, and once fell right in front of its face. When that happens, there is always a second or

* 391 kg. *en canal* was the exact weight.

two before any cape can arrive, even Antonio's, and in that instant Hiena had another 'life'. Just as the bull was about to drive the horn, he solemnly smacked its face! I saw him do it. The bull was so surprised that it stopped for a moment, and then Antonio's cape arrived for the real *quite*.

Perhaps the name 'Hyena' is not such a bad one. He has certainly had the last laugh often enough.

CHAPTER FOURTEEN

Brave Bulls and their Breeders

1 The Mantle of Aleas

The fight held in the Madrid ring on 27th May, 1951 ended
with an extraordinary spectacle. The audience were standing
up and cheering, the ring was full of hats and flowers, and a
man was being carried round the ring on the shoulders of
enthusiasts. His pockets were stuffed with cigars that he had
picked up on a previous round—on foot, after the fifth of the
six bulls had been fought. But the man was not a torero; he
was the bull-breeders' *mayoral* or head cattle-steward. The
breeders were Isaias and Tulio Vázquez, and they had sent
such a string of animals as the real bull enthusiast dreams of.
Of good size without exaggeration, handsome, tremendously
brave, and without a trace of malice. The first four were
each given a great ovation in the drag-out, and No. 5 and
No. 6 were each awarded a round of the ring. The *mayoral*
did a triumphal round of the ring alongside bull No. 5, and
as I said he was chaired and carried round again after No. 6.

Now a round of the ring for a bull, in Madrid, is something very unusual indeed, and I can only remember its
happening half a dozen times in the last eight years. But
what happened on this occasion was almost unheard of, and
one newspaper critic wrote that he did not know when such a
thing had occurred before, in the capital.

Actually, the last time was exactly twenty-five years
before, though what happened then was even more remark-

able; indeed it was a unique case. But the point was the same: a public tribute to a splendid breeder, a man so keen that he lived for his bulls alone, regardless of profit or loss.

The triumph of the Vázquez brothers was the more remarkable because bull-breeding today has got badly commercialised. The market is assured and prices are very high. Only a tiny minority of ranchers are scrupulous enough to keep to the highest standards of selection. It means endless patience and sacrificing a large proportion of your output, so as to offer only the very cream of the herd for sale. Every bull-calf you slaughter means 20,000 pesetas or more, roughly £200, that you don't make. Of all the breeders in Spain, perhaps only Pablo Romero and Urquijo —and possibly not even they—are as scrupulous as don Isaias and don Tulio Vázquez. For these magnificent animals, though of full size and weight, and several of them of full age, were fought in a *novillada* or junior fight, in which the bulls may legally be 'defective' or 'throwouts from the bravery test', that is, animals on which a breeder is not prepared to risk his reputation in a full-scale bullfight. Honour could hardly go further than that! These 'throw-outs' need take only three pics instead of four, but the Vázquez bulls got braver and braver under the iron. All took four pics, some took five, recharging harder and harder; the last bull took eight, throwing the picadors and their horses into the air in spectacular fashion. They all went on charging hard and fast in the second and third Acts, and they all died without opening their mouths, a sure sign of great caste.

The Vázquez bulls are always like this, and it is no accident. There is only one way to do it. First, you breed from the finest stud bulls and brood cows that can be got; second, you make the bravery test about twice as exacting as the average; thirdly, you slaughter every animal that fails to come through that test with the mark 'excellent' against its name. In that way you will probably sell, for fighting, less than a quarter of the animals you breed, and you will probably lose money, while all the less scrupulous breeders are rolling in wealth. But you will produce the bravest and noblest animal in the world, and your name will be a synonym for Honour.

It looks as if the mantle of old don Manuel Aleas had fallen upon the Vázquez brothers. Aleas was a breeder who died in 1950, aged seventy-seven, a grand old man, beloved of all who knew him. It was he who received the unique honour that I mentioned. It was on 24th May, 1926 in the old Madrid Plaza, demolished in 1934. The Aleas bulls came from Old Colmenar, north of Madrid, a famous breeding-ground of Castilian bulls from time immemorial. They were tough and formidable, and often extremely brave. On this occasion, No. 1 was so brave that the audience—much more bull-conscious in those days—appealed for it to be given the round of the ring. No. 2 was even better, and was given not one, but two rounds of the ring amid thunderous applause. But No. 3, 'Malagueño', was so superlative that after giving it two rounds of the ring they had its ears cut off and handed to old Aleas, a thing that had never been done before and assuredly never will be again.

Aleas was a striking figure, with his blue eyes, his bushy beard, once black but now white, his old-fashioned cloak and his flat broad-brimmed hat. He made no money at bull-breeding, indeed he impoverished himself even before his herd was destroyed. He always attended the *plaza* himself to see his bulls fight, and if any were not brave he suffered terribly; but when the crowd cheered a brave one, he would stand up to acknowledge the ovation with tears of joy in his eyes. It had been his great pride that his ranch, alone in Spain, still preserved in 100 per cent purity the ancient Jijona caste of red bulls; his family had owned the ranch

Below: '*Je toro!*' (see *Corrida* 1)

Above: Estatuario, *ayudado por alto,* or two-hander over the top (Andaluz)

Left: Right-hand *pase natural* (L. M. Dominguin)

since 1783, and he steadily refused to cross the breed. Yet one day, when the Belmonte brothers had fought six of his, and they proved, not cowardly or anything like that, but a bit soggy and with little fire in the last Act, Aleas never hesitated. He at once sacrificed his cherished caste, and crossed the red Jijona cows with a black bull of the dominant Vistahermosa blood (the Vázquez bulls are pure Vistahermosa of the best strain). Even so, for sentimental reasons, he still kept a small parcel of the Jijonas separate, to save the caste from being extinguished altogether.

To say that such breeders live for their bulls is a truism. To say that they would die for them may sound like an exaggeration; but in the case of old Aleas it is literally true and very nearly occurred. When the Civil War began, and the Reds started slaughtering bloodstock herds ruthlessly, Aleas consented, under heavy pressure, to let several bulls and cows be driven off to the slaughterhouse. But one day a party of Red militiamen—the same types that were operating the chekas on the Russian pattern and carrying out the nightly massacres in Madrid—turned up at Old Colmenar with the intention of driving off all the remaining animals. Don Manuel was sixty-three, but he went out to stop them. He took his stand at the entrance gate to the pasture, he surveyed them with the air of an ancient Castilian hidalgo, and he said this:

"You may be able to get the cattle out and drive them off, but you will first have to kill me where I stand, for as long as I have breath in my body I will stop you as best I can. This herd represents a family tradition, a calling, and a dedication of my life, to which I have sacrificed everything, including financial gain and my own fortune and that of my people. What this caste of bulls means to me, you will never be able to understand, but you can imagine it from my decision to stand here and prevent the herd from leaving, first by my words, and even, if need be, by a final appeal to force."

The old rancher's impressive bearing and fearless words staved off the danger for the moment, and the Reds withdrew. But he knew they would be back again, and I suppose that friends persuaded him not to throw his life away uselessly. He managed to drive a few cows in secrecy to a safer place, where they could remain hidden during the rest of the Red domination, and that is why there is still an Aleas breed today with the famous brand of the numeral 9 on their flanks and the right of seniority in the *plaza* of Madrid—the right to come out in first place if the string of bulls is a mixed one. But after that, life had little meaning for don Manuel. He never lived to see the herd rebuilt and a complete string of them fought again in Madrid; but two choice specimens, large, very brave, powerful and yet extremely noble, did appear in Madrid in June 1950. One was black and one was red, and the two big fellows with the 9 brand made the others look like calves. Each was applauded in the drag-out, the second one especially, for it was a real *toro de bandera*; and don Manuel stood up proudly in his seat on the platform over the bullpens, to receive the last ovation of his life. May he rest in peace; his soul goes marching on.

2 'Zamarrito', and the 'Terrorific Bulls' of Vázquez

The bravest individual bull I have ever seen was 'Zamarrito', who was fought in the Madrid ring on the Feast of the Assumption in 1948. He came from the small herd of Doña Andrea Escudero Calvo in Extremadura—a 'splinter' herd of the famous old herd of Albaserrada. The bulls were taking an average of five pics each that day, instead of the standard four and the all-too-common three, but none of them had done anything very special, except prove that no Extremadura bull is ever weak on the feet or 'easy meat', until the *toril* opened for the last time and 'Zamarrito' came out. No. 5

had been a substitute from Salamanca, for the regular No. 5 had got injured in the corrals. No. 4 had been loudly applauded for its grand appearance (it was a light grey, *cárdeno claro*, and most beautiful). 'Zamarrito' was also a grey but darker. There was no applause, for he had not the 'handsome' aspect of No. 4; but I was immediately impressed by his depth of shoulders and the breadth of his muzzle, and he had what is known as 'seriousness in the face'. His horns, too, were rather ugly: a wide half-moon in shape and rather blunt.

'Zamarrito' charged the horses from long distance in spectacular style, like the bulls of Arranz but with much more power. Eleven times he charged, and the balance sheet was nine pic-thrusts, five horses overthrown, and one killed. He did not kill the horse with a horn-stroke, but by throwing it so high in the air that it broke its neck on landing and died instantly. The photograph in this book shows 'Zamarrito' tossing another horse after just receiving his eighth pic; on seeing it fall, he was too noble to gore at an enemy he took for dead also, but turned in search of fresh foes. Twenty-five yards away, he saw the other picador, went at him like a racehorse, received his ninth pic, and overthrew him with equal ease, as the trumpet was finally blown for the *banderilla* act. Despite this formidable exertion, his mouth was still tight shut, and he charged the *banderilleros* so hard that they had their work cut out to place the sticks and reach the barrier in safety. In the last Act, he continued charging nobly and hard as before. The matador, Belmonteño, fought him bravely, in the dry Castilian style, but I should not like to say that he ever really dominated him; and he managed to kill 'Zamarrito' respectably, if I remember aright, with a couple of half-thrusts well placed. 'Zamarrito' died as he had fought, bravely and with his mouth shut. A grand bull.

But one bull does not make a string, and if I had to give a

prize for the bravest string I have seen, I should hesitate between two in particular. Of course, I have seen many strings of bulls which were brave; there was one string of Alipio Pérez Tabernero in the Madrid *feria* of 1948 in which five of the six were dragged out minus one or both of their ears, an ideal string from the matadors' point of view; but these Alipios were really super-noble rather than fiercely brave as a fighting bull should be, they did not take very many pics, and their horns were the reverse of formidable. There was no savour of danger in the air. No, the first of the two strings I am thinking of was that which was fought five days earlier, a string of Pablo Romeros which filled the audience with such enthusiasm that they made the ranch steward come down into the ring to receive an ovation after the fifth bull. But the sixth bull, also superb in appearance, was both silly and cowardly, and would certainly have been 'fired' had not the splendid *lidia* of Andaluz saved the breeder from that infamy by beguiling it into the picador's territory often enough to comply technically with the regulations. Again, though No. 4, 'Tejero', was an authentic *toro de bandera* from which Andaluz cut the ear after one of the grandest *faenas* and thrusts of his career, No. 1 was treacherous and dishonest in the highest degree. Nor did these Pablo Romeros take a great number of pics, though four of them went into the horses in the manner of real brave ones.

The palm, in my opinion, must go to a superb string of Tulio and Isaias Vázquez, which was fought not in the capital where it should have been, or by star figures as it would have been in the old days, but at the small town of Valdepeñas in La Mancha, famous for its bread and its wine, on Sunday 5th August, 1951, during the annual fair. I was living in Toledo, which meant a cross-country journey by rail, but I decided to travel the hundred-odd miles, first in order to see the bulls, and secondly because the senior matador announced was Andaluz, who, as I have related elsewhere, had been out of things for over a year through the old hip trouble which all dated back to the first Pablo Romero bull mentioned in the last paragraph. The other matadors were Cañitas the Mexican, brave enough but a man who had made little appeal to me in the past, and a third-class figure called Chaves Flores who had only recently taken the *alternativa*. In short, a pretty modest programme as far as the men were concerned, for Andaluz had hardly fought since an appearance in the spring in Madrid, and Cañitas, with nine years as a second-class figure behind him, was out of practice and also getting fat.

The description of that journey would make an amusing tale if I had space for all of it. I was short of cash at the time, and anyhow it would have been impossible to reserve a seat at short notice on a Saturday night for a cross-country journey in the fair season. The branch-line train from Toledo connected with the Andalusia express at a village station, and I foresaw difficulties in getting into it, so I attached myself to an Army sergeant and a civil guard who were sitting near me, thinking that they would be likely sort of people as regards know-how. We were travelling third-class. When the Andalusia express drew in, you could see that even the corridors were packed tight with people standing up; further, the doors into the train were locked, or at least the nearest one was. Of the hundred or so people on the platform, only about thirty managed to get on the train at all. Of the assault squad formed by the sergeant, the civil guard and me, the first-named managed to climb in through the window, aided by the good people inside, but until they had redistributed their luggage, it was physically impossible for him to make room for us to follow him, so the train drew out with the civil guard and me hanging on outside. After a minute or two we too crawled in through the window, but there was simply not the cubic space for us to stand inside, and the only place we could go was the swaying, bellows-enclosed platform of the coupling between this coach and the one in front. The middle section of the platform, moreover, was broken; but the 'bellows' was unhooked at one corner, so we got enough air, for it was very hot. The sergeant crossed the gaping void, through which you could see the sleepers whizzing past below, and calmly sat down, but there was not room for two to sit on our side without danger of breaking one's leg as the metal plate jolted and swayed. I had brought some bread and ham, and a bottle of wine; the civil guard held my handbag while with one hand I got out the food, the other hand being permanently needed to hold on to a bolt on the 'bellows'. In this way, helping each other to cut the food and hold the wine bottle, we spent the five or six hours of the journey, suffering chiefly from thirst after the wine was gone.

The train drew in an hour late, at ten o'clock, and I then faced the problem of finding lodging for the night, which is by hypothesis almost unobtainable at a small town on the eve of the Sunday in fair-time. All hotels, inns, and boarding-houses were naturally full, but at eleven-thirty I got a good clean bed in a lofty-roomed old lodging-house for muleteers such as Cervantes may have stayed at, and by midnight, though the hotels and restaurants were shut, I had even dined off ham and eggs and red Valdepeñas wine in a tavern.

Despite all this, I was in excellent humour, for these difficulties were quite expected; my only observation to tourists is that they should avoid making cross-country journeys third-class on Saturday afternoons in the fair-season. Second observation: the Valdepeñas wine sold as such in Madrid is a fake, or at least has been well 'christened'. The real stuff is quite different, very good indeed, but insidious, and has a delayed action. It seems so smooth and mild that you swig it off in bumpers, and next morning you feel you have been dropped from a great height, without benefit of clergy or parachute. What with this and having put in a spell at the fair till 3 a.m., the night passed all too soon.

Next day, after the pieces had joined up a bit under the soldering effect of good cold beer and veal chops and the excellent Valdepeñas bread, I went to the Town Hall to get my ticket, for the bullfights here are run by the municipality. I observed that they had built up all the publicity on the bulls alone. In the coloured posters advertising the fight, the usual phrasing of the headline, "Six handsome (or choice, or magnificent) bulls . . ." had been changed into "Six *terrorific* bulls of don Tulio and don Isaias Vázquez". The local paper carried an article about the bulls and a picture of one of them, an imposing-looking piebald (though I did not like it much, being outside the regular Vistahermosa type; in the ring, it was the least good of all); and on the back of the leaflet they gave me at the Town Hall, there was a short history of the ranch, which ended as follows: "These six superb specimens have a weight of THIRTY ARROBAS!, as can be verified by any *aficionado*, by attending the un-boxing, free of charge, on August 1 at 7.30 p.m." In fact, they were exaggerating slightly, for thirty arrobas is 345 kg. net, and in the event the average worked out at twenty-eight and a half arrobas or 1,160 lb. on the hoof; but the biggest was 1,275 (over thirty-one arrobas) and the 'smallest' was 1,120.

I went to call on Manolo Andaluz at the hotel, and was shocked when I saw him. He looked thin and ill, and he told me, in fact, that since his reappearance in Madrid in the spring after his absence of nearly two years, he had been ill once more, and had only recently been able to get about again. A poor preparation for such a testing *corrida* as this! I said, perhaps unwisely: "And I suppose this fight today is a crucial one for your career?" "It is, indeed," he replied. I said I was glad, anyhow, to see that he was senior swordsman, for that meant we should have good orderly *lidia* (Cañitas is very inferior at this), and again he had to disappoint me by saying that the posters were incorrect: Cañitas was his senior, outside Madrid, by virtue of his Mexican *alternativa* which was earlier than Manolo's. As it turned out, this fact did make a lot of difference, for Manolo was always one of those who take the job of senior swordsman very seriously, and used to intervene actively to straighten things out if a junior was getting into a muddle. Had he been in charge of the ring from the outset that day, the atmosphere of panic which at times prevailed would have been avoided, for Cañitas, while personally as brave as they come, has little idea of directing the ringcraft.

Manolo's uncle, who is also his manager, offered me a ticket, but I already had mine, and so, with a few more words of cheer, I shook Manolo by the hand and left him to rest before the fight. I was feverishly anxious for him to do well, but I feared the worst, for the sick man I had just seen was not the Manolo of the mighty 'benders' and the ful-minating *volapiés* that we knew of old.

As first comers had choice of seats in the *plaza*, I took care to arrive early, and got a seat in the third row, just behind the place where the toreros park their dress capes and watch the bulls being run, from behind a *burladero* in the barrier. The bullpen door was exactly opposite, across the ring in the sun. The *plaza* was small, holding only about 6,000. By a quarter to six it was nearly full. Over in the sun sat mostly cattlemen and farm and vineyard workers, with mahogany faces and the huge straw hats they wear while reaping wheat with sickles in the roasting sun on the vast La Mancha plain. Behind me, there were only seven rows in the *tendido*, and then a semicircle of boxes, all full of pretty girls and women, in high combs and mantillas. I've never seen so many together. A few black mantillas, not many, a lot of white ones, and still more of the *madroñeras*, the kind that is a net of wide meshes with hundreds of those little bobbles imitating the fruit of the *madroño*, which is like that of the plane tree.

The bobbles were in different colours, yellow, green, red, black or blue, and the effect was marvellous. Even the women without mantillas had great big red or white flowers in their hair, and some wore red-and-white flounced dresses in the Sevilian style. I only wish they turned out like that in Madrid; even quite a plain woman looks most attractive in that get-up. Whole bunches of them rolled up to the *plaza* in old-fashioned horse or mule carriages gaily caparisoned, and it all looked like a beauty contest as they drove through the narrow, whitewashed streets.

So the trumpet blew and the first of the 'terrorific' bulls rushed out of the red door opposite, which the toreros call 'the gate of fear'. And they were terrifying! In that little *plaza*, in Row 3, one was nearly on top of them. They came thundering out from the bullpen straight at us, and to me they looked like a cross between a racehorse and a rhinoceros. Once, the junior matador, who was standing in the *burladero*, involuntarily flinched back into the alleyway as No. 3 came racing across straight at him, although he was protected by the stout boards of the *burladero*. The programme had said thirty arrobas, and they certainly looked it. The weights I have given, I found out later on; I could not check them at the time, because there was no weighing-machine at the *plaza*; nor did they cut the carcasses up on the spot, for there was no butchery department there. I saw the carcasses afterwards in the horse-yard, and they looked less large than when alive; I reckoned about 1,100 lb. then, which was an underestimate. But they were only four years old; the tell-tale rings on the horns were not clearly marked, so I looked in their mouths, and there was the proof: the rear molar was a milk tooth still. I took off my hat to the old-timers who fought bulls like this at five years in the plenitude of their strength. Their speed was frightening, their power enormous.

In a show like this, everything depends on the picadors,

most of whom, fortunately, were up to their job, though two of them got a heavy and justified *bronca* from the crowd for screwing with the pole and other unpleasant tricks, which in fact can merely serve to wreck a bull that is really brave, not to temper it as good pic work does. The first bull (for Cañitas) took four pics, if you like to call it that, but it recharged seven times under the iron, overthrew thrice, and in the old days there would have been three or four dead horses. In the last terrible pic, with the picador screwing unmercifully amid angry protests from the crowd, the pic head snapped off and stayed in the bull. It was fought all wrong, the punishment was tremendous and unfair, the toreros were in fair terror of it, and it died without opening its mouth to pant. There was a real chill of danger, you could feel it in the air. The drama was intense, nothing faked here. The bull was out to kill every time, though it was always noble, never treacherous or crafty.

No. 2 unsaddled a picador and he fell on the bull's back, an agonising moment, I do not know how he got free; a peón did a marvellous *quite*. That bull took six pics with two recharges; it looked exactly like the photographs of its remote collateral ancestor, the famous stud bull 'Diano' which revolutionised the herd of Martínez from 1903 onwards. Its speed was something fantastic when it came out, despite its thirty-one arrobas. This was Manolo's first; he did a splendid *quite* to a fallen picador and some excellent *verónicas*, including two finished off over the horns, a most unusual pass; but in his *faena*, after some excellent 'benders' to start with (and a nasty wind had sprung up), and some respectable work with the right hand, he made a poor kill— he, the best swordsman in Spain, but only a shadow of himself today! And the crowd whistled at him, with applause for the bull. The third bull took four pics, but with three recharges, one of them shoving the horse and rider along for twenty-five yards with the picador giving it the works all the time. The fourth bull was the best of the lot, and was given the round of the ring. It turned away its face twice from the picador before the first pic, but once it felt the iron, it behaved very differently. It received three 'official' pics from old Boltañés, aged sixty-two, but they were all excellently placed, and the bull recharged eleven times under the iron. The fifth, the piebald, was less tough but took four pics, with five recharges including one of twenty-five yards. The sixth had a fearful swerving charge. It went into the horses five times from long range (the last time, from twenty yards), and overthrew spectacularly on four occasions, but did not insist under the punishment so much, and must therefore be regarded as less brave. But for the protector, it would have killed at least four horses.

In the circumstances, little brilliance was forthcoming from the men, with one exception. The junior man was all at sea, and only some timely aid from Manolo Andaluz enabled him to make the grade at all in the last bull. As for Manolo himself, his ringcraft was as good as ever, and he did some good *quites* and capework at times, but in the *faenas* he was only the shadow of himself, and the crowd was very hard on him, especially when he failed to produce the splendid sword-thrusts for which he was famed. Only the senior swordsman, Cañitas, distinguished himself. I certainly never expected it, getting on in years as he is, and distinctly fat and slow on his feet. But in No. 4 he risked his neck to save the fight from disaster, and he succeeded. Splendid capework in his *quite*, and *muleta* work enormously brave and artistic too, against the fierce charges of the bull. He started with three passes sitting on the *estribo* ledge followed by the breast pass (ovation); then, in the stiffish breeze, a set of left-hand *naturales*, again with the breast pass; all this cheered with *olés* and ovations. The tragic emotion was terrible, for the danger was all too obvious and his faculties were not what they had been some years before. A further great ovation for some excellent *manoletinas*, and then he tried the two-hander over the top, but was caught and heavily tossed. No blood, but a tremendous *varetazo*, or blow with the flat of the horn, in the groin. He got up in appalling pain, hardly able to walk. They tried to carry him out, but he shook himself free, returned to the bull almost fainting, made a couple of weak entries to kill, then got home a goodish thrust and passed out. Andaluz, out in the centre, finished off the bull with a spectacular *descabello* stab at the first attempt, and the ear was cut for the heroic Mexican, and taken to him in the infirmary while the brave bull was given a triumphal round of the ring.

That was the bravest and also the toughest *corrida* of bulls I have seen. The artistic result of the afternoon was not very high, but it certainly was a bull *fight* and not a ballet. I left the *plaza* all emptied out—purged with pity and terror, as Aristotle says concerning tragic drama. The second element was supplied by the 'terrorific', yet fundamentally noble, bulls of don Tulio and don Isaias. The pity was what I felt for my poor friend Manolo, recently risen from his bed of sickness to face such enemies, and finding himself physically unable to master them.

Manolo never fought again in the silk and gold uniform. Ill-luck and ill-health had been too much for him, and there is no armour against fate. But he had always chosen the biggest and toughest bulls, and he chose them to the end. That is the hallmark of his honour.

PART THREE

The Hour of the Truth

CHAPTER FIFTEEN

Eight 'Corridas'

1 *Andaluz Breaks the Hoodoo*

All the *corridas* described in this chapter were held in Madrid and were witnessed by me. All except the first are written up from actual notes made in the *plaza* at the time. I have seen good fights outside Madrid, but Madrid is the capital of the bull-fighting world and has a seriousness shared by few other rings and equalled by none. It is the most difficult *plaza* to succeed in, and its audiences, though only the shadow of what they were in the days of the *abono* or subscription-season, are still the most intelligent, discerning, and appreciative of what is really good, and the hardest to deceive with what is spurious; further, a reasonable degree of strictness exists in the enforcement of regulations and in the passing of bulls as valid for major fights.

Perhaps the best fight I have ever seen was the one of 3rd July, 1955, when Antonio Bienvenida killed six bulls single-handed in Madrid for the third time in his career, and scored the greatest triumph of his life. (See *Corrida* 8 below.) But if I had the chance to see any fight over again, then I think I should choose the one I saw in Madrid on 19th June, 1947. This was a normal show with six bulls and three matadors. I kept no notes that day, but I have often discussed the fight with friends and my memory of it is very vivid; besides, I have preserved the newspaper accounts, and in my album this fight is recorded by six photographs, two of each matador.

The first picture shows a bronzed, lean-faced man, no

longer young for a torero, since he is nearer forty than thirty. He is no film star, but he has the virile attraction of the Castilian soldier or rancher. His fine, high forehead bears the lines of a man for whom life has not been too easy, but at present those lines are relaxed, and his eyes have the smile of satisfaction which comes after a great effort—and success. His mouth is not visible, for he is holding up a small leather *bota* of wine and drinking from it. His fighting cape is slung over his left arm, and he has paused in his triumphal round of the ring to take a well-earned swig from the *bota* thrown in his path by some enthusiastic spectator. His name is Luis Gómez, nicknamed El Estudiante, because he abandoned his university studies to become a bullfighter. That was away back in 1928, when he was seventeen. He was a leading matador just before the Spanish War, and during the war he fought whenever he got a little leave from active service. After the war he had a good year or two, and then he seemed to get unjustly overlooked or shelved, and by 1946 he was practically out of things. The next year, 1947, after a successful beginning in a provincial fight, he was trying to make a comeback, in the only place that matters—Madrid. He had had two bookings there already. In the first he was still a bit stiff, and the bulls were Pablo Romeros of enormous size and power; on top of that, the junior man got caught and injured and Estudiante as senior swordsman had to kill a third bull. After a year and a half out of the ring, he did well to get through without disaster. In his second booking, he got an even tougher bone to gnaw, for there was a hurricane blowing, and the bulls were Salamanca ones of over six years old instead of the normal four. Salamanca bulls are seldom much good at five years, let alone six. El Estudiante fought them soberly and killed them clean. On the strength of these two showings, he was given his third and last chance in Madrid three weeks later; and he made the grade.

The bulls were the famous Gracilianos, also from Sala-

Left-hand *pase natural* (Antonio Bienvenida)

Pase afarolado (Estudiante)

Manoletina (Andaluz). The pass has some emotion when the horns are like this.

manca, but they look and fight like a good Andalusian breed, for their blood is identical with the famous Murubes. They were very well armed and were the regulation four and a half years old, except for Estudiante's second (it had to be his!) which was five and a half.

Estudiante had a splendid afternoon. He gained the first ovation of the day for a grand *quite* in the first bull, though later he was to do an even better one. With the red cloth he gave an excellent *faena*, followed by a good kill at the first thrust. Madrid was then more jealous of awarding the ear than it is now, but he was encouraged to take a round of the ring amid great applause. It was in his second that his full triumph came—with the older, more difficult bull, which he handled in masterly fashion. I remember the beautiful passes—not very many, for an old bull is not so easy to deceive; and how it cunningly retreated to the barrier as if to defend itself; and how it then suddenly charged out unexpectedly to catch him off his guard; and how Estudiante stood firm, and instead of the pass we expected, he sank the sword up to the hilt on the mathematical top of the shoulders —in other words, the sword-thrust *aguantando*, which is the same as the receiving method, but not deliberately prepared. A grand kill! This time there was no denying him the ear, for a *faena* and kill that will go down as among the best of his life. I have no photograph of that, but the second picture on my page (not the one in this book) is of a little treat he gave us in Act I, with that old and crafty bull.

You see the bull from behind, moving forward and to the right, but just beginning to swerve back to the left again. In this corkscrew manner it is attacking what looks like a giant butterfly, with a parti-coloured body, plain-coloured wings, and a black head. The butterfly is Estudiante himself, and he is doing the famous *quite* of the *mariposa*, which means butterfly. This hazard was invented by the great Marcial Lalanda, one of the supreme masters of the cape, who, in

1932, conferred the *alternativa* on Estudiante, one of the very few who have done the *mariposa* well since Lalanda retired. It is not a pass, but strictly a *quite* only, to draw the bull away from the horse or a fallen man. To do it, the matador holds the cape behind him, almost wearing it as a cloak, with the yellow lining visible to the bull as he holds out his arms sideways to form the 'wings' with the cape, with his own body as the body of the butterfly. As the bull turns and goes for one wing, he drops his arm and that wing folds up; the bull then swerves across and goes for the other, which in turn is closed and the first one reopened. This goes on alternately, with the bull nosing forward, tacking first to one side and then the other, and the man tripping lightly backwards, drawing the bull after him as it attacks each wing in turn but never the body in the middle. It is a marvellous sight to see well done, but very dangerous, and hardly any matadors can do it at all. The roar of applause for this beautiful hazard, from the old-time enthusiasts, was most impressive. I am glad I have that photograph; I have never seen the *mariposa* done since.

The second swordsman, the subject of photographs 3 and 4 on my album page, is a very different type. He is the brilliant but unreliable Pepe Luis Vázquez, who could electrify the *plaza*—when he felt that way inclined—with a couple of *verónicas*. Short, fair-haired, pink-faced and a bit plump, he does not look in the least what he is, namely a Sevilian from the classic San Bernardo quarter, which one associates with dark-eyed beauties, guitars and castanets. Perhaps he has Vandal blood, which is responsible for the quite numerous ash-blondes to be found down south among the normal dark type, for not all of that Germanic tribe crossed over to Africa; some stayed in Vandalusia. Pepe Luis on the programme was always an unknown quantity. Like the little girl in the nursery rhyme, when he was good he was very very good . . . I have heard him called a 'white gipsy', and certainly, of the non-gipsy toreros, he was the only one who could reach the inspired genius of the gipsy when the gipsy lets himself go. On this occasion, after Estudiante's fine work in Bull No. 1, the show went downhill badly in Bull No. 2. Pepe Luis did not feel confident. Fine capework, yes, but in Act III he hesitated, faltered, and was lost. He pricked and poked about with the sword for a long time, and when the bull—not a good one—was dragged out, Pepe Luis received a fair-sized ration of whistles and boos. However, when that happens in his first bull *and is justified*, he often rises to the tops in his second—as he did today!

He started off in Bull No. 5 with some *verónicas* that no one past or present, with the possible exception of Gitanillo, could have improved on, and the audience got steamed up at once. His first effort was forgotten or forgiven. This put him on his form, and when it came to his solo in Act III, he started off in the way shown in my photographs 3 and 4. In No. 3 (reproduced in this book) you see the diminutive figure of Pepe Luis alone, for the bull is out of the picture. He holds the sword in his right hand and the *muleta* in his left, but furled, like a flag not yet unfolded to the breeze. He is advancing towards the invisible bull holding out the tiny red lure, and his mouth is open as he shouts "*Jé, toro! Jé, toro!*" The bull's tail went up and it charged; and in the other photo, Pepe Luis has let the cloth unfurl just as the bull arrived, and is starting off his *faena* with a perfect *natural*, the most beautiful, sincere and dangerous of all the regular passes—and executed nearly face on to the bull, not edgewise which is a modern trick. That was how he began, and the rest was a little poem such as he alone can write. He killed beautifully at the first thrust, and there was his triumph complete, with all his faults in No. 2 wiped out, and the ear of No. 5 in his hand as he went round the ring amid ovations.

The last two pictures are of my own favourite, Manuel Alvarez, nicknamed El Andaluz, from the Triana quarter of Seville. I have said a good deal about this torero elsewhere and will not repeat it. But until that day, despite brilliant successes everywhere else, he had always been dogged by ill luck in the capital itself, where, despite plenty of good and indeed brilliant work, complete triumph always seemed to escape him.

Today we saw his grave, classical work with cape and *muleta* at its best, yet his victory came only at the very end when both the other men had their laurels already secure. But it was he who pulled the afternoon round when things had gone downhill in Bull 2. In Bull 3, his first, he did a masterly *faena* but failed to win the ear when it came to the sword. Though he was the best killer in Spain at the time, his bad luck came in again. Twice he entered immaculately at the *volapié*, but each time the point struck bone. On the third entry, what should have been a superb thrust to the hilt went in less than half-way because the point struck a *banderilla*-shaft *en route* and had to cut through the wood of that. Bad luck again!—but still he got a great ovation and a round of the ring.

Bull 4 was Estudiante's triumph, and Bull 5 that of Pepe Luis. At last came Bull 6, Andaluz's one remaining chance, and it came out of the pen with seven devils in it, goring at the barrier, hooking and swerving right and left. Brave, yes, but a bull needing great science and skill to dominate it. He gave it some marvellous *verónicas*, but in one of them he got so close that the distance was nil, and he was tossed violently. My fifth photo shows him lying in a heap on the sand, and the bull with its head down going for him, and a torero dashing to the rescue. He got up, in evident pain, and went on with the *verónicas* where he had left off. All through Acts I and II he was limping. This was the first injury to his hip, which was repeated twice next season, once by a Pablo

Romero and once by a five-year-old Alipio from Salamanca,* which both got him in the same place. This hip ultimately, years later, put an end to his career. Now it looked as if triumph was going to slip through his hands once again, as usual. The hoodoo of Madrid was at work.

The trumpet blew, and Andaluz took up the red cloth and the sword for the final Act of the afternoon, in the failing light. He flexed the sword hard against the planks of the barrier in the old-fashioned style, to give it just the right curve in the first twelve inches, known as *la muerte*, 'the death'. Most people, in view of the bull's temperament and the man's injury, thought he was just going to line it up and kill it quick. They were wrong. This bull was a good one, if you knew how to master it, reduce it, teach it to charge straight, lure it on, dominate it. He did all that, with grand *natural* passes both left and right, with low backhanders to bronco-bust it, with high two-handers to give it confidence to charge straight; grave, scientific, thrilling and artistic work, always with the tragic emotion that this torero imprinted on his *faenas*. A beautiful and intelligent job.

Only at the moment of the kill did he make a small mistake—if you could call it that, for the result was the most sensational and brilliant sword-thrust of the year. It is shown in my sixth photo, which is also reproduced in this book. It shows man and bull in the middle of the encounter, both going all out: Andaluz in his famous 'flying-feet' *volapié*, and the bull at full charge. Of the six feet, his and the bull's, only one is on the ground. His mistake was in under-

* In this latter case there was bad luck again, for he was senior matador and it occurred in the first bull. By some extraordinary oversight the ring had not been watered before the fight. The wind blew the sand in his eyes and blinded him in a *verónica* and he got a fearful toss. His face was all grey with pain and it was two minutes before he could go on— with more *verónicas*. After Bull 1 they did water the ring. He cut the ear of Bull 4 with the best sword-thrust of the year. But the damage was done.

estimating the amount of gas the bull still had left, and also in entering from rather too far. His rule was to kill at the *volapié*, which implies a stationary bull. But this time, as he launched himself forward, the bull did the same, and they met in the middle, which is called *a un tiempo*. Here there is no chance to get out of it, you have to improvise like lightning in the middle of the hazard; and he did so. In the picture, the cross-over with the left hand holding the cloth has been performed to perfection, the bull's head is down and to its left, his flying body has passed the horn, and the sword is already half-way home before the hazard has been consummated. Four seconds after that exposure was taken, the bull fell dead on the sand. And then at last the hoodoo was broken. Twenty thousand handkerchiefs were waving, and the ear was cut for Andaluz, and enthusiasts jumped into the ring and carried him round the ring and out, together with Pepe Luis and Estudiante, shoulder-high through the big gates and up the *calle de Alcalá*.

2 Gitanillo is Unlucky

The former account was of a fight on a warm summer day in a packed *plaza*. Here is the other side of the picture. Here the interest largely shifts to the first Act. Apart from Llorente's valour, the highlights were the splendid bulls and the gipsy's amazing *verónicas*. The account is jerky, for in a fight like this everything happens fast and you have to keep your eyes skinned.

1st May, 1949. 6.30 p.m. by the clock, 4.30 by the sun. Six bulls of Arranz (Salamanca, but this breed is also one of my four or five exceptions to the rule), for the gipsy Gitanillo de Triana (Seville) and Rafael Llorente and Manolo Navarro, both of Madrid. The *plaza*, half-empty, and a cold, strong wind, sometimes so strong as to make fighting well-nigh impossible. The bulls were excellent in general, as always with this breed (but occasionally weak on their feet). They are not enormous, but very brave, with a long straight charge, and very fast. Almost all were applauded in the drag-out. There was no sun, and those in the cheaper 'sun' seats, including myself, saw the best part of the fight. I omit the opening ritual.

Bull No. 1, for Gitanillo. Bull 'Buenas Tardes', weight 937 lb., smallish, handsome, sharp horns. Slow to take capes at first, then does so eagerly. Applause to bull from intelligent crowd (it is a day for enthusiasts only). Trumpet.

First pic. Bull knocks horse over with a crash, showing great power. Chases riderless horse across ring, an unusual sight. Second pic, well placed, bull recharges hard under the iron. Crowd whistles at picador for screwing with the pole, a dirty trick. The bull is very brave; that pic equals at least two ordinary ones. Third pic, bull charges from long distance. Fourth pic, knocks horse over, but comes away loose without *quite*. Fifth pic, good and hard, bull insists under the iron, some whistles at picador, but also some applause, for apart from that first screw he's pic'd well, and bull's power is enormous despite its moderate size. Trumpet. *Banderillas*, first pair very good, second very bad. Trumpet.

6.45, *faena* starts. Despite all those pics, the bull's mouth is shut tight and it is charging hard. Gitanillo the gipsy starts with four low passes to get bull under control; good. Tries to give the left-hand *natural*, but the cloth, even after wetting, simply blows out horizontal, and he has to desist. A pass over the top, a *natural* at last after much trying, three nondescript ones and another *natural* and breast pass. Half a dozen more flaps of one kind or another, then loses the cloth, hooked out of his hand by the bull. 6.50 he squares the bull with two more flaps, and then 'enters' to kill. . . . I say 'enters', but really he throws himself outwards so far that he delivers a full thrust, up to the hilt, into the air—the point just touches one rib of the bull. Loud laughter from audience. These gipsies! More passes to square the bull again. 6.52, a half-thrust, on top this time, but throwing himself outwards and lengthening his arm. The bull, notably, goes and takes a *querencia* in the middle, sign of exceptional bravery, when mortally wounded. *Descabello*, right first shot. A few whistles, not many. In a wind like this, not too bad, for a gipsy. Hearty applause to very brave bull in drag-out.

Bull No. 2, for Rafael Llorente, of Barajas (Madrid airport). This is a tough guy if there is such a thing. Doesn't care two hoots for wind or rugged bulls or anything. The bull, 'Rompelindes', weighs 967 lb. Handsome, with wide horns, needle-pointed and turned upwards. It is well and bravely run right away by a peón standing firm on the ten-yard line, no dodging and messing about in *burladeros*. Applause for man and bull. Trumpet.

Pic 1, overthrows horse. Bull eager and strong. Picador No. 2 looks worried but does well. Pic 2, horse over again. Pics 3 and 4, very good indeed, applause to picador, not a common thing, and quite a light, slender picador too. The *quites* were strictly business ones, no fancy capework. Trumpet. *Banderillas*, first pair good, second fair, third good; all in orthodox style, on the arc. Applause to peón who places first and third pairs. The crowd is very fair and generous when conditions are like this. Trumpet.

7.03, *faena* starts in a very high wind. Llorente begins with five 'benders' of great power. Applause. Two curtain-raisers over the top, magnificent, very difficult in such wind, shouts of *"Olé!"* from the crowd. Then, to our amazement, five beautiful *naturales* in a string, rounded off with the breast pass. Huge ovation, 'palms fairly smoking' as the Spanish say. Llorente is *rabioso*, crazy keen. He challenges the bull from long distance and it goes through nobly for another fine *natural, Olé!* One pass low, and

Above: Pepe Luiz Vázquez in a breast pass to the biggest bull of the year (a Miura of 1,330 lb. on the hoof), to which he did one of the best *faenas* of his life

Left: Plastic rhythm in a breast pass by Andaluz

Above: The *ayudado por bajo*, or two-handed 'bender', most powerful of all passes (Andaluz)

Right: Gitanillo in a excellent 'bender' to dominate a tough bull

another *natural*. Gets his capemen out to steer the bull back to the only place where there is some lee from the wind—just under my seat, hence my good view of detail. Another pass low, three of decoration, all fine, cheers by the crowd, and the bull is squared. Llorente enters at full *volapié* for a fulminating thrust which kills instantly, the bull crashing dead on the spot. But the sword went in a trifle low because the bull had shrugged sideways at the critical instant, so the President will not grant the ear. Triumphant round of ring, picking up flowers, sampling contents of wineskins. 7.08, applause to brave bull in drag-out. Trumpet.

Bull No. 3, for Manolo Navarro. Bull, 'Tendero', looks small but proves heavier, 1,038 lb. Good horns. Very fast and eager. Old Gitanillo, standing in a *burladero*, looks frozen: his brown Hindu face has gone bronze-green with cold. Spectators are feeling it too, now they have stopped applauding Llorente.

Pic 1: a long straight charge, frank and noble. Picador connects well. Pic 2, knocks horse over. Pic 3, charges from far, recharges twice and thrice under the iron, a tremendous pic but a fair one. Bull is weakened but keeps mouth shut. Trumpet. *Banderillas*, good. Trumpet.

7.19, *faena* starts. Three low passes to get bull fixed. Some more, both high and low, with right hand. The bull falls in turning sharp, not too strong on its feet. Manolo continues with mostly high passes for that reason. Then decorative stuff, not well done, not to taste of crowd. In flapping to square bull, loses cloth. Eventually kills with three pricks, a half-thrust and the *descabello*. Not much good; silence. Applause to brave bull, 7.29.

Bull No. 4, Gitanillo's second. The bull, 'Caribello', is very fast indeed and most beautiful. Weight, 1,056 lb. Applause to bull for its superb appearance. Gitanillo is rabidly keen to retrieve his honour after failure in No. 1. Without waiting for his capemen to run it, he steps out himself to the ten-yard line in the howling wind, and gives the brand-new, unfixed bull four and a half *verónicas* as good as any he has ever given in his life, *cargando la suerte* marvellously. The bull is as eager as can be and charges furiously: the gipsy just stands there and deflects the express train as it is about to crush him. Grand ovation: people rise from their seats and cheer. The green face is brown again, and grinning. Trumpet.

Pic 1: the bull charges like a racehorse from twenty yards, the picador connects, but over goes the whole outfit. Gitanillo does a superb *quite* to the prostrate picador in danger, then adds three and a half more *verónicas* of his very special vintage, even better than the first. I have never seen any *verónicas* better, from anyone, on any day. All in a few square yards, in half a gale. It seemed that the bull could not fail to catch and kill the man as it charged straight at him, from in front, and then the gipsy, legs wide a-straddle, *cargó la suerte*, turned on the power, and bent the bull's trajectory so as to miss his thigh by inches each time. Colossal cheers. You see *verónicas* like this about once a year, if you are very lucky, on a calm day, and then only from Gitanillo himself. Pic 2: the bull goes in hard and recharges harder against the iron, and now comes Gitanillo's wretched luck. When 'Caribello' first came out, it charged madly across the *plaza* and smashed into the barrier, knocking two neat holes through the thick planks. This weakened it, of course. Then the terrific charge and recharge in the second pic took more out of it. Gitanillo saw in a flash that it had had enough pics, and hastily appealed to the President, hat in hand, to have the trumpet blown. But the President, high up on the opposite side of the ring, hadn't seen so clearly, and refused. Gitanillo turned away in distress. The picador saw it too, and tried his best to give 'Caribello' only a token pic next time. But the bull was so brave and charged so hard, the picador simply had to lean on the pole to avoid going over, and the pic-point, which was resting on the hide only, slipped into the old hole. Still the bull insisted, and so it got a full pic, twice as damaging as a normal one. Gitanillo looked miserable; his beautiful bull ruined for him! Trumpet.

What a shame! Gitanillo tries everything, but the bull was played out. Nothing to do but just kill it. 7.47, two pricks, then a three-quarter thrust well on top, and *descabello* at the first shot. Some applause. Ovation to magnificent bull, sadly wasted through President's mistake and obstinacy. It is very rare for Presidents to refuse an appeal by an experienced matador.

Trumpet, Bull No. 5, Llorente's second. Bull 'Jasmín', 1,045 lb., fast, but weak on feet. Less power than the rest, less caste too. Run by peones, then some indifferent *verónicas* by Llorente. First pic, bowls horse over with a great crash and gores furiously at fallen horse, which is saved from certain death by the mattress-protector. Second pic, round and round in a circle, equal to three normal ones. President has trumpet blown quick this time, taking no chances. *Banderillas* good, applauded.

7.57, trumpet, *faena* starts. Wind bitterly cold now. Bull being weak on feet, all passes are over the top or gentle ones with the right hand. All good stuff, but the animal is not worth much, best to kill it quick. Four good righthanders to square it, and a fine *volapié* but struck bone. At second entry, wind blew cloth out of line, very dangerous; Llorente did well to get a half-thrust on top. *Descabello*, second shot. Ovation, and Llorente salutes from barrier, making signs of annoyance with the wind. No applause to the bull.

8.05, the last bull, 'Escurrido', for Manolo Navarro. The name means 'scrawny' but this bull is the reverse. Walked out slowly with a ferocious look in its eye. Took five pics, two recharges, with tremendous power. It just stands and eyes the picador, then goes in like a battering ram. Bowled picadors over three times. They pic'd well, but had their work cut out to remain upright. *Banderillas*, fair. Trumpet, 8.15, for last Act. Not many spectators left now. Manolo was out of form and discouraged. His *faena* was nothing, and the kill was bad, a crooked half thrust and no less than seven *descabello* stabs. A few whistles from the remains of the crowd, and some applause for the fine bull. Manolo can do better than this, the conditions got him down. An uncomfortable fight, just those seven marvellous *verónicas* from the gipsy, Llorente's lion-hearted work, some good pic'ing, and the splendid bulls of Arranz. Ah, if only the President hadn't made that mistake, with the best bull of the day, and a gipsy mad keen to do the *faena* of his life, what things we should have seen! And so home, walking fast to keep out the chill, and looking forward to a good tot of Fundador.

3   *Forty Years On: Luis Miguel's High-water Mark*

I have already quoted the account, which I heard from an old-timer, of one of the best performances ever seen in the old Madrid *plaza*, when Vicente Pastor cut the first ear awarded in the capital.

But that took place in 1909; I did not see it myself; and since then the bulls have changed greatly, and naturally the style of fighting has changed too. Today the bull is younger and lighter, and no doubt it takes less dominating as a rule. On the other hand, far more is demanded of the matador than just to dominate and kill it.

Here, then, is an account of the modern counterpart to that old-time performance. It was a fight which I saw myself, and I have a detailed record of the fighting of all six bulls, from notes made in the *plaza*; but it would take too much space to describe the entire *corrida*, which was thoroughly disappointing except for the fifth bull, so I will confine myself to that.

This was certainly the best performance I had ever seen in a single bull. Moreover, conditions were about as adverse as they could be. It was the big show of the year 1949, the Hospital Charity fight in Madrid, with the Head of the State present. The first two bulls gave very poor play; two brilliant Sevilians, Manolo González and Pepe Luis Vázquez, had failed in Bulls 3 and 4, which were the best two in the string. The crowd, which had paid high prices, was cross, and the fight appeared to be petering out. Worst of all, a strong wind was blowing, so that the danger of everything was doubled. That was the state of affairs when the trumpet blew, and out came Bull 5, the largest and heaviest of the lot, 1,047 lb. on the hoof.

The matador was Luis Miguel Dominguín, then Spain's Number One ace. I say ace, not idol, for the crowds always treated him with great rigour and judged him by very different standards from the rest. In his first bull, No. 2, he had received some rather cool applause, mixed with whistles, for a fine performance with a very bad bull; Pepe Luis, on the other hand, in No. 4, had received warmer applause and less whistles for what seemed to me a failure with a formidable but fundamentally good and brave bull.

Well, here is 'Peregrino', *cárdeno oscuro* or dark grey, from the Extremadura ranch of Juan Antonio Alvarez like all the rest. For the love of Mike, let's hope he's brave. This is our last chance to see anything decent today, and the crowd knows it. 'Peregrino' is rather ugly, long-bodied and well armed. He turns left as he comes into the ring, which is unusual and is called a *salida contraria*. The very first thing he does is to jump the barrier, and once back in the ring again, to attempt a second jump; a bad sign. He takes the capes uncertainly. This bull is going to take some fighting. Here come the picadors now.

Good! 'Peregrino' is not so tame after all. Over goes the first picador's horse with a crash, and Luis Miguel saves the man with a timely *quite*. 'Peregrino' has caste after all, for Pic 2 is a good hard one, and the bull recharges three times under the iron. This pic equals at least two normal ones, but Extremadura bulls are never soft, and 'Peregrino' needs at least one more. Yet, while González does the *quite*, Dominguín appeals to the President for the trumpet to be blown, and he is not a matador who misjudges a bull. All right, that means two things: one, he is going to place the *banderillas* himself and he wants to leave the bull with some surplus power in hand; two, he is out for something extra special in Act III. And so he was, but none of us can have guessed quite what.

Trumpet for Act II. *Banderillas* by the master, completely alone in the ring. Just the bull, and Luis Miguel with two sticks in his hands. First pair, normal style, *al cuarteo*, running in an arc—but running *slowly*. An exciting piece of work, a lovely exercise in geometry, and a grand pair of *banderillas*. Ovation. Second pair, head on in the style called *poder a poder* or power to power, magnificently placed, but one stick fell out later. The third pair was amazing, *al quiebro*, in which the bull charges the stationary man. This is normally done out in the open, but he chose to do it with the bull beside the barrier and himself also, about a foot out from the planks. He challenged the bull from twenty yards. No charge. Now he's walking slowly along the fence, one yard out, in the sun. No charge; nor at fifteen yards; nor at ten yards. The crowd gets agonised: you just can't do the *quiebro* at under ten yards, it needs a long straight charge from the bull. He's too near, it'll smash him against the boards, he'll never get it to swerve in that space. Now he's at seven yards, and a woman shrieks, now at five yards, my God this is awful. At five yards it charged, and he did a perfect *quiebro*, both sticks plumb on top, just swaying outwards enough to deflect the bull's trajectory twelve inches to miss his chest with the horn, and with its ribs bumping his as its long body rushed past. If it were not a physical impossibility, I'd have said that he never moved his feet. An amazing *quiebro*, I've never seen one like it. Colossal ovation. Trumpet for the final Act, with the *plaza* fairly seething.

As we've seen, 'Peregrino' does not charge too honestly, and of course it is one pic short. It needs torrying and it needs dominating. I expected some 'punishment passes' to soften it up a bit. But no. One testing flap with the cloth, then two of the curtain-raisers over the top, both magnificent, shouts of "*Olé!*" The strong wind makes this sort of work twice as hard, too. Now the *muleta* is in his left hand for a *natural* pass, not easy, the bull's charge is still uncertain. Two more testing flaps, then four colossal *naturales* and the breast pass, classic style, grand ovation. The bull is growing more obedient under the magical cloth. Two more testing flaps, and then, the sensation. I had read newspaper reports of this astounding pass of Dominguín's, but found them hard to believe. But he did it. A right-hand *natural*, often called *en redondo* or 'in a circle', because the pass is an arc of a circle, so that after three passes the man and bull are back where they started; but this one was not merely an arc of a circle, nor merely a semicircle, but a full circle of 360 degrees in one pass, and oh! so slowly, the man gyrating in slow motion in the centre, and the bull charging round the circumference like a toy horse on a merry-go-round. This he did three times running, without a stop, except to engender a fresh pass each time, and finishing off with an *afarolado* with the cloth swirling up around his head, and a *desplante*, kneeling on one knee, back to the bull, and looking up at the audience as if to say: "What do you think of *that*?" It was 'the delirium', as the old-fashioned reporters say. The *plaza* went mad cheering. Then, three enormous *naturales* with the left hand, each of 180 degrees, roars of "*Olé!*" The bull won't come in for the breast pass, so he gives it a breather (I see now why he wanted the pic act cut short), and when it does charge, the prepared breast pass and a right-hander of 180 degrees; and then, the final, fantastic pass, a right-hand *natural* of 540 degrees, a full circle and a half all in one, revolving very slowly with the bull charging right round him and round again. The audience, all standing up now, shouting, cheering, throwing hats into the ring.

Now he withdraws the sword for the kill. "No, no!" shouts the audience, some because they want more, others because they see that the bull is not properly squared. But he knows what he's at. He just nods firmly, as if to say: "Yes, this is it, just watch, you haven't seen this either." He challenged the bull, waved the cloth at it, stamped his left foot forward, withdrew it, the bull charged and he stood like a statue and sank the sword up to the hilt in a perfect thrust *recibiendo*, the ancient, classical kill, hardly ever attempted today* because it is too dangerous and too difficult and the sword goes in crosswise unless it is perfect. The kill *recibiendo* is the most beautiful sight in all bullfighting, and this was done the way it is described in the old books. Afterwards, one quick stab with the *descabello* sword and the bull was dead. The *plaza* was a madhouse, a snowstorm of 23,000 handkerchiefs waving. The ear. The other ear. Two rounds of the ring, with our hands sore from clapping; hats, cigars, flowers, wineskins raining down into the ring. And at the end of the day, a rush into the ring to hoist him shoulder high and carry him out through the big gates and all the way up the *calle de Alcalá*. Dominguín, successor to Joselito! Dominguin does the *faena* and kill of his life, to a difficult bull on a windy day! I have tried to describe it, but I think I have failed. You can't describe these things. You have to see them, and then, perhaps, you can believe them.

---

* Until Antonio Bienvenida, in the second half of 1955, started killing bulls *regularly* that way, after the famous fight of 3rd July.

There is the tragedy of Luis Miguel Dominguín. For he could do such things; and he could dominate any bull, however tough—I have seen him dominate bulls far tougher and more dangerous than 'Peregrino', and heavier, too. Nor was he ever daunted by needle-sharp horns, when his bulls had them. Yet, when the integral bull, with integral horns, was restored for all fights instead of merely for some, he retired. And thereby he rejected the right to be called a second Joselito. He could have shown that the weight of the bulls meant nothing to him, and the sharpness of their horns meant less. But he turned down the chance.

Interlude: Noblesse Oblige

Earlier on I mentioned photographs from my album. This time also I refer to photographs; but these ones are not in my possession, except as they appear on a certain page of a bullfighting review, in which, the owner tells me, they appeared without his permission.

The first photograph shows a bull, sideways on, at the end of Act 3 and exactly as it ought to be at that moment: completely dominated but not exhausted, head a little lower than horizontal, mouth shut, feet exactly squared; a perfect position for the kill. The matador stands facing the camera; his left hand is holding the bull's right horn, not by the tip but the base; yet he is in no special danger, for the bull is so intent on the red cloth he holds low down in his right hand, that for it nothing else on earth exists. As a photograph of how a bull should be prepared for killing, it would be hard to surpass.

In the second and third pictures you see him delivering the thrust, in fact the sword is almost home. But things have changed. The actual position in the ring is different. The bull's attention is now fixed not on the cloth but on the man.

From the angle of the second photograph, you can appreciate the length of the bull's neck, so typical of the older type of Miura bull, of largely Cabrera caste, with their trick of lengthening out the neck and hooking hard for the man's body at the critical moment. That is what it is doing now, in picture 2; in picture 3, which is a poor exposure and blurry, details are not clear, but it is evident from the unnatural angle of the man's right thigh that something has gone amiss. And in picture 4, the man has fallen almost under the hind-feet of the bull, which is staggering off mortally wounded with the sword-hilt sticking up on top of its withers.

The contrast between the first picture and the second is so glaring that it is hard to believe they come from the same fight. The obvious and complete domination of the bull by the matador in the first has vanished. The bull is no longer squared. It has changed its terrain. The man's position is hopelessly compromised. How in the world could he have thrown away the perfect position he had in the first picture?

The result, according to the medical report by Dr. Garrido of Linares, was the following: "A horn wound in the lower corner of the Scarpa triangle, with two trajectories: the first, 10 in. long, upwards and inwards, damaging the fibres of the sartorius, facio-cridiformis and rectus externus muscles, cutting the long saphenous vein, and skirting the vasculo-nerve packet and femoral artery for two inches: the second, about 8 in. long, downwards and outwards. Intense hæmorrhage and traumatic shock. Prognosis, very grave." (Note that the femoral artery was not cut; also that the prognosis was not *gravísimo* or critical.) They gave him a blood transfusion while doing the first treatment, and three more during the night. That was Thursday to Friday, 28th–29th August, 1947.

For some reason I had not bought a paper on Friday morning and I knew nothing of all this. I was very busy all day, and in the evening I turned up at the Spanish National

Radio, where I was then working as a temporary announcer in English. They gave me the sheets I was to read, and I started glancing over them in the few minutes before the broadcast started. The first news item to be read by me began thus: "We announce with great regret that at six minutes past five this morning, the world-famous bullfighter Manolete died at Linares, as the result of a wound he received yesterday afternoon in the ring from a bull of Miura . . ." I had no idea that he had even been fighting on Thursday, and it can be imagined with what emotion I found myself broadcasting the first English announcement to the world of the tragedy which had occurred.

After the first collapse, the great horn-wound specialist Dr. Jiménez Guinea had been sent for from Madrid. He arrived at four a.m. after breaking records over the 180-odd miles. Manolete recognised him and spoke to him, but there was nothing to be done. The feeling was already leaving his legs. At five the priest gave him the Last Sacraments, and six minutes later, as they were preparing the fifth trans-fusion, Manolete died. It is most unlikely that Jiménez Guinea could have saved him if he had been there at the start, for he died not of the injury but of the shock. Rafael Ortega and the Portuguese Dos Santos have both had worse wounds than that—Ortega's was far worse—but they simply refused to die. In Manolete's case, for some psychic reason, the organism failed to react.

Later on, the photographer who took these pictures, and who is a friend of mine and is himself an ex-bullfighter, showed me the complete set of the whole fight, bull by bull, and particularly a very full series of this *faena* of Manolete to No. 5. From what he told me, and from the pictures, I have pieced together an explanation of one mystery: How did the world's most famous matador get himself killed in such a way?

First, here is the explanation of the radical difference

between the scenes in picture 1 and picture 2. Among other objectionable innovations, Manolete was responsible for the practice of using a sham sword for the *faena*. His slavish copiers simply did it to save themselves trouble, but he had a reason, namely an injured wrist, which, if operated on, might have left him useless for bullfighting. He therefore used a sham sword for the passes, and then switched over to the real one just before the kill. This destroys the unity of the *faena*, and there are also graver objections; but for him it was a *pis-aller* at the time; meanwhile, he used to carry a heavy iron walking-stick on country walks in an effort to re-educate his wrist muscles.

In the fighting of this bull, 'Islero', he began as usual with the sham sword. The bull, which had been so villainously and abusively pic'd by Atienza that the President actually fined him on the spot (a very rare occurrence) had become crafty and wised-up, and at the beginning of Act III it had established a *querencia* at the bullpen door, which is reckoned about the most dangerous spot in the ring; its being permitted to do so is further evidence that the *lidia* given to this Miura bull was very bad. The photographs my friend had taken showed clearly how Manolete had to go into the heart of the bull's terrain, at the risk of his life, in each pass, to draw it gradually away from its chosen haunt. Then, once out in the open, he had the opportunity of changing the sham sword for the real one; but his *mozo de estoques* stated in an interview afterwards that he twice offered Manolete the killing sword and it was twice refused. Having got the bull into the open, Manolete then gave it a better *faena* than it deserved, even including left-hand *natural* passes and decorative effects. All this is proved abundantly by the complete set of exposures, which has never been published. 'Islero' received the sort of *faena* that is normally given only to a brave, noble bull, not to a crafty *manso* with obvious ill intentions. Manolete was the outstanding figure in the bullfighting world, and he charged fees two or three times higher than had ever been dreamt of before (though less than his inferior imitators demand today); accordingly, the public had the right to demand much more from him; or so he may have reckoned.

However that may be, there he had 'Islero' so completely mastered that he could stroke the base of the horn and look at the audience while the bull simply stared hypnotised at the red cloth. That was the perfect moment for the kill, and if he had had a sword in his hand, he would have sent 'Islero' rolling over dead without much trouble and would still be alive today. But all he had in his hand was a piece of wood covered with aluminium paint.

So he went over to the barrier to get the real sword. And by the time he had exchanged the stick for the steel, the magical red cloth was forgotten; the spell was broken; 'Islero' was back in its *querencia*, and was waiting for him there. All the lovely *faena* was thrown away, all the risks had been taken for nothing. "This was where we came in," at the beginning of Act III, only with the bull still more wised-up now. Did he realise the terrible lapse in ringcraft, and just go on in a spirit of fatalism, or was the whole thing a sort of mental blackout such as the greatest experts suffer from at times? We shall never know. But what he cannot have failed to realise was that a decent kill in the new position entailed overwhelming risk. The 'intelligent' thing would have been to give the bull a *bajonazo*, or at least (as the sword-handler shouted out to him from the barrier) to "take it easy and lengthen your arm", without going in too close or too straight. But Manolete was a killer of bulls, not an assassin. On the sword his fame had been built, and his position demanded that he should kill all bulls, including this one, as well as he knew how. His reputation, in the ring, was that of an honourable fighter and a killer who never faked. So he killed the treacherous 'Islero' in the honourable way. He is dead now; his influence on bullfighting, almost uniformly disastrous, has now nearly evaporated; but his personal honour, as an individual swordsman, lives. It was a case of 'Noblesse oblige'. *¡ Que Dios le haya perdonado!*

4 The Rise of Rafael Ortega

I seldom bother to keep notes of junior fights in the off season. But this one looked worth it. The then crack *novilleros*—Aparicio, Litri, Ordóñez—were going round the provinces, fighting four or five times a week against small three-year-olds, 'selected' and certainly 'shaved' as well. At Headquarters, that stuff does not go down.

Madrid, 21st August, 1949. Six *novillos* of Manuel Arranz, the best of Salamanca though occasionally weak on feet, for Jesús Gracia (Saragossa), Jerónimo Pimentel (Madrid) and Rafael Ortega (Cádiz).

Gracia had done well at his début in Madrid; Pimentel also, and likewise last time out, with an elderly *manso*. Ortega (no relation to the great Domingo Ortega), a brilliant début in Madrid, carried out shoulder-high at the end. He is a more sturdy blond lad of twenty-five who knows plenty and kills beautifully. Only his second fight of the year; none last year; in '47 fought thirteen times and did well. Here was his big chance. Great expectancy: the *plaza*, recently half-empty, was full up despite terrific heat. At the sorting-out in the morning, a good intelligent crowd, much impressed by fine appearance of *novillos* (almost *toros* in truth, bigger than a lot of the animals fought in provinces as full bulls) and by their exceptionally long horns. The two most formidable are for Ortega, who doesn't seem to care how big they come.

Start, 6.45 summer time. Stifling heat, even in shade seats. I was in No. 3 Block, sun-and-shade, where at this time of year you get full shade for the lower price. *Verb. sap.*

Bull No. 1 for Gracia. Bull's weight, 838 lb. on hoof. Sensation, as it emerges, at size of horns. Man and wife next to me comment. I said: "Madam, there are five more inside and most of them have bigger horns than that." Old-timer near, delighted. No horn, no enemy; no enemy, no emotion; no emotion, no bullfight, only ballet. Alas, this bug, though very brave, is dicky on forefeet. Falls twice in pic act (three pics), also in capework and in *banderillas*. Great disappointment at weakness of brave bull (it was the only weak one).

5.59, *faena*. Dedicates to audience, unwise with such a bull; mixed reception. Gracia takes his time, gives it a rest. A brave but feeble bull is a problem indeed. Half a dozen passes with the right, gently so as not to ground it. Draws it out to centre where terrain favours bull, then stupidly gives a low pass, grounding it (whistles). Muddled work with the right, then left-handers, but in the breast pass the long horn hooks hip of breeches and up he goes, swung round and round. General fright but no consequences. Some more passes, not worth much. 7.04, hands in his wooden sword and gets the real one. Torries with precautions to square the bull. 7.05, a *pinchazo* a bit low. 7.06, a fine thrust to the hilt, right on top. Bull falls, dagger-man connects. Applause for good will and fine thrust. Whistles to bull in drag-out. Not too good a start.

Bull No. 2, for Pimentel. Bull looks tougher, horns respectable but shorter. Weight 948 lb. on hoof, more than regulation minimum for full bull in any ring, then. Has plenty of gas. Pimentel, six *verónicas* and a half, not bad, applause.

Pics: 1, good, shoves horse round in a circle and nearly over. In turning short, bull trips and falls accidentally. Howls from crowd, but they're wrong this time. Pic 2, goes in hard from fifteen yards, impressive; good pic, giving bull its natural exit on off side. *Quite* by Ortega, business only; he fears this bug is weak on feet too. Pic 3, charges furiously and knocks horse over, coming away loose without *quite*. Storm of whistles at President for not sounding trumpet after three pics, the official *novillo* ration. But President is dead right; this is a full *toro*. Pic 4, recharging hard twice, a good pic. Trumpet. Whistles at picador and also a strong ovation from those who appreciated his good work. All round me clapped.

Banderillas: 1st pair by good peón Escudero, good; 2nd, by notable peón Faroles, also good. Chasing him, bull smashes hole as big as a man's head through stout boards of barrier. After four hard pics! 3rd pair, a false run. Trumpet.

7.17, *faena*. Did all the work on the ten-yard line opposite Block 9 in the shade: excellent linking-up. Preliminary flaps; then draws bull a bit further out. Some right-hand *naturales*, insufficient follow-through, bull reaches cloth. Walks away. (Division of opinions.) Challenges from far as before: three with right hand and the breast pass, applause. Turns bull neatly by swopping cloth to left hand, then cites for left-hand *natural* from far, face on, classic style: 1, good; 2, had to move feet; 3, good; 4, 'taking it' courageously when bull stops in middle of pass and has to be 'sent through' in two tempos. Much emotion. Another, colossal, cheers and big ovation. Three *manoletinas* and a swirl flourish. Changes sham sword for real one (pity he uses that silly thing!); then, 7.24, a *pinchazo* a bit forward. Three more *manoletinas*, applause. Then an ugly thrust, three-quarters, in the neck, and far from straight. Dagger. Very good *faena*, poorish kill, to a bull that had gone sticky and difficult, probably through that fearful whack against boards, which was no one's fault. Round of ring, 7.26. Applause to bull in drag-out.

Bull No. 3, for Ortega. Smaller in size (810 lb. on hoof), but with very wide horns. Lady next me comments.

("Madam, when you see Number Six, you will regard this one as *cubeto!*") Ortega, ovation for fine *verónicas*; feet pretty nearly together, so not classical, but a 'gesture' all right against an unpic'd bull with such horns. *Plaza* fairly seething with excitement; last time they saw this lad was a week ago and he went out shoulder-high.

Pic 1, bull swerves in an S as it goes in (may have been tested as a calf, but this is very rare in Salamanca). Pic, on top, but picador does a 'White Knight' act, nearly unseated. *Quite*, Ortega, one classical *verónica, cargando la suerte* beautifully, and one *chicuelina*: ovation. Pic 2, on top, but a token only; bull recharges, and picador then 'places' the point on stationary bull (whistles from crowd) and gives bull the works with unnecessary savagery (*bronca*). *Quite*, Gracia, by *gaoneras*, elegant, ovation; gives a swirl and walks airily away in best gallant style, but bull wasn't as 'fixed' as he thought, and was after him in a flash; opportune *quite* by a peón saved him from a fearful *cornada* in the backside. Pic 3, in the ribs, picador doing everything dirty he knew. Trumpet. Picador had to ride round three-quarters of ring to the horse gate, and he received one of the heartiest *broncas* I've heard, with shouts of "Assassin!" etc. *Banderillas*, 1st pair good; 2nd, by grand peón Migueláñez, excellent, ovation; 3rd, bad.

7.36, *faena*. Three flaps low down and then draws bull out to centre. Cites for left-hand *natural* right away, from far, face on, classical. Gives four, excellent, and breast pass, ovation. Bull is now facing the other way, so Ortega, without needing to move, gives another series starting in the opposite direction, excellent again, ovation. Still without moving from the spot, two right-handers plus change of hands plus a *molinete*, applause. In same spot, three *manoletinas* (very exciting with such big horns, which come out under man's armpit each time), and another change of hands, ovation. Squares the bull with one single steady flap. Ortega, naturally, uses the real sword, so is ready to kill. A near-*volapié*, up to the hilt on *todo lo alto*, bull falls stone dead in four seconds. Tremendous enthusiasm. Ear, round of ring. Applause to brave bull. 7.50, out comes watering-cart and waters the sand. Everybody happy now. My wineskin is going round and I have made some new friends.

Bull No. 4, for Gracia. Bull very handsome, deeper of shoulder, looks powerful (weight 915 lb. on hoof, just on the weight for full bulls). Gracia, applause for moderate *verónicas*.

Pic 1, lifts horse and rider four feet off ground and over-turns outfit with a crash. The pic was low. Gores at fallen horse. Pic 2, on top, a stab only; recharges and takes pic 3, with another crashing fall (*batacazo*) for picador. *Lidia*, very bad. Pic 4, recharging, but comes away loose without *quite*. Pics 5, 6, 7 and 8, bull goes in well each time; pics, weak. Horse dies, after leaving ring on its own feet (not same horse as in pic 1). Bull's mouth, still shut tight. *Banderillas*, two pairs and a half, with considerable difficulties.

8.00, *faena*. Despite all those pics, bull has still plenty of strength. Gracia starts well and intelligently with 'benders' *por bajo*. Then cites for right-hand *naturales*, face on, on ten-yard line by Block 10; gives one, then one over the top, gets a fright in middle, bull nearly catches him. More with right hand: one poor, two good, change of hands, breast pass, and is caught and tossed, without consequences. Four more right-handers (two good), nearly gets caught again in same way. Despite the 'benders', the bug is not dominated. A hair-raising *molinete* on his knees. Sheer bravery but not much science. *Manoletinas*, exciting, three, plus a swirl. At 8.04 a half-thrust, a bit forward, but entering well. Peones with capes (*enterradores*) do their stuff in hope of a *descabello*, but not a chance, the bull has plenty of vigour left and its mouth is shut. Shouts of "Get out the long sword!" So he does, but there is more capework by peones, not liked. 8.07 a short thrust not entering well; 8.08 a whole thrust, good, and this time bull falls. Dagger-man has a dangerous job, as he has to kneel in front of bull and stab down over its horns. Gets it right. Applause to Gracia for bravery. Big ovation to bull. Gracia retires to infirmary with contusions and slight hurt to arm.

Bull No. 5, for Pimentel. Bull, with very large horns, weighs 985 lb. on hoof, would make a respectable *toro* in any major fight.

In running the bull, expert peón Escudero loses cape. Bull has lots and lots of gas. Pic 1, a miss, bull overthrows, gores at horse. Pic 1 again, bull swerves in an S like Bull 3, picador misses but then 'places' the point on bull as it shoves against the mattress. Incorrect of course, but not so bad, as he placed it on top. However, is bowled over just the same; bull gores at horse. Business *quite* to prostrate picador by Ortega. Pic 2, horse now very leary; picador, a fine rider, has work cut out to control it and stand up to bull. (Horse not damaged; I saw it later; just no more use for ring work, had 'had enough'. Not common for horses to get like that; as a rule, nowadays, they're all right after they've been knocked over a few times and discover that the *peto* saves them from being wounded.) Pic 3, hard again, good pic, very skilful in view of horse difficulty; bull recharges and round they go in a circle, out in middle of ring. *Alguacil* is standing by near picador for final pic, and tells him that if horse won't take it, he must go and get another. However, he manages the job just once more, a good hard pic, very skilful. Applause for picador. I was just over the horse gate and I saw him ride out cursing horse for folding up under him. He dismounted in a rage, so I clapped hard and called down "Well torried!" Horse was led away, scared but not hurt, I saw it at the end of the afternoon, quite calm and cheerful, in the horse-yard, and the carcass of the one killed by Bull 4 was lying there waiting to be carted off.

Banderillas: 1st pair (Escudero) excellent, ovation; 2nd (Faroles) good; 3rd, fair.

8.21, *faena*. Some low passes. Then cites for left-hand *natural*. Has the same trouble as in his first bull: it sticks in middle of pass; dangerous and awkward. At last he finds the remedy. If challenged from far, bull will come right in, then stop in middle. But if he then gives it a half-pass low down with the right, and quickly changes over to the left while bull is still turning round, it will go through like anything for two *naturales* and then he has to force the third one. Does this several times, most intelligent, brave and skilful; crowd fully appreciates difficulty and tactics. He is fighting a bigger animal than many front-rank full matadors tackle in any but about three *plazas*. In this way he gets in about fifteen *naturales* in series of twos and threes, sometimes with breast pass as well. Constant *olés* and applause; big ovation at end. Gets real sword, 8.27, more passes, good. 8.28, a full thrust to the hilt, well placed. Bull falls, dagger-man connects. Great ovation, and well-deserved ear for fine *faena*, well linked-up, brave and resourceful. Applause and also whistles to bull; the former were deserved.

Bull No. 6, for Ortega. Great sensation as bull comes out. You see horns like this about once a year. Highland-cattle type, but needle-pointed. Bull is a full *toro*, for those days, weight nearly 900 lb. on hoof. Is magnificently 'run' by tubby little Migueláñez, who gives a lesson in efficient and artistic torrying by *largas*, casting the cape full-length in one hand as it should be cast; four *largas*, all classical and all different, test the bull perfectly (ovation). Then Ortega gives three splendid *verónicas* and attempts a '*recorte* with cape over arm' (as one carries a folded mackintosh)—a pass not seen for about fifteen years, which calls for a bull with 'comfortable' horns. He did it fine, but the horn was so long, it just whisked the cape off his forearm. He was rabid, but got a big hand.

Pic 1, a miss, horse nearly over, bull shoves hard. *Quite* by Ortega, *gaoneras*, sensational on account of horn width; I didn't see how the horn could get through, in this pass. Huge ovation; Ortega acknowledges, cap in hand. Pic 1 again, good, recharges hard, round in circle, bull very brave, picador skilful. *Quite*, Pimentel, three *verónicas*, excellent, and a *larga* (ovation). Pic 2, a scrape, then 'placed' on stationary bull as it shoves and shoves, 'going to sleep under the iron' while picador shoves back. At last *quite* by Ortega, by . . . *chicuelinas!*—the pass of all passes which needs nice neat little curving horns. This time, he had to sway body back each time (without moving feet), to make it physically possible for horn to pass (huge ovation). Pic 3, nothing. Trumpet. Enormous ovation to both matadors, who have to salute cap in hand from centre of ring, while peones keep bull quiet.

Banderillas, 1st and 3rd pairs satisfactory; 2nd pair, by Migueláñez, colossal, by the power-to-power method, running straight at the charging bull, method seldom used except by champion matadors. Grand ovation.

Faena. Hush of expectancy. The mere physical conformation of this bug makes every *muleta*-pass an achievement, if done at all close. Ortega alone in ring, banishes capemen. Whole *faena* is done on ten-yard line at Blocks 9-10. Three good low passes to get control, then two *ayudados por alto*, in the old style, the 'pass of the Celestial Empire' as it used to be called, following through with arms and *cargando la suerte*, not the modern dead-statue type; now given only by Gitanillo, Ortega the Great, and a few other old-timers. Ovation. Having removed sword arm, challenges now for left-hand *naturales*, from far: 1, *olé*; 2, *olé*; 3, *olé*; 4, *OLÉ!*; and draws bull out towards centre a bit. Cites with right hand, gives three *naturales* that way, a nasty hook by bull at third one. This bull is not easy meat, to say nothing of its 'timber'. Cites again with left hand from far off: bull slow to come in, Ortega jips it up by running quickly towards it and stopping short; through it goes for two good ones and a swirl, plus a *molinete* but given *slowly*! Ovation. Cites for *manoletinas* (with this bull!) and gives one (great emotion); then, as horn really can't get through properly, changes to the *lasernina* which is the same pass but without holding cloth with left hand behind back. Applause. Bull now tossing head much, and what a head! Not easy to square. Tries hard, still in same area of Blocks 9–10, and gets it squared twice in the 'contrary *suerte*' (bull facing towards barrier), but that is not advisable, and he keeps trying for the 'natural *suerte*' with normal terrains. Once he is about to enter, but audience shouts "NO!" as bull is not well enough squared for a *volapié*. At last, he equalises it in the natural *suerte*. He profiles. (How *is* he going to get past that telegraph pole sticking out to the bull's right?) He raises sword, looks round with a gesture, dedicating bull's death to audience in old-time style as Mazzantini might have done, then in for a colossal *volapié*, fulminates bull on the spot. 8.53, the delirium. Ear, round of ring on shoulders, and both matadors carried out through the big gate. Ortega's name is made. He is ripe for the *alternativa*. What cape! What *muleta*-work! And what a killer! The best, since Andaluz.

5   *Rafael Recovers his Cartel*

Third *corrida* of San Isidro week, Madrid, 16th May, 1950. Six bulls of Buendía for Manolo González, Manuel dos Santos of Portugal, and Rafael Ortega.

These bulls, the famous Santa Coloma herd of old, had gone off badly in recent years but have been coming up again recently. These ones today were not very large, but they were handsome, respectably armed, and good on the whole. No. 2 was a *toro de bandera* and No. 6 was also very brave.

The most splendid-looking was No. 5, which was never fought.

González, Sevilian airy-fairy style but has yielded to vice of doing nearly all his stuff with feet together, consequently has got knocked about a lot, looks gaga or punch-drunk, and in my opinion has gone off a lot. Has the cheek to ask bigger fees than L. M. Dominguín at times. Madrid public loves him, but he's done nothing here for some time now, and has badly overdrawn his credit; left the *plaza* amid a hearty *bronca* yesterday, not for bad luck, but for simply not trying.

Dos Santos, the tough Portuguese who got wounded in the same way as Manolete but much worse, and refused to die; was suicide-merchant at first but now scientifically brave and knows how to torry. Usually kills well. Ortega has a blot on his copybook to wipe out, from the 14th.

Weather cloudy, some raindrops before start. Sand damp, conditions not cheerful, but thank heaven hardly any wind. *Plaza* full.

Bull No. 1, for González. Bull 'Currito', black, weight 941 lb. gross, 590 lb. net. In running, González gives poor *verónicas*; then more, also poor. Whistles.

Pic 1, bull recharged very bravely twice. *Quite* by González, nothing. Pic 2, poor, whistles. *Quite* by Dos Santos, *gaoneras*, but shuffling feet, poor. Pic 3, good, bull brave but not too strong. *Quite* by Ortega, two sound *verónicas* and one bad one. Whistles.

Banderillas, 6.10, amid some drops of rain: a half-pair, then two pairs good. 6.11, *faena*. Two flaps and a right-hander *por alto*. Three left-hand *naturales*, fair; one *alto* with feet together (division of opinions). Then, right-handers: two low, two normal, one low, two normal and a spinner (division of opinions) and two flaps. Changes *muleta*, why? Flap, then left-hand *naturales*: one bad, three more, fair; a left-hand *molinete* (applause), two flaps, and bull is squared. At 6.16 a *pinchazo*, bad, throwing himself outwards. Three more flaps, bull falls down (whistles), gets up again. 6.18, a similar *pinchazo*, more whistles. Bull is buzzed round hard by gravediggers; heavy whistles and shouts of "*Fuera!*" ("Get out!"). 6.19, third *pinchazo*, as before, never facing horns, and this time not even going in, but at arm's length. Catcalls and tango clapping (this is, after all, the torero who headed the list last year, alleged rival to Dominguín who can do everything). 6.20, a half-thrust, fair. Bull lies down after being buzzed round again (heavy whistles), *puntillero* stabs it dead. Heavy whistling and shouts of "*Sinvergüenza!*" ("Scoundrel!"). Bull applauded in drag-out. 6.22. It was brave and noble, no difficulty to torry if one had the essentials, and not even large.

Bull No. 2, for Dos Santos. Bull 'Balconero', black, white belly; 957 lb. gross, 591 lb. net. Is well run. Dos Santos gives four *verónicas*, fairly good but cheered with *olés* and ovation, more for man than his work. Last time here he was never seen, he gave one *farol* to first bull in his *quite*, and got a six-inch *cornada*. Crowd shows sympathy and encouragement.

Pic 1, bull brave, eager, overthrows. *Quite* by Dos Santos, applauded for rescue part, then one *verónica*, one *chicuelina* and one *serpentina*; showy, ovation. Pic 2, overthrew again. *Quite* by Ortega, two *verónicas cargando la suerte* and a half (applause). Pic 3, bull very brave indeed, shoves and shoves regardless of punishment. *Quite* by González, one *verónica*, one *chicuelina* and one nondescript (division of opinions).

Clapping, invitation to Dos Santos to place *banderillas* at which he has high reputation. First pair, good (applause). Second, after showy preparation, half-pair in compromised terrain. Third pair, good. All *al cuarteo*. Ovation.

6.34, *faena*. Three *ayudados por alto*, not bad. Two right-handers of sorts, then draws bull out into middle. Cites from far for right-handers, face on, classic, gives four and breast pass. Ovation. More right-handers, and much better ones, two and a Villalta-type spinner, ovation after *olés* (all this work nicely linked together). Left-hand *naturales*, face on, three good, one fair. Ovation. Then three *laserninas* and a *molinete* and change-over of hands. Grand ovation. Bull squared. 6.37, good *pinchazo*. Ovation. Three right-handers to square bull: a three-quarter thrust but not dead on top. *Descabello*, first shot. Great ovation, petition of ear, not granted. Ovation to brave bull in drag-out; it was very brave and noble. Dos Santos, well-earned round of ring for excellent *faena* and very competent kill.

Bull No. 3, for Ortega. Bull 'Caribello', looked smallest at *apartado* in morning, but was not. Black, white belly. 968 lb. gross, 578 lb. net.

No 'running'. Trumpet. Ortega then gives one poor *verónica*, three good ones with *olés*, and a half. Then three and a half more, good. Ovation. Bull looks fine; long, straight charge.

Pic 1, charges from far, nearly overthrows but not enough power. *Quite* by Ortega, half-*farol*, two *gaoneras* and a *serpentina*. Ovation. Pic 2, good, recharges thrice; picador good, bull better. *Quite* by González, three *chicuelinas* (two good) and a *delantal*. Big ovation. Pic 3, good, recharges and goes on shoving, finally overthrows. Bull very brave but has taken a lot of punishment from pics. *Quite* by Dos Santos, *farol* and *gaoneras*, rather clumsy. *Banderillas*, fair.

6.51, *faena*, dedicated to audience. *Ayudado por alto*, then two more good ones. Applause. Draws bull out to centre. Left-hand *naturales* from far, one *olé*, two more, fair. Bull a bit slow now. Right-hand spinner and one *por alto*. Three more *naturales* and a breast pass. Applause. Bull gives only half-charge now, very *aplomado*, difficult. *Natural?* No, bull won't come in, scraping feet, difficult. Three right-handers; bull now discomposed, pity it got too much pic, but this President doesn't change the Act quick enough, as in the Pablo Romeros two days ago. Two more passes; crowd shouts "Kill it!" Flaps. Squares, 6.56, but with head down on sand, useless to enter like that; two flaps and some good *bajos*. 6.57, a thrust, on top but a bit *tendida*, entering well; kills outright, 6.58. Petition for ear, but *faena* not well enough linked for that. Round of ring. Spots of rain.

Bull No. 4, for González. Bull 'Bizcochito', handsome *cardeno*, big horns. 7.01. Weight 568 lb. net. Running, not good, losing cape. González, some messing about. Trumpet.

Pic 1, good, bull brave, *burladero* saved horse from going over. *Quite* by González, none. Catcalls. Pic 2, very hard and with three recharges under iron. *Quite* by Dos Santos, poor, losing cape. Pic 3, excessive (like No. 2, both well above washer). Recharged. *Quite* by Ortega, *chicuelinas*. President is behaving as if these bulls were five-year-olds. These pics equal about eight normal ones. *Banderillas*, satisfactory, bull still charging well, despite lots of capework.

7.09, *faena*. No *brindis*. Near barrier at No. 10, flap, three *por bajo* (one good), flap, draws bull out towards middle, flap. Then four right-handers (applause), but some use of the 'invisible line'; three more, good, and a *molinete* and a flap. *Olés* and ovation (crowd ready to forgive and forget). Now on *tercio* line of No. 10: three flaps, a *natural* that didn't occur, and some odd passes. And that's all, thanks. 7.14, a *pinchazo*, throwing himself outwards. Whistles. 7.15, ditto, ditto, more ditto. 7.16, a three-quarter-thrust, forward through not entering properly. *Enterradores*; whistles. Bull lies down. *Puntilla*. Loud whistling and shouts of *"Fuera!"* So much for the phenomenon! Crowd getting bored and annoyed.

Bull No. 5, for Dos Santos. The *barbas* of the afternoon, a magnificent bull, black, heavy, very well armed. But it walked out, unable to run. Back legs gone amiss. I remember it hardly moved in corral this morning; man next me said it was already lame last week when on show in Venta de Batán. Green handkerchief, out come steers.

Substitute bull, of Escobar, a decent Andalusian breed. Handsome. Name 'Africano'. Black. Big: 1,078 lb. gross, 655 lb. net. Is slow to take capes. *Manso?* (Some drops of rain, sky dark, day cheerless.) Bull unfixed, running all over ring despite good *brega*; probably has been in corrals some time and needs exercise. Looks *manso*, no eagerness at all. Dos Santos, a bad *verónica*, trying to fix. At last they got it to notice a horse.

Pic 1, *batacazo*, over she goes. Pic 2 (reserve man), point in bull's shoulder, lousy; bull shoves fit to burst. *Burladero* keeps horse upright. *Quite* by Dos Santos, poor. Pic 3, bull eager now, goes to sleep under iron, describes semicircle under pic, then recharges and another semicircle the other way. This pic equals four normal ones. No *quite*. Trumpet. This bull, brave for horses, doesn't care for capes. Head down on sand now, and scraping. Difficult. Clapping for Dos Santos to place *banderillas*. Accedes: 1st pair good, after difficulty; 2nd, good, applause; 3rd, very good, ovation.

7.34, *faena*. This *toro* is a problem. Far from easy: one has to go very close to get a charge, and take big risks; yet it will sometimes charge from far, unexpectedly. However, *brindis* to audience. Applause. 7.35, bull's head, on sand just before, is now in clouds, got to get it down. Two *por bajo*, then out to the middle. Left-hand *naturales*, from far, one good, one not; bull is discomposed and needs much dominating. Two more; dangerous *colada* in second; Dos Santos cool as cucumber. One right-hander 'taking it' at great risk. One flap. Two right-handers, good; a spinner (he is torrying scientifically and well); one *por alto*, one flap; applause. Now the bug has head on sand again. Draws it back to centre, most dangerous place. One right-hander *por alto*, then four *en redondo*, excellent, *olés*; change of hands, applause. Now he has it dominated and obedient. In centre, tries for left-hand *natural*, walks all round bull challenging it, very brave, profiled all the time on contrary horn, no faking or invisible-line stuff; gives his body as lure every time, but nothing doing (it might have charged on the *tercio* line; but in the centre the bull 'weighs very heavy' as they say). Three flaps, lost cloth the last time; still, has bug properly dominated now. 7.42, trying to square it, always cool and elegant, but not easy job; bull, with head on sand, won't follow lure; useless or worse to enter now. At last it attends: 7.43, excellent *pinchazo* on bone; 7.44, a good half-thrust to bull not perfectly squared. Lies down; *puntillero* kills it at third stab. Ovation, salutes from *tercio* line. Dos Santos has been brave and unlucky once again.

Bull No. 6, for Ortega. Public now bored a bit, want to see something spectacular, and not much chance now. Some fools start filing out. Light failing. 7.46, bull 'Cazolejo'. Black, white belly; 1,012 lb. gross, 660 lb. net (over sixty-five per cent, very high power/weight ratio). Shouts of "*Cojo!*" by some more fools. Nonsense, it is not lame at all, but they are bored. Bull well run by Migueláñez, but he lost cape in last *larga*. Ortega applauded in *verónicas*.

Pic 1, bad, low, bull loose. *Quite*, by Ortega, *gaoneras* and *serpentina*. Ovation. Pic 2, good, bull recharges twice very hard (equals three pics). *Quite* by González, indifferent *verónicas*. Pic 3, as above, bull is very brave. *Quite* by Dos Santos, four *gaoneras*, applause. *Banderillas*, one pair good by Migueláñez, others fair.

7.54, the eleventh hour. Shall we see anything? Bull by no means easy. One *por bajo*. Right-hander? No, bull won't charge, has learnt a bit. Flap, *bajo*. Draws it towards centre. Right-hand spinner, good; *bajo*, good. Right-hander? No, won't take it *en redondo*. More domination needed, some of *old* Ortega's stuff. Right-hand spinner, good. Left-hand *natural*: one good, then bull hooks right round at Rafael's face, knocking sword and cloth from his hand. Rafael remains cool. One right-hander, one *por bajo*, now it's better. Left-handers: three *naturales* and breast pass, very good, applause; four more and *pecho*, standing up and 'taking it' with considerable risk. Great ovation. Bull now under control. (All this work linked together, or at least all together in same territory.) Three right-handers and change of hands, much applause; two more *naturales* and *molinete*. Ovation, this is fine. To get it to charge he has to profile on the contrary horn, making it feel sure it will catch him each time, then lead it past as it charges, and make it swerve outwards and round. Beautiful work. Now is the hour of the truth. Two good *bajos* to square it; then, with a gesture of *brindis* to public, old-fashioned style, enters from two yards, straight as arrow, for most beautiful perfect *volapié*, one of the best I have ever seen, buries the blade to the hilt in *todo lo alto*. Bull falls dead at once, without *puntilla*. Enormous enthusiasm, two ears, round of the ring, another round shoulder-high and so out through the big gates. The first ear cut in the *Feria*, at the 18th bull! And well cut. Fine finish to *corrida*. Bulls good but needed torrying. Rafael Ortega has recovered his honour and his cartel. *Olé!*

6   100 *Minutes of Sound Lidia to Bad Bulls*

22nd April, 1951. Reappearance of El Andaluz after two years virtual absence from ring through hip injury. Six bulls of Benítez Cubero of Seville, for Andaluz, Rafael Ortega and Alfredo Jiménez who is to confirm his *alternativa* in Madrid.

I had not seen Jiménez, a second-rater who took *alternativa* in Seville late last season and did badly in Seville Spring Fair this year.

Before May you seldom get a good programme in Madrid nowadays. This one looked all right as regards the first two men, though Andaluz was not likely to be in his best form after his long absence. The bulls were not a breed to inspire confidence but at least were not Salamanca stuff. At the *apartado* I did not think much of them. Armament was all right, but they didn't seem very big. An expert reviewer later admitted in print that he too had estimated them at far below their real weight. Origin of this breed is Vistahermosa-Parladé, but the caste has gone down a lot. This string were all more or less *manso*, mostly *bronco* too, with only a half-charge, and dangerous in general. No. 2 ought to have been fired, as some people near me were observing. But nowadays, with these silly black *banderillas*, it makes no difference. About time they restored the rockets, which do serve some purpose. The *corrida* was very quick, that is something: all over in one hour forty minutes, including a *cornada* and a substitution. *Lidia* was excellent at all times, as always when Andaluz directs it. Weather good. Sun seats full, shade half-full. Normal order altered by *alternativa* in first half.

Bull No. 1, for Jiménez (for *alternativa*). Weight 1,084 lb. on hoof. In running, clearly tends to hook to the right. Jiménez applauded for good capework. Pic 1, fair, horse overthrown. *Quite* by Jiménez, three *verónicas*, a *chicuelina* and a *serpentina*, all good. Ovation. In Pic 2, picador screws with pole. Whistles. *Quite* by Andaluz, three and a half good *verónicas*. Applause. Pic 3, bad, low. Whistles. *Quite* by Ortega, half-*farol*, *gaoneras* and *serpentina*. Applause. A nice *tercio* of *quites*. Bull looks a bit soft to me. *Banderillas*, nothing special.

Faena (after *alternativa* ceremony by Andaluz). Jiménez dedicates to audience. Bull needs one or two 'benders', is hooking right. The lad starts out for glory or the oilcloth. On barrier of Block 9, two *por alto* given kneeling. Three two-handers (*ayudados por alto*), good. Right-hand *naturales*, challenges from far: two fair, in third he has to step back, *as bull is hooking right*. Some applause. One flap, then challenges for left-hand *naturales*, from far, face on, the good way: 1 fair, 2 fair, 3 good, 4—no, bull won't take it. He should then have started a fresh series; instead, tries to force the breast-pass on an unwilling bull *which is hooking right*. When the bull does take it, the inevitable: up he goes, falls on sand, bull goes for him again. The *quite* is made; Jiménez gets up, staggers to barrier but can't go on. Carried to infirmary. Hard lines in first bull, very sorry; but the lad did not dominate the bull; secondly, should have noticed it was hooking to the right; thirdly, should not have forced the breast pass. (Wound, 10 in. deep, in left thigh, upwards, from the toss; running *puntazo* only from the goring, lucky not worse in the latter case. Prognosis, 'grave', i.e. serious but not dangerous.) Ovation to Jiménez as he is carried out.

Andaluz steps forward to kill the bull. Dominates it with four powerful benders, fixes it, squares its feet, and kills quick with two respectable *pinchazos* and a good half-thrust on top. No buzzing of bull round by capemen. It falls. *Puntilla*, first shot. Applause. It is 5.16 (all this, plus the parade, in sixteen minutes).

Bull No. 2, for Andaluz. Weight 1,078 lb., looked less. Is not well run. Seems to give only half-charge, much inferior to last bull. Andaluz gives it two *verónicas*, ordinary, then three more, good, and the bull does a nasty *colada*. Bad intentions from start! Pic 1, flees at first touch; Pic 2, refuses, turns face away; then a poor pic, in two *tempos*; bull thinks of recharging, then flees: a *manso de solemnidad*. Token *quite* by Ortega, three *chicuelinas* and a *media-verónica*, ovation. Turns face and flees from Pic 3, approaches other picador, flees from him too. *Lidia* good, thank heaven. Pic 3 again, after being well put in *suerte* by Andaluz: a fair pic, bull comes away loose. So far, has taken equivalent of one full *puyazo*. Pic 4, never taken, turns away twice. Should be fired. A year or two ago, there'd have been a general shout of *Fuego!*, but no use today. President gets bored, shows handkerchief.

Banderillas, two pairs poor, one pair satisfactory. This *toro* is plain bad, *manso*, *bronco*, dangerous, hooking and tossing.

The *faena* lasted just four minutes. The bug got exactly the *lidia* it needed, as all the papers and radio critics said afterwards. Andaluz starts with four benders *por bajo*, of great power. The *manso* stands there, whacked, and the matador does a *desplante* with back to horns. Great ovation from the real knowledgeable bunch of *aficionados* in Block 9. Then he tries a right-hander. Bull doesn't take it well. All right then, you so-and-so, more benders then: 1, 2, 3, 4, 5, 6, all really hard, all good, all given in twenty-five square yards of ground; got to bust this *bronco*, mustn't let it get its breath, for it is three pics short and has most of its power left. One flap to square it. Enters beautifully at full *volapié* for three-quarters thrust, a shade to left of top centre, which kills outright. Great ovation for most intelligent and able *faena*. Whistles to bull in drag-out. Ovation repeated, Andaluz comes out and salutes from *tercio* line. Critics later all said this was the best *faena* of the day; but of course, you don't cut ears for this.

Bull No. 3, for Ortega. Bull is run and takes a pic, then is clearly lame in one foot, probably two. Green handkerchief, steers remove it.

Substitute bull, of Alicio Tabernero, a bad Salamanca breed (since improved a bit); heavy (1,130 lb.), very wide horns, long and sharp. An old bull, at least five years completed, maybe six; Lord knows how long it's been knocking around in the corrals waiting for a job. Ugly, too. Is well run. Ortega *verónicas* with precautions and I don't blame him, with this prize packet.

Right: This matador described himself as Manolete's successor. Unerring killer Rovira (hatless in *callejón*) observes the exhibition.

Below: When the bull will not follow the cloth only the full *volapié* will do. Andaluz left a piece of shirt-front on the horn.

Pepe Bienvenida killing *recibiendo* in Madrid

Pic 1, horse falls, *quite* nothing. Pic 2, lifts horse, comes away loose, pic O.K. *Quite* by Andaluz, one *verónica*, fair, then hands bull back to waiting picador: not good to give elderly Salamanca cattle too much cape, especially when not your own bull. Pic 3, very hard, recharges, lifts horse, but comes away loose. Applause to picador (Hiena II). Pic 4 (by Reserve), good, comes away loose. Pic 5 (Hiena) good, recharges.

Banderillas, all good, applause. Bull has lost most of its gas now; mouth open, tongue out. Poor caste.

Faena starts on barrier of Block 9 with two passes *por bajo*, fair; the fourth is in front of bull's face, it won't pass now. Two flaps. Bull has less than half-charge. Nothing to be done but kill it. Squares it up, and enters well, but not at full *volapié*, for half-thrust nearly on top. Bull goes down. Dagger. Ovation, not so strong as Andaluz's. Whistles at bull. More applause, Ortega salutes from *burladero*. Correct *lidia*, quick and efficient, to a bad elderly low-caste bug.

Bull No. 4, for Andaluz. Bull seems smaller than last but weighs more (1,148 lb.). Appearance not impressive. Is run by Andaluz himself, with seven purely 'business' *verónicas*, then two and a half more, of artistic type. Some applause.

Pic 1, low, overthrows horse, comes away loose. *Quite* by Andaluz, with yellow side of cape, two *chicuelinas* and a half-*verónica*. Some applause. Pic 2, overthrows; loose, but picador in danger; Andaluz does the business end of the *quite*, and hands bull over to Ortega who does the trimmings: two and a half *navarras*, good, ovation. Pic 3, good, then recharges, picador misses, bull comes away loose. Andaluz puts it back in *suerte* without wasting time. All the *lidia* very good, a pleasure to watch. Pic 4, weak, recharges, gets a good hard one, recharges again. Unjustified whistles from crowd. *Banderillas*, fair.

Brindis to audience. Andaluz starts *faena* on barrier of Block 10 with four *ayudados por alto*, good. Bull is woolly, doesn't charge hard, little life; bad luck, for Andaluz is in fine form and very keen to make a comeback. Cites for right-hander and gives one *por alto*. Left-hand *naturales*: 1 fair, 2 and 3 good; breast pass good, applause. Cites again, jumping up and down to incite woolly bull: 1 fair, 2 and 3 good, 'taking it' from bug with half-charge. Breast pass, good. Some whistles from audience: but why? It's the bull that's dull, not the man. Now with the right-handers: 1 fair, 2 good, 3 good, 4 good, then Domingo Ortega's slicing *cambiado por bajo*, and an *afarolado*, all good, and two *molinetes* on knees; much emotion, for this bull passes so slowly. Mild applause; crowd didn't seem to appreciate. The bull was not worth all this; but it was Andaluz's only chance of the day. Cites for *ayudado por alto*, gives four, but in the style of *manoletinas*, gyrating each time. Finishes with a *kikirikí*. Division of opinions. Two flaps. Left-hand *naturales*: 1 fair, 2 good, 3 poor, breast pass good; two flaps and a *desplante*. Squares bull: a good *pinchazo*, then a good thrust, *todo lo alto*. *Puntilla*. Division of opinions. Applause to bull (unjustified). What a pity it hadn't a little more pep in it!

Bull No. 5, for Ortega. The one fairly decent bug of the day. Weight 1,040 lb., the lightest. Bull emerges kicking with hindfoot, looks bad caste. Is run well and seems eager. Ortega, fine *verónicas cargando la suerte* well, classical, great ovation. They were really excellent. Hats fall in ring. He salutes, *montera* in hand.

Pic 1, overthrows, comes away loose. *Quite* by Ortega, a spectacular and classical *larga afarolada* (*olé!*) and *gaoneras*. Big ovation. Pic 2, good, overthrows horse, picador in danger, grand *quite* by Andaluz, plus two *verónicas*, only fair; whistles. (First time I have heard a matador whistled at after rescuing a comrade from a goring. There are some fools in the audience today.) Pic 3, good, but overthrows; *quite* to picador by Ortega, then two *chicuelinas* and a *serpentina*, good, ovation. He appeals to President for change of *tercio* and

President agrees. (Last time Andaluz did that, the President fined him for it!) Trumpet.

Banderillas, by Faroles; one pair, excellent; pair by other peón, good. Applause. The bull is buoyant, in good condition for *faena*.

Faena begins with three *por bajo*. One right-hander *por alto*. Cites for left-hand *naturales* from far, face on. Has to challenge twice, then: 1 *olé!*, 2 *olé!*, 3 *olé!*; breast pass fair. Ovation. Again: 1 fair, 2 fair, flap, breast pass fair; this series a bit muddled. Applause. Bull now has only half-charge and is tossing head high; awkward. It didn't take long to run out of gas. Ortega cites for pass on *tercio* line at Block 10; loses cloth. Ditto again: right-handers, 1 good, 2 and 3 *por alto*, breast pass good. Three more with the right hand, 'taking it' from stodgy bull, a bit dangerous now. Really time to kill. Three flaps. *Manoletinas* (pretty stale now, toreros have about given best to this pass in good-class circles); fair. Ovation. One flap to square, in middle towards Block 9. Good half-thrust, *todo lo alto*, to bull *arrancando*. Bull is buzzed around by peones, but not much. *Descabello*, first shot, in middle. Great ovation, very weak petition for ear, round of ring. Is given a prepared bunch of flowers in cellophane, looked bad as Ortega is a burly virile fellow and appeared thoroughly unhappy with the thing. This is a bad Barcelona fashion and looks sissy; the classic thing to throw down to toreros is cigars.

Bull No. 6, for Ortega (Jiménez's second bull—Andaluz killed his first). Bull appeared bigger, wider horns. Weight 1,122 lb. Seemed five years old. In running, a nasty *colada*; Ortega runs out from *burladero* to do *quite* to his peón. Pic 1, good but overthrows. Business *quite* to picador by Ortega, then 1 *verónica* and another *colada*. Pic 2 very bad, almost left stuck through skin on shoulder-blade. Bull falls. Andaluz puts it back in *suerte* well. Pic 3, good. No *quite*. *Banderillas*, fair.

Faena dedicated to plaza impresario (good business, but

certainly this firm has treated Ortega well). On barrier of Block 9, three *por bajo*, fair. One *por alto* with right hand, and a third *colada*. Breast pass. Some odd flaps. Now more towards centre: left-hand *natural*, fair. Bull now discomposed and tossing head about. Four flaps. Three passes with right hand and a *molinete*. Brave but not very good. Bull now visibly running out of gas like all the rest: half-charge only. Eight or nine miscellaneous passes with right-hand, applause. Cites with left hand (shouts of "No!"); gives one, not good; another, not good; a third, is apparently caught in the face by the horn, horrors! No, it's only a *banderilla*-shaft. Three flaps and bull is square. Good thrust, a bit forward; three *descabello* stabs. Applause. End, 6.48.

The bulls, of poor caste, with little gas in tank. Not of much respect despite their weight, yet dangerous and nasty. Little chance to shine. Best thrust, Andaluz in No. 2. Best *faena*, ditto. Best cape, Ortega by far. Public, apart from Block 9 in No. 2 *faena*, a bit silly. Interesting *corrida* for those who knew something and were acquainted with the men's styles; Andaluz was working outside his real style in No. 4, in a desperate effort to prove he hadn't lost his old skill. Jiménez, bad luck and bad management; after all, a man who is a full matador must learn not to do certain things, and any fool could see the bull was charging short and hooking right.

Andaluz was evidently all out to get booked for the big May *feria*, especially in the Pablo Romero fight, his favourite bulls although the stars make faces at the idea of tackling them. He was omitted, and the Pablo Romero fight was a mess. The management left out Ortega from the *feria* too, inexplicably. It was dull that year. Andaluz never fought in Madrid again. I saw him fight his last *corrida* later, in July, with huge bulls of Tulio and Isaias Vázquez, after a further bout of illness.

7   Six Bulls in Madrid

There is one enterprise so difficult that few matadors ever
attempt it, because to fail (which in this case means anything short of resounding success) implies the permanent
lowering of their reputation. Actually, in the last fifteen
years, it has only been attempted six or seven times. This
enterprise is to fight six bulls in Madrid, as sole matador.
Even in Madrid you may get away with shoddy work at
times, or you may have a fluky but sensational success in one
bull, or you may be very lucky on several occasions (there
are such men, I can think of one very easily) in drawing the
best bulls of the day; but if you fight six bulls running on the
same afternoon, you show up your true class and resources
unmistakably, and the Madrid public, though it will be
generous and always anxious to applaud, will simply not
accept brass for gold.

The matador who most often fought six bulls single-
handed was Joselito, but even he only did it once in Madrid,
despite the overwhelming triumph he scored. That speaks
for itself. Apart from the natural danger, and the difficulty
of handling six bulls which are all different and require to be
fought each in the right way, the mere physical strain is very
great. If the matador does very well, he will require rather
more than an hour and a half as a rule; if he gets into trouble,
he may take two hours or more. During that time, he never
has a moment off duty. He must direct the *lidia* at all times;
he personally must do all the artistic capework and all the
quites. By regulations, he must carry three complete fighting
teams, one for each two bulls; two of these teams will be
unknown to him, and he must get them to do the work his
way. In practice, he will do most of the *brega* or routine capework himself; in fact, he will not only be sole matador and
director of *lidia*, but probably chief peón as well. In hot

weather, the sweating that a man does—even a well-trained man—under the weight of the heavy gold-braided jacket, is prodigious, and being 'on duty' continuously from start to finish, he will never get a moment to cool off. Any mistakes that he makes will stand out all the more because there is no other matador to divert the audience's attention. He cannot afford to ease up in one or two bulls, or the whole afternoon may go sour on him.

The first attempt since World War II was made by Morenito de Talavera in spring 1947, and he failed, as most people expected. Of course he actually killed the bulls, but that was about all, and he proved beyond dispute that he was a very mediocre torero. His retirement was not long delayed after that. The second occasion was in the same year, by Antonio Bienvenida, shortly after the death of Manolete. He fought without pay, in aid of the Toreros' Benevolent Society, and he proved beyond dispute that he was a first-class torero, despite weakness with the sword at times. The third was the former Argentine, now Peruvian, Rovira, who had built up a great reputation for cast-iron courage and as a sure-fire killer (he is of Basque origin). The fight, which I saw, took place on a broiling July day in 1948, with the temperature at 100° F. in the shade—and no shade, but only a heat haze which later turned into a dust storm. Rovira got his chance because the Marquess of Albayda, a scrupulous rancher of Old Colmenar near Madrid, had sent a string of very handsome and high-caste bulls to Madrid, and the management tried to contract three fashionable stars to fight them. As the blood of these animals is pure Vistahermosa, they were almost certain to prove brave and honest, but the management found it impossible to get the matadors they wanted, though the bulls were not very large. The explanation of the mystery leaked out later. This was in the full ballyhoo period, about which I have written elsewhere, when the horn-mutilation racket was at its height. The Albayda bulls were exceedingly well armed, with needle-sharp horns, and it appeared that none of the self-styled aces would agree to fight them unless the Marquess would have the horn-tips blunted in advance, a thing which he refused point-blank to do. So there were the bulls, and no one of the star class to fight them; and Rovira took the opportunity and offered the management to fight the whole lot himself as sole matador. He scored a memorable triumph, for the bulls, though brave enough, were strong and had nerve, and were nobody's easy meat, but required proper dominating. Rovira proved that day that he was mediocre with the cape, good at the *lidia*, a brave, dominating though rather monotonous torero with the *muleta*—and a superb killer, for he killed every bull with a single magnificent thrust. He was awarded four ears and five rounds of the ring, and was carried out on the shoulders of a large crowd of enthusiasts.

This fight was followed three days later by another of the same kind, when the unchallenged Number One of the Spanish ring, Luis Miguel Dominguín, also appeared as sole matador of six bulls, in the big annual *corrida* in aid of the Press Benevolent Fund. No one fights free for the press; indeed, on this occasion everyone charges the absolute maximum so as to get a little of his own back, for the sums a torero has to spend annually on the press are very considerable. I am not referring to actual bribery of critics, which is another matter; I merely refer to the free seats and the routine sweeteners, and the advertisements he is expected to buy in the papers. However, the fee paid to Dominguín for fighting six not very terrifying bulls of Villagodio (a distinctly flabby breed) was a million pesetas, and for that record sum the public expected plenty from a matador who was an acknowledged master of the art in its various departments. I should not like to say that Dominguín wholly failed, which would be unfair, for after a good start, and an ear rather generously awarded in the second bull, a violent storm of rain, thunder and lightning occurred, and continued for the rest of the afternoon. Dominguín, for the first time in his life, got rattled: his killing went to pot; the last bull, a substitute of Montalvo and five years old, proved a 'block of marble'; and at the end the matador left the *plaza* amid boos and catcalls.

The fifth occasion was the fight I am now going to describe, and the sole matador was Antonio Bienvenida, for the second time in Madrid. Since Antonio had broken the horn-mutilating racket in 1952, he had been the victim of spite and injustice. In 1953, six of the leading figures clubbed together to boycott him, and succeeded in getting him excluded from fight after fight, to the great indignation of the public. So as not to prejudice the success of the charity fight for the Toreros' Benevolent Society, he even resigned from the presidency of that body, which he had held for some years; but was promptly re-elected. Even so, it looked as if the Society was going to lose its biggest source of revenue; for the boycotters were left to arrange the fight, and the cattle they chose were thrown out by the vets as unworthy of Madrid, and the fight was called off. At the last minute, Antonio, aided by the good offices of the Old Master Domingo Ortega, managed to organise a substitute fight in the Madrid suburban *plaza*, which was a howling success, and so the Society survived. In 1954, it appeared that the hatchet had been buried; but then, at the start of the season, in the big April fair at Seville, Antonio's bookings were cancelled by the 'hidden hand'. After that came the still bigger Madrid fair in May, with eight or nine fights in a row, and again Antonio's name was simply passed over, despite the fact that he charges modest fees and is an immense draw with the crowds, who are well aware that if they have a real bullfight today and not a pantomime and a swindle, the credit is his.

All right; so if the mountain won't come to Mahomet,

Two superb *volapiés* by Andaluz to a big Pablo Romero. First entry struck bone (elbow up, sword bent) but got a great ovation. At second entry, bull refused to lower head, but *volapié* succeeded.

Thrust *a un tiempo* by Andaluz (see *Corrida* 1)

Grand thrust *arrancando* by Rafael Llorente; not right horn tip

Mahomet will go to the mountain. On the day that the big Madrid fair ended, Antonio announced that he would fight six bulls in Madrid, single-handed, one week later, on 30th May. So far, I think, he had had only one booking that year on Spanish soil; the other two or three were in French territory which is not taken very seriously. Out of practice as he was, he just had to force the Spanish promoters to accept him and what he stands for; namely, bookings on merit alone, without trusts or closed stables or intrigues. The only way was to appeal to the Supreme Court, the public of Madrid. That public was all for him—but he simply *must* deliver the goods. He was not in practice yet, and his weak spot had always been the kill (he mastered this weakness in the second half of 1955 only, after thirteen years in the ring, and by reviving the almost forgotten *recibiendo* method which his father had practised successfully fifty years before). In Madrid, you may be as brilliant as anything in the course of the *lidia*, but the bull must be killed decently. Otherwise, no ears and no triumph. And with six bulls running, if it is not triumph it is disaster.

The six bulls were from the ranch of Graciliano Pérez Tabernero, of which I have already spoken. This string were brave, all but one, and some of them put up a spectacular fight in Act I. They charged the picadors twenty-nine times with seventeen recharges under the iron, took twenty-seven pics and overthrew seven times, with one horse actually killed—a rare event nowadays. A fine showing for a Salamanca breed. But their bravery was the nervous bravery of the bull of caste: they were not easy meat, they needed dominating by science and art. The flash 'phenomenons' would not have liked them much. With bad ring-craft and excessive cape-flappings they might well have turned *bronco*. Antonio however is a master of the science of *lidia*. He never forgets the old adage: "The hazard of the kill begins with the first cape-flap".

We saw a lot of very good things in the fighting of those six bulls: good pic work (by no means common), splendid *lidia*, a superb display of art with the cape, several admirable *quites* which saved fallen picadors from a goring, a complete range of sincere, classical work with the *muleta*, including two or three really beautiful *faenas*, and even two nice pairs of *banderillas*—all, except of course the pics, being done by Antonio alone, for he hardly used his capemen. I have a complete note of everything that took place, but I am not going to give a detailed account of everything, for there is another fight of Antonio's to come later, in which he reached his absolute zenith. What I would prefer to do is to try to convey an idea of the drama behind the drama going on in the ring.

In itself, Antonio's work is not very 'dramatic'. He is a gay, exquisite, effortless torero of the so-called Sevilian school (though he was born in Venezuela and the family comes from Extremadura). His work does not inspire that deep, tragic emotion which was so notable in that of the real Sevilian El Andaluz. But in this fight today, the passion and emotion is in the audience. Antonio cleans up the bullfight. Antonio boycotted. Antonio defies the boycott. Antonio stakes his reputation on an appeal to Madrid. Madrid fills the ring to bursting; the House Full notices are pasted up outside. Madrid is longing to pass judgment in his favour. He has just got to succeed today—on merit. If he fails, he'll be all washed up, he'll have to retire, and it will be a tragedy, not only for him, but for what is good and true and uncommercialised in bullfighting. And he is out of practice.

That is what thousands of us were undoubtedly thinking when the big red gates swung open, and out walked one solitary little figure, for Antonio is very short, followed at an interval by the immense array of subordinates that compose the three fighting teams of a lone matador. He is greeted with a rousing ovation, which is repeated, twice more, before the first bull comes out, and twice Antonio has to step forward into the ring to bow. The public is eager to cheer him, to award him trophies of victory, if he will give them the chance.

And that is exactly what he does not give them during the first half of the fight. Capework, yes, clamorous and richly deserved ovations for glorious pieces of plastic art and scientific torrying. *Muleta* work too, beautiful sincere passes, domination, good taste. *Faenas* admirably linked together. We cheer you again and again, Antonio, for your lovely work with the cloth lures, for your masterly *lidia*, for your courage: now, dear Antonio, just kill the bull clean and quick, and help yourself to trophies. We know you aren't a Rovira or a Rafael Ortega, we don't expect fulminating *volapiés*; just a decent thrust or half-thrust, respectably placed. We'll allow you a margin of striking bone once or even twice first, on the strength of your other talents; but do just kill respectably.

But he could not. In the first bull, one prick on bone, two, three, four, this is getting bad; five, six, seven (the President must be getting ready to send a trumpet-warning now, which would be a terrible start for the day). Seven times without getting the blade in; and not entering well to the bull himself either. The eighth attempt is a very short thrust. And then three *descabello* stabs. A sorry finish; after the Lord Mayor's Show, the dustcart. Applause for the lovely *faena*, and some whistles. A generous audience.

In Bull No. 2, things were better. Capework superb, two separate ovations for the opening *verónicas* and others for the two *quites*; something really grand. A bad strong wind in the *faena*, which is efficient but not outstanding, and he kills quickly with a moderate half-thrust. Ovation and salute from the ten-yard line. But in Bull No. 3, a big heavy animal, which he torried beautifully with the cloth, the kill was worse again; four bad pricks not entering straight, and then a defective thrust. Silence. Things are beginning to look black. Half the fight gone, and not even a round of the ring to show for it. The wind is getting stronger and stronger. The shadows are right across the arena now, three bulls are dead and triumph is much further away than at the start. Antonio has already overdrawn his credit with the public. If he cracks now, he is finished for good. I begin to feel very sad.

Bull No. 4 is very brave, overthrowing horses and riders. Antonio saves two picadors from a goring by excellent *quites*. At the public's request he places *banderillas* himself. Ovation. Here is a grand bull (the *banderilla* act is the best time of all to size a bull up). His killing simply must not fail this time. The *faena* is glorious. No one could fight closer than this. Four grand 'benders' to get control. Shouts of "*Olé*" for seven beautiful *naturales* with the right, challenging the bull face on with his actual body, then leading it out and around him with the cloth. A two-hander over the top, then still more thunderous *olés* for ten magnificent *naturales* with the left, in the wind, followed by a clamorous ovation; three more *naturales*, and he pricks with the sword twice, on bone, yet nobly, going in straight and putting his heart behind it. Then a fine deep thrust in the right place and the bull falls. Twenty thousand handkerchiefs wave, and the President unhesitatingly grants the ear. Round of the ring amid wild enthusiasm: hats fall in the ring, coats, even shoes, plus flowers, cigars and a wineskin. Antonio takes a long, long drink out of this. He has got going at last!

Bull No. 5 is ugly, with horns like a buffalo. It is of poor caste and rather cowardly. The wind is very nasty. Antonio does a scientific *faena* of domination and kills briefly though not brilliantly. Applause. But still he must get it right in No. 6. One swallow doesn't make a summer, and one ear doesn't make a triumph. No. 6 is medium-sized, well armed and brave. Antonio excels himself with the cape, amid roars of applause. Grand ovation as he dedicates the bull to the audience as a whole. The *faena* is a little jewel, mostly impeccable right-hand *naturales*, in the strong wind and the failing light. The bull is squared and he wants to kill it but the audience won't let him. Just one or two more passes, please, Antonio! Then it squares again, and he goes in beautifully, straight and sincerely, for a thrust which kills outright. The dagger-man draws back his hand, for the bull is already stone dead. O Antonio, why didn't you start like that, you'd have made bullfighting history! But this is the authentic triumph now. The ear, of course, two rounds of the ring with frenzied ovations, and as he departs, a crowd of youthful fans bursts in at the horse gate and carries him twice more round the ring on shoulders (with the audience still standing in their places to applaud) and out through the big gates. How happy we are! Antonio, in a high wind and out of practice, has done it again. No other torero can say the same. His ship has come home.

8 *The Best of All*

3rd July, 1955. *Corrida* in aid of the Toreros' Benevolent Society, which has recently doubled pensions to aged and disabled members, to meet increased cost of living, and needs money badly. Six bulls of Galache (Salamanca), for Antonio Bienvenida, sole matador.

There is always difficulty in organising this fight, in which it is a point of honour to charge no fees. A few years ago, Antonio Bienvenida, who is president of the Society, could not get any men of the front rank to join him, and therefore fought the six bulls himself and scored a great triumph. Since then he has always had trouble with the programme, but in 1952 it was this fight which led to the abolition of the horn-shaving racket. This year, he had been promised support from the leading stars Girón and Aparicio; but when the time came, somehow neither of them was available. Result: Antonio once again offered to fight the six bulls himself. This makes the third time he has appeared alone in Madrid with six bulls, a feat never achieved by anyone before. People said the *plaza* would not fill, for Antonio has been seen a good deal in Madrid, and is now in his fourteenth year as a full matador; also, he is not a good killer, and he did very badly, with *broncas* and all, in the big May *feria* in Madrid this year.

The fight started at 6.30 B.S.T. All toreros fought free in aid of their aged, sick or injured companions. Fine weather, hot, almost no wind. *Plaza* full to the limit; House Full notices pasted up outside. Prices moderate: a good seat in the shade, twelve shillings. President, I don't know who. Technical assessor, Vicente Pastor. This fight was such a historic one, by common consent the best seen in Madrid for many a long year, that it deserves to be recorded in detail.

Gates open: Antonio, in green and gold, walks out alone, followed at interval by the supernumerary matador (an unknown junior) and then his three fighting teams (two bulls each). Huge ovation as he appears; at half-way across *plaza* he already has to doff his *montera* to acknowledge it. Ovation does not stop; increases while they change capes. A three-in-one ovation. All advance into centre to acknowledge. Still another as *alguacil* takes key to bull pen.

Bull No. 1, 6.36. Plain black, fair size, well armed. Comes out *abanto* (leary, scary). Handsome. Antonio gives it one testing *verónica*, then: *verónicas*, 1 and 2 good, *olé*, but with a dangerous inward swerve (*colada*); 3 good, given low down to cut bull's speed; 4, and a half-*verónica*. Ovation. Bull is 'fixed'. Antonio puts it neatly in *suerte* before picador.

Pic 1, good. Bull recharges in circle, carrying horse round. Pic 2, lifts horse twice without overthrowing; comes away loose. Antonio looks after it carefully, no unnecessary cape-flaps. Pic 3, good; recharges three times; the bull grows under punishment, for the moment, but this is deceptive, see later. On coming out of pic, bends forefeet. Trumpet. Applause.

Banderillas: bull doubles forefeet in first pair, falls down in second. Trumpet, 6.40.

Faena. Problem, difficult: bull has caste (good or gone bad, but caste), yet no strength in feet; will therefore defend itself with its head (horns, formidable). Needs dominating; but 'benders' will merely make it fall down.

Antonio starts on boards of Block 10. Two *ayudados por alto* (two-handers over the top), good; one right-hand *alto* (right-hander over the top), good; breast pass, good; then loses cloth on needle-pointed horn. Then: right-hand *alto*, and a *cambiado por bajo* (Ortega's slicing right-hander), applause. The bull is *de cuidado*, a dangerous customer. Needs whiplashing with low passes to reduce it, but impossible to give these for reason stated. So: *ayudados en redondo* (two-handers but in circle like *naturales*; Joselito was a master of this pass, which is of great domination but not so violent as the *ayudado por bajo*, low down); three of these, *olés*, very good. One *alto*. Two right-handers and a breast pass, excellent. Grand ovation. (The whole *faena* linked together in twenty-five yards of terrain.) A valiant *desplante*, kneeling and touching horn. Ovation. Right-hand *alto*, a *bajo*, trying to square the bull, which gives trouble. 6.43, squared. Short thrust *a un tiempo*, man and bull meeting in middle. Bull spits out sword. 6.44, squared again: a low thrust, not fully his fault, bull shrugged sideways as he entered. Dagger, first shot. Much applause.

Bull No. 2, with shorter horns, seemed smaller and not handsome, but grew in the fighting and proved brave.

Antonio runs it himself with five *verónicas*, excellent (in fifth, bull slits cape in half). Great ovation. Antonio's *lidia*, perfect.

Pic 1, overthrows; *quite* by Antonio, very good, to picador; then one *verónica* and two *chicuelinas galleando* (running lightly and doing a sort of dance with the bull) and a half-*verónica*, all excellent. Great ovation. Pic 2, good, with two recharges. *Quite* at Antonio's invitation, by the supernumerary: two and a half *verónicas*, applause. Pic 3, light. Trumpet. In the *quite* Antonio looks after bull carefully so as not to give it one flap too many.

Banderillas, by Antonio himself. Alone in centre: first pair, *al cuarteo* (running in arc), right-hand side, very well placed but one stick fell out. 2nd pair, ditto, but left-hand side, very good, ovation. Bull is 'growing', getting braver and better. Its own caste, of course, but also the admirable *lidia* it is being given, with everything useful and nothing wasted. 3rd pair, out near centre: exciting preparation, then *al cuarteo*, left-hand side, beautiful pair. Great ovation at end of Act. Trumpet.

Faena, dedicated to whole audience, starts 6.57, with right-hand *naturales*, challenging face on and *cruzándose mucho* (i.e. not merely in front of bull, but even over towards its opposite horn, so that when it charges, it will hit the body if it goes straight; the 'phenomenons' do this a lot when bull is exhausted and won't charge, but they don't start *faenas* that way—unless bull is already moribund from abusive pic work). First pass, a try-out; second, *olé*; third, *olé*; fourth, *olé*, and changes hands behind back. Great ovation. Again the same: four right-handers and change of hands, all excellent, *olés* and great ovation; *kikirikí* or *abaniqueo* (opening and shutting 'fan') with left hand in which cloth now is; beautiful; thunderous ovation. And bull emerges ready squared. Eleven passes 'of anthology' and bull ripe for killing. Antonio never wastes opportunities when he is master of the situation. So, he furls *muleta*, profiles, sights along sword, and goes in on bull (poor Antonio, the kill is his Achilles heel, do let us hope he gets a respectable thrust!) . . . at the pure *volapié*!—a thing I've never in nine years seen him do yet. Magnificent, but alas! (I thought) for he hits bone. Top centre, but bone. *Pinchazo* only. Deep sigh of disappointment from crowd, for when Antonio doesn't get it right first time, he's apt to 'eternalise himself with the sword'. But great applause for fine execution of the hazard. "What a pity!" says a man beside me. I agreed; but we didn't know we had been lucky.

Instead of squaring bull again, Antonio decides to do another *faena* for the brave bull has grown in the fighting and still has the gas. So far, apart from the fanning pass, all has been with right hand. Now he starts again with right-handers, two over the top, but then changes to left hand. Now, four left-hand *natural* passes, incredibly close, *olé*, *OLÉ!* Breast pass, magnificent, the real one, not the prepared version. Grand *desplante*, old style. Enormous ovation. More work with either hand, crossing to the limit on the contrary horn. Roars of "*Olé*", palms smoking. 7.05, bull emerges squared. Antonio advances the *muleta*, withdraws it again, bull charges, and he takes it *recibiendo* with a superb thrust to the hilt which kills outright without a dagger. 'The delirium'! Two ears, two rounds of the ring, hats, flowers, cigars. Salute from centre of ring. Colossal!

Bull No. 3, 7.10. Bull is heavy, fat, old, ugly, horns a bit downswept. Much power (it is five years old), but little real bravery. Antonio fixes it with three 'business only' passes.

The picador is 'Hiena II'. Pic 1, overthrows with mighty crash. Great power. Antonio does lightning *quite* to Hiena, then three *verónicas* (second is very good). The *lidia* to this bull is difficult, but is very well directed. Pic 2, charges hard from fifteen yards, wallop go horse and rider again. Bull certainly has power. While Hiena remounts, Antonio keeps bull busy, then puts it back in *suerte* with just one flap of cape. Masterly! Pic 3, overthrows sensationally before picador can get pic properly home, but comes away loose without insisting. Not very brave. *Lidia* by Antonio, excellent: again one wave of cape and it is back in *suerte*. Pic 4 (No. 2 picador), almost overthrows. Good *quite* by Antonio. Grand directing of *lidia* (old style) to old-fashioned bull, which scrapes with forefeet; little bravery, but spectacular long charge. Applause for *lidia* itself, a thing not often heard outside Madrid or even in it. Pic 5 (Hiena), over with a crash again. Hiena, with bull right on top of him, *slaps its face* as a self-*quite*; a split second later, fine *quite* by Antonio. The public is relishing this, just like the old days. Pic 6, over again before pic goes home. Real old-fashioned emergency *quite* by Antonio. Old-fashioned *lidia* with a vengeance! Pic 7, lifts horse in air twice, but comes away loose; distinctly *manso*. Antonio makes No. 2 picador return to his station now, not crossing the other one and going clockwise in muddled fashion, but riding all the way round, anti-clockwise in correct way. This is 1910 *lidia* and the public enjoys every bit of it. Nothing wasted. Meanwhile Antonio himself puts bull in *suerte* with effortless elegance. Pic 9, lifts horse. A good pic. Bull actually recharges, for first time. Trumpet. Applause to picador Hiena, who has pic'd splendidly and suffered five *batacazos*, for which he will collect no fees. It is 7.18; eight minutes for this act; with bad *lidia* (e.g. that of the fashionable 'phenomenons'), it would have been fifteen, and the bull probably spoilt.

Banderillas: 1, a false run. Bull charges furiously when it sees a capeless man (typical of Pablo Romeros, this). 1 again, fair. Bull still has lots of power. 2, good. 3, a half-pair, bad. Trumpet, 7.20.

Faena starts 7.21, on boards of Block 6 (sun), but after one pass has to desist on account of wind which has sprung up. Draws bull to Block 10, under President, then four right-handers and change of hands, very good; tempering (*templando*) excellent, bull never reaches cloth but is always just about to. (Second norm of Pedro Romero: *templar*.) Then, out on ten-yard line: one right-hander, good, then, face on and *cruzándose mucho*, 2, 3 good, 4 *olé*, 5 followed by *ayudado por alto* in centre (wind). Right-handers (alone in centre) 1, 2 *olé*, 3 *olé*, 4 *OLÉ*, and an *ayudado por alto*. Ovation. Great domination; the bull doesn't ever pass as *it* wants to, it comes out of each pass *torried*, steered and made to do just what Antonio wants. Two more *ayudados por alto*, *olés*. Trying to square now. 7.25, square. (All this *faena*, only four minutes, because no time wasted and no messing about.) A grand thrust, right on top, to the hilt. The bull is tough, resists death, but totters, retrocedes and at last falls. Dagger. Great ovation, petition for ear, granted. Retired bullfighters of the Society jump into ring with a banner expressing thanks to Antonio, go to him, shake hands and embrace him. The little child of one of them brings Antonio a bunch of flowers, he kisses the child. From Block No. 3, Nicanor Villalta also jumps into ring and embraces Antonio warmly. They represent about the opposite poles. Nicanor, very tall, awkward, no grace, but admirable killer. Antonio, short, elegant, true artist, but generally weak killer. Triumphal round of ring. Repeated ovations. Watercart comes out and does its round of ring. Another ovation afterwards.

Bull No. 4, 7.35. Bull walks out, very slowly. Handsome, tall at shoulders, deep-chested. Dead black. Peón tries to run it with *largas* and gets the fright of his life, bull makes a fearful swerve to the right. Peón loses cape and streaks for barrier, just makes it, over head first into alleyway. Is this *toro* a 'Barrabas'? Antonio at once steps forward and gives it its 'running' with five and a half *verónicas*, not just 'business' ones but the best vintage stuff, *cargando la suerte* marvellously; corrects bull's 'error' (*olés* and applause). Leaves bull in *suerte* for picador with just one flick of cape.

Pic 1, lifts horse, but comes away loose. *Quite* by Antonio, business only. Pic 2, good. Bull recharges, but comes away loose. *Lidia* by Antonio, lovely: puts bull back in *suerte* with . . . one *chicuelina* (of all passes!). Pic 3, light. Bull comes loose. Pic 4, poor, too far back. Antonio does marvellous *quite*, removing bull from horse, bringing it all the way round him, and leaving it in *suerte* again, all with one single cape pass. He in the middle like Aristotle's motionless mover, and all the *lidia* revolving around him. What a treat this is! Pic 5, good. Bull loose. Pic 6, poor. Antonio, one *verónica*. The motionless mover has not budged a yard from where he was before Pic 1.

Banderillas, by Antonio at public request: 1, from centre, preparation very artistic; *al cuarteo*, left-hand side, very good. Ovation. 2, the same, execution excellent, applause, but one stick a little low. 3, he seems to be preparing for a pair 'from inside outwards', from boards towards centre; but then, as bull starts, he stops, waits, and plants a superb pair *al quiebro*, a *suerte* which I've never seen him or any member of his family attempt before. (*Olé* and a gasp from the crowd, then a clamorous ovation: as good a pair as Antonio has ever placed.)

Faena, 7.43. Boards of Block 9. Right-hand *alto*, then three *ayudados por alto*, *olés*. Then left-hand *naturales*, seven and the breast pass, shouts of *"OLÉ"*, louder and louder, the *plaza* fairly rocks; a magnificent string of *naturales*, the best *muleta* work of the day so far, and we've seen some grand work. Colossal ovation. One over the top and the breast pass (wind). Ovation. Four more grand *naturales* with the right hand (*olés*), and Ortega's *cambiado por bajo*, beautiful, and a grand *desplante*. Superb! Roars of applause, this is THE *faena* of the day, perhaps of the year. ("Kill it well, Antonio!") The bull is squared, the audience is at boiling point, all is waiting for two more ears. But for the first time, Antonio, flushed with his last two kills (*volapié* and *recibiendo*) is *too eager*, like a young apprentice and not a matador of fourteen years' standing. He goes in at the full *volapié*, yes really, but too far and too hard, and as the sword strikes bone he trips and falls in the face of the bull, which goes for him on the ground. As it puts down its head, Antonio *pats its muzzle*! *Quite*, like lightning, by the peones (and by about eighteen retired toreros and *monosabios* too, the ring was half full of them). Gets up, holds hand to right temple (he got wounded here in South America last winter); apparently some concussion. Rests a minute. Then, two flaps, to ten-yard line of Block 10. Two more, to square. 7.46, from very close, a good *pinchazo* right on top. Applause. One flap. Three more *pinchazos*; Antonio is a bit hurt, what a shame he couldn't finish off that marvellous *faena*! Obviously has concussion. On fourth *pinchazo*, falls in front of bull again: *quite* by peones. *Descabello*, O.K. first shot. Huge ovation for grand *faena*, and big petition for ear. Not granted, of course, and rightly.

Question: at that first entry, was Antonio 'pressing', in the golfing sense? I myself think so; it was the only moment of the day when he wasn't quite cool and collected, but hasty. Applause to noble bull in drag-out; grand ovation and two rounds of ring for Antonio, who seems a bit better now, step springy again. But in fact that *cogida* shook him up a lot. Two more bulls to go, this is where the strain tells. He's achieved his triumph already; now to finish decently.

Bull No. 5, piebald black and white. Quite unlike other bulls in type. This one is a typical example of the degenerated herd of Sánchez Cobaleda, the 'horned dough-nuts', beloved of the 'phenomenons', because they charge slowly and straight; but they have no caste and seldom stand up to more than one pic. The breed of today is called 'Galache de Cobaleda'; I don't know if two strains have been mixed, but this object, No. 5, is obviously a Sánchez Cobaleda, there is no mistaking them: coarse *morucho* type, thick ankles, large feet, flabby appearance, cowlike face. Looks like a Swiss milch cow, not a fighting bull. Daft, too: wanders all over ring as Antonio tries to 'run' it. 'Pics' (so to speak): No. 1 is not a pic, but bull caught horse with feet crossed and made it fall over with a gentle shove. *Quite* by Antonio, and the brand-new 'fighting bull' falls down during a plain cape flap. Yes, this is real Sánchez Cobaleda stuff. Pic 1, too far back, but very light, point hardly enters. Bull recharges. *Quite*, and its legs collapse under it. This animal is fit only for a *nocturno* without picadors. Antonio is far too good a *lidiador* to do anything so vulgar as to doff his hat with a flourish and request the President to change the Act. But he did glance up at the presidential box and lift an eyebrow. Almost at the same instant, the trumpet blew (old Vicente Pastor is assessor today!)

This 'bull' is worthless. A doughnut for phenomenons only, not for serious toreros. Maybe they gave it a pair of *banderillas*, maybe two; I did not bother to note. The correct *lidia* for the bug is half a dozen flaps to square it, and then send it back to the butchery department where it ought to have been sent in the first instance. Antonio proceeds to do just that: three low passes, applause; three flaps in the centre, to fix it; four more to square it; two *pinchazos* and a clever half-thrust in the Lagartijo manner. "No doughnuts for Mr. Bienvenida!" Much applause for him, and whistles to dead doughnut, whose entire *lidia*, all three Acts and the drag-out, lasted just twelve minutes.

Bull No. 6, 8.08, final bull; black, and with much more presence than the last. Antonio runs it himself with five and a half magnificent *verónicas*, *olés*. Today he is not only sole matador, sole capeman and director of *lidia*, but chief peón as well. Great ovation as picadors ride out for the last time. Bull, scraping with feet. Antonio, complete master of ring, directing every man just what to do and where. What a relief after the *capea* (village cape-fight) exhibitions given by flash stars who know nothing except the *muleta* and stunts! Antonio, just to show he knows the entire art, puts bull in *suerte* for first pic with three splendid one-handed *largas*, all different. Ovation.

Pic 1, fair. Pic 2, lifts horse (against barrier), recharges. *Quite* by Antonio: one *verónica* (*olé*), one *chicuelina* (*olé*), then four more *chicuelinas galleando*, out into the middle again, pirouetting each time as the bull charges through, and the final pass so timed as to leave the bull precisely in front of the picador for the next pic. Marvellous! Huge ovation, Antonio has to doff *montera* to acknowledge the cheers. Pic 3, good, recharges twice; brave. In *quite*, Antonio first rests bull after effort, then one flick and it is in *suerte* again. Grand *lidia*, brains and art combined. Picador's horse now gets a bit out of hand. Antonio signs across ring for No. 2 picador to take over. Meanwhile, Pic 4, light. New picador arrives; Pic 5, good, recharges. Applause to bull. Trumpet.

Banderillas: 1 and 3 good; 2, bad.

Faena, 8.16. Starts sitting on *estribo*-ledge of barrier at Block 10 and gives an exciting pass over the horns (dangerous: Ignacio Sanchez Mejías got killed doing this). Public on foot. Then, one high, one low and one more low. Bull bends a foreleg, not too strong on feet? Two gentle right-hand passes. No, bull's feet seem all right. Domination passes: *ayudados por bajo*, two-handers low down, most powerful of all passes, two very good. One-hand ditto, three or four, excellent. Bull is squared, and Antonio no doubt thinks 'This had better be it'. (Six bulls in Madrid is a very exhausting affair, to say nothing of the *cogida*.) Excellent three-quarter thrust, right on top, and bull falls. Grand ovation, Antonio is paraded round ring on shoulders of retired toreros and out through the big gates amid clamorous ovations, and so up *calle de Alcalá* right to his house; even there, I understand, a crowd assembled and he had to say some words from the balcony. In ring, after he left, all the peones and picadors, who had also fought free, come forward and are given a big hand by audience, which leaves the *plaza* delighted. One of the great fights of history, certainly the best I've seen, not for profusion of ears cut, but for perfect *lidia* all through; one hour and fifty minutes for six bulls, with all those rounds of the ring. We have seen as good cape-work as the most exacting purist could demand, all through the day; Antonio excelling himself with the *muleta* (that *faena* to No. 4 and the double one to No. 2!). We have seen *lidia* such as has not been seen since the days of Marcial Lalanda before the Spanish War. And a magnificent pair of *banderillas al quiebro* (in the street half an hour later I passed two men still discussing it). We have seen the 'weak killer' kill magnificently at the *volapié*, and still more superbly *recibiendo*. And lots more. And never the slightest breach of regulations or of good form all day. And the empty coffers of the Benevolent Society are full again.

Antonio left the ring, not quite so debonair as usual, for he had had a *cogida* and also a fall. But his hair was not really rumpled, and his nice green and gold suit was innocent of any blood. The only blood he got on himself, ever, was in the right place: on the first two fingers of the right hand, on driving the sword home. The flash stars love to get their bellies all covered with blood off the bull to show how close they work. They do it by leaning in after the horns have gone past. Antonio is not like that.

Descabello (Manolo Navarro, who cut the ear of this bull in Madrid)

The *puntillero*. The matador holds the bull's attention.

A Portuguese *rejoneador*

The last resort. When the bull felled Adolfo Rojas of Peru in the centre of the ring, he wrestled with it until his capemen reached him.

CHAPTER SIXTEEN

The Hour of the Truth

How the Integral Bullfight Was Restored

I

The 1953 season in Spain opened a new epoch in bull-fighting. This is not a mere personal opinion but a plain hard fact—so hard that half a dozen leading matadors, including three of the top stars, retired from the ring. The eldest of the three was just twenty-seven years old.

What had occurred since the close of the 1952 season was quite simply the normalisation of the bullfight; and when I say normal, I am not referring to mere style. In that respect, Pedro Romero was 'normal' in 1780, Montes in 1840, Frascuelo and Lagartijo in 1870, Guerrita in 1899, Joselito and Belmonte in 1917, and Domingo Ortega in 1936, to name the leading figures of each period. Only the period since the Civil War, dominated by the figure of Manolete, had not been normal.

By normal, I mean that the bullfight was what it purported to be: the fighting of a bull. The word *toro*, bull, has just as precise a meaning in bullfighting as the word *horse* has in racing. The first means the entire adult male of the bovine tribe, the latter the entire adult male of the equine tribe. The words 'entire' and 'adult' are both significant. For animals not yet adult or full-grown, the respective words *novillo* and *colt* exist. But what had come about since the

233

Spanish War of 1936–1939 was first the blurring and then the disappearance of this vital distinction. Indeed, apart from Madrid, Seville and a few other rings such as Bilbao and San Sebastian, well-fattened three-year-olds were freely served up as 'bulls', in open defiance of the regulations; but even when the regulations were strictly observed, the public still had no guarantee of seeing genuine bulls, for the minimum weights had been reduced below the point at which even a four-year-old could be truly called a 'bull'.

In the days of Joselito and Belmonte (World War I), the minimum age for a 'bull' was five years completed, and the minimum weight admitted in a first-class ring was 570 kg. on the hoof, that is, 1,254 lb. In 1919, a Royal Order permitted the fighting of four-year-olds, provided they could draw the weight and satisfy the other conditions. Naturally, few four-year-olds could qualify. Then, in 1930, a new code of regulations was drafted, which authorised the regular fighting of four-year-olds, rising five, as *toros*, and reduced the minimum weight to 470 kg. or 1,034 lb. This is a big drop, but it does about represent the minimum at which a modern, precocious four-year-old can really be a mature *toro*. This state of affairs continued until the Spanish War.

During that war, the Reds slaughtered vast numbers of thoroughbred fighting cattle—sometimes to eat, more often out of sheer spite against the ranchers—and by 1939 the situation was chaotic, with an acute shortage of bloodstock cattle, just when everybody all over the country wanted to hold bullfights again. A few months later, with the outbreak of World War II, the devastated state of parts of Spain, and the subsequent droughts, it was very hard to get fodder. So it was announced that "some latitude would be tolerated" in the matter of weights. This was an invitation to commit every sort of abuse, and things got so bad that calves of 650 lb. and even 550 lb. on the hoof were being fought as *toros*. Finally, in spring 1943, it was announced that as conditions had improved, a provisional minimum weight of 423 kg. (930 lb.) would be demanded in first-class rings, 401 kg. in second-class, and 370 kg. in third-class.

This was still 100 lb. short of the regulation weight, but even so it was seldom obeyed outside Madrid. The rancher (especially the new commercialised kind who had largely succeeded the old aristocrats) knew the amount of the fine that was coming, added it to the price of the bulls, and the promoter raised the price of the tickets accordingly; thus the public paid the bill for the underweight animals it had just protested at in the ring. In any case, the fines had been fixed before the war, when one peseta would buy what now cost ten. In 1949 it was attempted to improve matters by making the fines per kg. underweight increase in arithmetical progression up to a given limit; thus the maximum fine for a complete string of undersized *novillos* served up as *toros* became 33,000 pesetas instead of 6,000. But as the undersized *novillos* were selling for 25,000 to 30,000 pesetas a head, and were precisely the breeds most popular with the star matadors who charged the highest fees, the net result was negligible. You still got decent cattle in the four *plazas* I have named, and also elsewhere when the star men were not engaged. But it was quite legal, even in the capital, to call an animal of four years and 930 lb. a bull; in other words, there was complete confusion between *toro* and *novillo*. I myself have seen a junior apprentice in Madrid, an inexperienced newcomer, tackle a big bull of Aleas, rising five years and dressing out at 303 kg. net, i.e. 1,100 lb. on the hoof; and in 1948 I saw Spain's Number One ace matador fight a three-year-old calf weighing 198 kg. net, 660 lb. on the hoof, at Saragossa, a first-class ring, in what was supposed to be one of the big fights of the year. And not only was it a miserable three-year-old calf, but it had practically no horns . . . which brings us to the second 'abnormality'.

All this business of undersized cattle was bad enough in

itself, but there was something much dirtier going on as well. The star men were not content to fight *novillos* instead of *toros*; they also wanted artificially blunted or shortened horns into the bargain. This abuse had occasionally occurred in the past, just as racehorses are occasionally nobbled or doped; but it did not become generalised until the time of Manolete's supremacy, when he and the Mexican ace, Arruza, got together. Their two managers, Camará and Gago, are extremely astute business men; and as the two toreros were the biggest box-office draws, a sort of trust or 'closed stable' was formed, led by the two stars, which could dictate to nearly all the rest of the bullfighting world. The practice of having the bulls' horns 'shaved' or 'arranged' then became more and more widespread.

There is no need to emphasise the dishonourable nature of this racket, which is only too obvious. But as far as the fighting is concerned, the mere filing down of the horns is not the worst of it, unless it is done so viciously as to cause acute suffering, inflammation and even fever to the bull. The worst of it is the preliminary operations, above all when they are carried out on the same day as the fight. A thoroughbred fighting bull is not going to let you simply walk up with a saw and remove the business end of its defences. It has to be immobilised first, with ropes and pulleys and a team of men playing it to a standstill. When the animal emerges from the 'barber's shop', it is half-dead already. Your ropes have done half the matador's work for him. When it comes into the ring (if the job has been done that day), it has only a fraction of its normal power; it also knows that its natural defences have been spoilt, it has just taken a physical thrashing followed by hours of misery and thirst, and psychologically it is not the proud wild animal it was the day before. In addition to this, there were other and darker reports of purges, sandbags and similar methods of sapping the bull's natural strength. . . .

The public knew that some of this went on at times, but they did not know how much. With a few honourable exceptions (notably 'Selipe' of the weekly *Semana*, and Armiñán of *A B C* in a special investigation), the press critics kept very quiet about it, and one need not be a Sherlock Holmes to guess why. Even the honest ones could not always be sure. In Madrid, which is what comes before the public eye most, the 'shaving' was not always done by any means, and when it was, it was done discreetly. Again, many bulls were sent ready-shaved from the ranches. An occasional Civil Governor in the Provinces banned a fight in advance because the bulls were obviously shaved; an occasional bribe-proof vet reported the matter on examination of the carcasses afterwards; but these were rare exceptions. Young Litri, the star who retired at the end of 1952 a rich man after only two years as a full matador, switched over, during his earlier career as a *novillero*, to Manolete's old manager, Camará. Upon this, Litri's former manager, Fernández, sued him for moneys due. The accounts of his stewardship were published in the press: they included one item of 15,000 pesetas in one year, "for arranging the horns of the bulls fought". When Litri retired after two years under Camará's administration, he had had seventy-eight tosses without a single wound. The thing was now quite naked; it was a riotous farce and could hardly last much longer before something blew up. It now remains to describe how the 'gaff' was first publicly blown in a way that could not be ignored; and thereafter how the racket was laid so wide open that it was impossible to keep it up any more.

2

The first scene is Barcelona, where the impresario, señor Balañá, has a string of bulls of the Conde de la Corte which

237

are now over five years old. He bought them in September 1951 as four-year-olds, but all autumn he tried in vain to book first-class matadors to fight them. This is odd, for these bulls are as good as any in the country. They are very brave as a rule, and noted for honesty, without the great weight, power and speed which makes the Tulio Vázquez breed so formidable. Balañá swears that someone is going to fight those bulls, if he has to keep them all winter in the corrals, and in fact he does keep them there. Naturally, they are now much more formidable at five and a half than they were at four and a half. But, people ask, what is so special about these bulls anyway?

In April 1952 the secret leaks out. It appears that the Count of La Corte strongly objects to having his bulls' horns tampered with. So, when he sells a string, he sends a steward and a trusty cowboy with them, not only to deliver them safe, but to stay near them, day and night, until they are fought, so as to prevent any jiggery-pokery. And the Count's men have been camping out at the Barcelona bullring corrals for eight months. That is why no one of the first class wants to fight the bulls.

All this gets plenty of publicity, and the name of the Count becomes popular with the public and unpopular with certain toreros and their omnipotent 'managers'. At last, one star matador, Aparicio, volunteers to fight the bulls. By this action he makes some atonement to the public, for in the past he has been one of the most notorious fighters of shaved bulls. Two other men also volunteer, one of second rank, Carmona, of whom we shall hear again, and a third-class man, Marín. The bulls were fought on 25th May and did not give good play owing to their eight months' lack of exercise. But they were five-and-a-half years old and with horn-tips like daggers. Aparicio cut an ear and Carmona was justly applauded.

The public now started to ask: How many other ranchers

take similar precautions with their bulls? From the fact that top-rank matadors went stone deaf when anyone mentioned Tulio and Isaias Vázquez, it was correctly assumed that this ranch also refused to stand for any tonsorial activities. Then came the bombshell.

One month after the Barcelona fight, a conference was given at the Madrid Press Club by the famous ex-matador (since returned to the ring) and bull-breeder, Domingo Ortega. His bulls are very good, and close blood-relations to those of Conde de la Corte and the Vázquez brothers; only they are fought in all the chief rings and are very popular with the star figures. Whatever Ortega's motives were, he certainly spilt the beans. In answer to a newspaper man's question, he said that (1) the practice of shaving bulls' horns had been pretty general for the last ten years; (2) speaking for himself as a breeder, he could say that with a few exceptions only, *all* the bulls he sold were shaved on the ranch before delivery to purchasers; (3) the few exceptions were precisely the ones that had caused wounds to toreros.

There was the evidence, straight from the horse's mouth, or the bull's horn. No one could pass this over in silence. Some commentators got indignant, and called Ortega a scoundrel for thus trumpeting forth his own disgrace. Others called it "the best *faena* of his life", and he certainly received an ovation at the Press Club. My own view is that Ortega is neither a scoundrel nor a fool. I think he knew exactly what he was at; and I admire his sense of timing, which is what you would expect from a great torero. He had obviously known the whole set-up for years, but until that moment, when things had come to a head, it would have done no good to blurt it out.

The first immediate result was a meeting of bull-breeders to decide what to do. (Incidentally, press statements were published from Tulio and Isaias Vázquez and from señor Urquijo, owner of the famous Murube herd, to the effect that they also prohibited shaving.) At the meeting, it was unanimously resolved to issue a statement deploring the shaving racket, into which they said they had been forced by financial pressure; and petitioning the authorities to put a stop to it.

This sounds rather like Satan rebuking sin, but it may not have been as hypocritical as it appears, for not all breeders have the financial solidity of Vázquez, Urquijo or the Count. And if they know their animals are going to be mutilated in the *plaza* corrals, better to file the horns discreetly on the ranch weeks ahead, rather than have the animal brutally smashed a few hours before the fight. Anyhow, there were all the bull-breeders (except the three mentioned, and a few others who were known to be 'pure' such as the Marquess of Albayda and señor Pablo Romero) begging the government to stop the practices of which they confessed themselves guilty. It was all rather funny. It was funnier still because Ortega, who admitted having filed horns regularly for years, was not actually caught, whereas the famous Juan Belmonte (also a bull-breeder now) was fined a large sum of money the very next week for doing just that. Belmonte, however, forfeited many people's respect by openly supporting the racket in an interview, on what he called 'humanitarian' grounds.

As the season advanced, interest grew. In particular, an open campaign against 'shaving' was started by the daily paper *A B C*. At the same time, the radio critic Curro Meloja, who had regularly denounced shaving for years like a voice crying in the wilderness, began a still more ardent campaign for positive action against it. This critic is the editor of a sponsored programme, but in it he reserves one section which is not sponsored by anybody, and in that he says just what he thinks, and some very good things he says too, for he is a real expert and an old-time enthusiast of forty years' standing. 'Selipe' also turned on the heat in *Semana*, with a blind eye to the large coarse notes which were doubt-less offered him.

Finally, at the end of the season, came the big charity fight in aid of the Toreros' Benevolent Society. This fight, the best seen in Madrid for several years, will go down to history, and was the key piece in the pattern that was gradually assembling.

3

Antonio Bienvenida, who had been president of the Toreros' Benevolent Society for several years, had a lot of trouble in organising this fight. He had announced the date and the bulls, and invited applications from matadors who wished to offer their services; but nobody wished to do so. The bulls were in fact a string of the Conde de la Corte, and by now everyone knew that the Count's brand on a bull—the barred circle and coronet—meant 'untouched by hand'.

When the announcement of these bulls was greeted with what Kai Lung would have called "a strong feeling of no enthusiasm" by the leading matadors who should have volunteered, Antonio declared that the show would positively take place, and if necessary he would fight all six bulls himself, a feat, as we already know, of which he had proved himself capable on an earlier occasion.

Eventually, two men not of the star class did offer. One was young Carmona, who was not scared of these bulls at four and a half years, because he had already fought them at five and a half in Barcelona. The other was the Mexican Silveti, who was not likely to be scared of anything on four feet, because in the Madrid May festival that year he had had to kill four large Pablo Romeros all alone, with both his companions lying in the infirmary wounded. So there were Antonio's comrades, and most suitable ones too. The

Mexican's gesture, in risking his life for a foreign society to which he did not belong, was regarded as very fine.

For this historic fight, the *plaza* was packed, the expectancy tremendous. The teams were cheered on the parade, and then called forward by the audience to salute. Every single man was fighting or serving without pay: the three matadors, the eight picadors, the nine peones, the dagger-man, the sword-handlers, the ring servants, even the carpenters and muleteers; all in aid of the aged and disabled toreros supported by the Society. The bulls were known to be formidable, and the audience was prepared to be indulgent; but this did not prove necessary. Though not very large, the bulls were magnificent-looking, with long, needle-sharp horns. They were very brave but very noble. The general *lidia*, directed by Antonio, was masterly. The bulls were applauded, and two were actually awarded the round of the ring, a very rare occurrence in Madrid. All the matadors did brilliantly, cut ears, and were carried out shoulder-high at the end.

Well, there was a fact like a skyscraper, which nobody could ignore or deny. It had been demonstrated beyond doubt, in the strict *plaza* of Madrid, before the most knowledgeable audience in the world, that men who were not topline stars could triumph *in the modern style* with the unmutilated bulls which the stars would not touch. Everyone felt that something was bound to happen now, and sure enough it did.

As can be imagined, Curro Meloja's broadcast that evening was fairly jubilant. His attitude had always been the same: if you want a bullfight, you must start off with a bull; otherwise you get a swindle or a ballet. A week or two later, after ramming home the lessons of this *corrida* in the interval, he announced that the main feature in the programme that evening was going to be an interview with Antonio Bienvenida, who was to make some special statements. And were they special! Briefly, he said this (I heard the broadcast myself): he thought that horn-mutilation was a smear on what purported to be a brave and honourable profession, and also a swindle against the public. He confessed that he had fought a number of 'shaved' bulls in the past—who hadn't?—but he was never going to fight another.

"In future," he said, "I'm going to the sorting-out of the bulls on the morning of the fight, and if I find that the bulls are shaved, I'll refuse to fight them. So, any promoter who books me from now on knows where he stands. If the public want it the other way, that's all right with me, and I'll retire from the profession. But if I'm booked, then I fight the integral bull, and no other, from now on."

Antonio is a small, slight, cultivated man with charming manners, not a tough guy by any means. Curro Meloja asked him humorously if he was trying to set up as the bravest of the brave. Antonio, also with a chuckle, replied: "I don't think anyone who knows *me* would say *that*. No, I look at it this way: if the bull has long, sharp horns and all its natural power, then you get extra credit if you do well. And if you feel funky that day and get out of the way—well, after all, you've some excuse for it!"

After this classic interview, which millions heard from Radio Madrid and Radio Valencia jointly, things fairly hummed. The papers *A B C* and *Semana*, which had broken the conspiracy of silence, started publishing red-hot articles, accompanied by sensational photographs, some of which were reprinted in the United States press. From the matadors, with one exception, there was a 'deafening silence' (admittedly, one or two were in South America or Mexico by then, such as the excellent swordsman Rafael Ortega). One second-class man, Llorente, wrote in to say that he had never had a bull shaved for him, a thing that no one had ever suspected, for Llorente is as tough as they come and has always fought the most 'uncomfortable' bulls. But the star men just did a Brer Rabbit act. Antonio's declaration was about as welcome to them as a pig to a Rabbi or a bottle of whisky to a Quaker. But the racket had now been forced into an untenable position. The authorities proceeded to hold conferences with all affected parties. Nothing was done with precipitation, but no time was wasted either. Then they acted, and with decision. The new chief of the Police Department, General Hierro (which means 'iron'), did not belie his name.

4

On 10th February, 1953, General Hierro gave a press conference, and handed each reporter a copy of the new ordinances. He explained that they had been drafted after hearing the views of bull-breeders, toreros, promoters, vets, the National Stockbreeders' Union, and his own technical and legal advisory boards, and he reckoned the new rules would produce the desired results. He added that the vexed questions of the pics and the design of the horse-protector were still under review, but no final action would be taken till it was seen how things worked out with the new bulls.

The following is an adapted version of the ordinance, which I have merely boiled down slightly and turned into plainer language. It begins with a preamble, followed by three Articles.

The so-called National Fiesta of Spain is based on the factors of courage, skill, grace and danger. These confer a high artistic value on what might otherwise be regarded as a mere butchery of a brave and noble animal. What gives this National Fiesta its chief æsthetic element is the gallantry of the fighters, calmly and intelligently defying the danger offered by powerful and aggressive animals. In the bullfight, the decisive element is undoubtedly the risk to the performer.

However, the bullfight is passing through a crisis, caused by artificiality, unbridled ambition and fraud, to which the authorities are in duty bound to put a stop. For years a large number of bulls fought in Spain have been subjected to treatment that breaks down their power and tampers with their natural defences, and methods of real brutality have even been employed for this. Accordingly, since the powers placed in the hands of the government authorities by the existing Code of 1930 have not sufficed to protect the rights of the public, the Ministry of the Interior, at the suggestion of the Police Department, has issued the following ordinance:

Article 1. The 1943 provisional relaxation of Regulations 26 and 27, on age and weight of bulls, is hereby cancelled, and those Regulations are restored to full force. (In other words, as already explained, the bull must weigh 100 lb. more on the hoof, making the bull of today equal to that fought before the Civil War, by Belmonte and others.)

Article 2. As from the present season, the bull-breeder's sworn guarantee must also carry a clause that the animals' horns have not been tampered with in any way. When the dead bull is cut up, a government official will take possession of the horns. They will later be examined by veterinary specialists, who will report on their condition. For every animal whose horns have been interfered with, the breeder will be fined 10,000 pesetas, without prejudice to any other punishment inflicted on other persons who may have tampered with the bull after it has left the ranch. In the case of a second offence, that breed of bulls will be banned for a year, if the breeder or his employees have been a party to the mutilation.

If the swindle has been carried out by order of ring managements or toreros against the will of the breeder, the same fine will be inflicted on them; for a second offence, toreros will be banned from performing for six months, or managements forbidden to hold fights for one month, or else fined whatever the Ministry may think fit.

Article 3. The Police Department may make whatever orders it thinks necessary to enforce these ordinances.

All quite short and sweet, and leaving the authorities with all the aces. The first 10,000 pesetas per bull may not seem much, being in fact half the price of the animal or less, if of a good breed. But this is only a warning. The banning of a breeder for the whole year is the real punishment, for a second offence; the warning just tips him off to tighten up his precautions, unless he is prepared for the credit side of his ledgers to show a total of nil for the next twelve months. Such a punishment would indeed be exemplary; besides, it would have a positive advantage for bullfighting, because in that case a ranch's whole output would remain 'on ice', and next year they would be large and powerful and five years old. Further, as five-year-old bulls are not popular with toreros, they would have to be sold cheap, and that would be an advantage for the public. This regulation shows plenty of intelligence in the drafting.

Again, for second offences, fines are no good, as has been abundantly shown in the past. The public always ultimately pays the fine in increased ticket prices. The only way to hit offenders where it hurts is to ban them. A star torero out of action for six months will lose up to two or three million pesetas, apart from letting all the other men get ahead of him. The month's ban on ring managements would work only in Madrid and Barcelona, where there are fights oftener than once a week. In other places, once they have had their festival week, it is nearly all over till next year. So in those cases provision is made for a thumping fine, of un-limited amount, so as to be able to cancel their profits.

The results were positive and immediate. First, real bulls started appearing, not runts. One civil governor banned a whole string in advance, at Palma in Majorca, a tourist resort where anything used to go. The same management runs the Toledo ring, and here there was a fine of 20,000 pesetas for a string of bulls that would have got by as respectable the year before. Secondly, the difference in the horns was most striking; it just shows how one can be gradually bamboozled, a little more each year, until one forgets what a bull really looks like in its natural state.

During the winter preceding the new ordinance, half a dozen well-known toreros had announced their retirement. After the publication of it, several others, not positively retired in theory, have in fact ceased to appear, including Spain's undisputed Number One ace, Luis Miguel Domin- guín. He may yet make a comeback, for he is perfectly capable of fighting the integral bull, even if it were five years old, and he has never shown lack of courage in the past. On the other hand, the Old Master, Domingo Ortega, who first 'blew the gaff' at the Press Club, and who had announced his positive retirement after in fact being out of the game for three years, made a most successful comeback at the age of forty-seven, after first trying out his faculties privately, before a dozen friends only, with a five-year-old bull of his own ranch, which he fought brilliantly and killed as well as ever.

During 1953 the disgruntled 'phenomenons', flash stars who depend more on ballyhoo and their picadors than on their own capacity for domination, attempted to put the veto on Bienvenida, by refusing to appear on the programme with him, and even clubbing together to get him excluded from important festivals. The whole shady manœuvre came out, and the result was the best free advertisement that Antonio could have had. In 1954, the same procedure was attempted again, though less clumsily, for there are some people too stupid to learn. Antonio's reply, after being excluded from the big spring fairs at Seville and Madrid, was to appear in Madrid one week later to fight six difficult bulls single- handed. He scored a resounding triumph, ·and made himself the idol of the Madrid public. At the moment of writing, the boycott is completely broken and a thing of the past; all but one of the 1953 conspirators (who has more or less retired) have been freely alternating with Antonio in all rings. In short, the 'normal' order of the integral bull of full weight and age is now accepted by all, and with this we have apparently seen the last of a cancer that had been under-mining the Spanish bullfight for a dozen years, threatening to reduce it from a virile spectacle and a tragic drama to a quaint old piece of folklore for tourists only.

Index-Glossary
of Technical Terms

Index-Glossary of Technical Terms

Where the term is fully explained in the text, page references only are given here. Only the chief mentions are cited.

ACOMODADOR, ring usher who shows you to your seat. It pays to use him. Tip, in Spain, one peseta.

ACOSO Y DERRIBO, 40.

ADORNO, any pass or other action done for show only, without bull-control.

AFAROLADO, 86.

AFEITADO, 'shaving', artificial blunting or shortening of horns. Illegal, cowardly, cruel and dishonest, but very widespread in Spain in 1942–52. See Chapter 16.

AFICIÓN, keenness. AFICIONADO (1) amateur; (2) bullfight enthusiast, 'fan' or connoisseur.

AGUANTANDO, 94, 169.

ALGUACIL, mounted constable in dress of reign of Philip IV (end of seventeenth century). Two *alguaciles* open the fight by riding out to salute President; then make the DESPEJO (q.v.); then one of them collects key of bullpen from President and delivers it to bullpen-keeper (*torilero*); then both lead ritual parade of toreros from horse-gate to President's box. During fight, an *alguacil* remains in *callejón* to receive orders telephoned down from President and to transmit them to fighters. In some *plazas*, *alguacil* supervises cutting of ear for successful matador and hands it to him.

ALMOHADILLA, cushion hired for afternoon in *plaza*. On no account throw it into the ring in Spain, or you will be fined 250 pesetas.

ALTERNATIVA, full matador's grading, giving former *novillero* right to 'alternate' in major fights with full matadors. Ceremony takes place at beginning of Act III of first bull. Senior matador, as sponsor, formally hands neophyte *muleta* and sword and embraces him, wishing him good fortune. Neophyte then kills first bull, and hands back theoretically lent sword and *muleta* in Act III of second bull, which senior man kills. In second half of fight, normal order of seniority is restored; thus the neophyte kills first and last bulls of day. *Alternativas* conferred in provincial rings should be confirmed in capital, otherwise not valid for Spaniards in Mexico or Mexicans in Spain. An *alternativa* once taken can be renounced, and matador will revert to rank of *novillero*; can take it again if he likes. *Alternativa* is deemed taken, even if neophyte gets wounded and retires before ceremony takes place.

ALTO, PASE POR, 80, 81. EN TODO LO ALTO, right on top (of bull's shoulders), the correct place for pics, *banderillas* and sword-thrusts; also known as *la cruz, los rubios, las agujas, las péndolas*, etc.

ANDANADA, 31, 70.

APARTADO, 36.

APLOMADO, 51, 53.

ARRANCANDO, 94–5.

ARRASTRE, drag-out of dead animal by mule-team.

ATRAVESADA (sword-thrust), askew, crosswise, not parallel with nose-tail axis of bull. Bad fault.

AVISO, 75–6. AVISADO, of bull, 'wised-up', bull that has now learnt to distinguish man's body from the red cloth.

AYUDADO, 80–3. The right-hander given with cloth and sword both held in right hand is *not* an *ayudado*, though sometimes ignorantly so described.

BANDERA, TORO DE, bull of quite exceptional bravery and honesty.

BANDERILLA, paper-decorated wooden stick 70 cm. long, with barbed steel point of 4 cm. by 16 mm. wide. B. DE FUEGO, 71–3. BANDERILLERO, the peón in his capacity of placer of *banderillas* in Act II.

BAJA, of sword-thrust, low, well below right spot. BAJONAZO, scandalously low, amounting to foul blow.

BAJO, PASE POR, 80–3.

BARBAS, EL, the big fellow, biggest bull of a string.

BARRENAR, to drill; screwing with pic pole to enlarge the wound. A foul trick, always protested at by audiences, but only now beginning to be punished by heavy fines. The proper punishment is disqualification *of the matador who permits it*. That would stop it quick.

BARRERA (1) inner barrier; (2) front-row seat.

BATACAZO, crashing fall of picador. Also called *caida de látigo*.

BECERRO, bull-calf. BECERRADA, show (generally amateur) in which such calves are fought.

BERRENDO, piebald, skewbald. B. EN NEGRO, black-and white; B. EN COLORADO, red-and-white; B. EN CÁRDENO, grey-and-white. The colour black dominates in heredity; thus a mating between a black bull and a red cow, both pure-bred, will give a majority of black calves.

BICHO, bug; slang for bull.

BRAGADO, having white belly.

BRAVUCÓN, blusterer, bull that makes great show of aggressiveness but does not show up too well under the pic.

BREGA, the tactical cape-fighting, and in general all work done on bull without the use of any weapon.

BRINDIS, 77-8.

BRONCA, quarrel, row, e.g. between impassioned spectators; also, especially, angry noisy protest by audience at what happens (or fails to happen) in ring; a gilt-edged *bronca* is highly picturesque and some of the Mexican ones, even today, have been truly memorable.

BRONCO, bull that charges irregularly and with sudden violence, either by nature or because spoilt by bad *lidia*. Not incompatible with bravery; good *lidia* will smooth down the harshness and bring out the latent honesty of the bull.

BURLADERO, 52; also, seats affixed to outer wall of *callejón*, for use of fighters, authorities, medicos, pressmen, etc.

BURRICIEGO (bull) that sees badly from near, or from far, or both. The first kind is the worst; one such killed Joselito.

CABESTROS, trained steers. Also called *mansos*.

CACHETERO, see PUNTILLERO.

CALLEJÓN, 31–2.

CAMBIADO, 80–1, 82, 84. The CAMBIADO POR ALTO is the breast pass; the CAMBIADO POR BAJO or *trincherazo* is Domingo Ortega's slicing right-hander, a pass of great domination and basis of all his *faenas*.

CAMBIO, pass in which bull is made to swerve across man and exit from *suerte* on other side of him. The word implies necessarily the use of a cloth lure. AL CAMBIO, incorrect term for *al quiebro*. The *cambio* is extremely dangerous, but most spectacular, and very meritorious; not an *adorno* at all, for it implies the highest degree of bull-control.

CAPA, CAPOTE, cape, 56, 61. CAPEA, village cape-fight; often shouted derisively by audience when *brega* is muddled and ineffective. CAPOTAZO, cape-flap or cast.

CÁRDENO, grey (bull). I do not know why, but *cárdenos*, besides being handsome, are nearly always good, especially among the Pablo Romero bulls.

CARGAR LA SUERTE, 58–9.

CARIOCA, otherwise 'the *suerte* of Atienza' because invented by picador of that name. Consists in swinging horse round so as to block bull's exit from the encounter, then slackening pressure and paying out pole but not withdrawing pic point. The bull, relieved, recharges, picador swings horse further round and gives bull the works again, pic point being still in original wound. Repeat as often as President will stand for. Can half-kill a bull with one pic if bull is brave but not too powerful and goes on shoving, while horse and bull do a sort of slow waltz. Invented, says Atienza, to deal with cowardly bulls that would never take a second pic; but for such bulls the fire-*banderillas* exist, and anyway, there is a correct *lidia* even for a *manso* and it is interesting to watch, being scientifically right. The *carioca* has become common with picadors working for stylised matadors who are unable to dominate a bull not half-killed for them in advance by their picadors. With a bull even half brave, it is just a cowardly trick. Audience generally protests strongly. Fines have been getting plentiful, but do not work since matador pays them. Remedy: *peto* reform, and suspension of picador and his matador for, say, a month at a time. That would work like magic.

CARRIL, TORO DE, bull so noble and smooth that it seems to run 'on rails'.

CARTEL (1) bullfight poster; (2) repute enjoyed by matador in given town.

CASTAÑO, chestnut (colour).

CASTIGO, punishment, e.g. by pic. PASES DE CASTIGO (also called *doblones* or 'benders'),82–3, 130–1, 208.

CHICUELINA, 60–1, 86, 197, 224, 231.

CHIQUERO, see TORIL.

CITAR, to challenge or cite a bull for a pass or other hazard by attracting its attention by voice or gesture.

CODILLEAR, keeping elbows close to sides when giving a pass. Bad defect, ruins bull-control.

COGIDA, being caught by bull.

COLADA, inward swerve by bull, between cloth and man's body. Alarming.

COLEAR, to pull bull's tail. Can cause great pain and injury if done with a twist; hence banned, except in emergency *quites*.

COLETA, torero's pigtail (since Belmonte, sham one).

COLORADO, red (bull).

CONTRABARRERA (1) outer wall of *callejón*; (2) second-row seat.

CORNADA, horn-wound. Usual place, upper thigh.

CORRER AL TORO, 51–2, 56.

CORRIDA (1) bullfight; (2) string of bulls to be fought.

CRUCE, 93, 96, 122.

CRUZ (1) see TODO LO ALTO; (2) crosspiece of sword. In a perfect kill, the matador is said to perform the 'three *cruces*'; in other words, he does the *cruce* perfectly, and buries the sword up to the *cruz* on the *cruz* of the bull.

CUADRAR, 87.

CUADRILLA, team of assistant fighters.

CUARTEO, AL, 69 70.

CUBETO, having horns so inward-curving as to be nearly incapable of wounding. Such animals are fit only for *novilladas*, being evidently *defectuosos*. A lesser degree of *cubeto* is called *brocho*.

DEFECTUOSO, see DESECHO.

DELANTAL, pass of *verónica* type but holding out cape like apron.

DELANTERA (thrust) too far forward; (seat) front row in *grada* and *andanada*; ditto in upper bank of *tendido*, if any; in lower *tendido*, row behind *contrabarrera*.

DENTRO AFUERA, DE, 70.

DERECHAZO, right-hand *muleta* pass.

DESCABELLO, 97.

DESECHO, throwout (from bravery test); animal admissible for *novilladas*, as is one that is DEFECTUOSO, having minor defect, e.g. in horn formation, which disqualifies it for major fight.

DESPEJO, 'clearing', ritual ride round ring by *alguaciles* after saluting President. Today symbolical only; formerly, public strolled about in ring before fight, listening to band, and *alguaciles* really did 'clear the ring'.

DESPLANTE, 86–7.

DESOLLADERO, 32.

DIESTRO, matador.

DIVISA, colours of breeder, ribbons affixed to bull's shoulders by tiny dart, through trap-door, immediately before bullpen door opens.

DOBLÓN, see CASTIGO.

DOLOROSA, 57.

DON TANCREDO, SUERTE DE, a living-statue act, first put on by one Tancredo López in Spain, in 1899. Not part of proper fight; permitted only in *novilladas* and *becerradas*. The man, dressed in white and whitewashed, stands on low white pedestal in middle of ring, and bull is let out. Man stands motionless, and if all goes well, nothing occurs: bull approaches, sniffs, decides the thing is inanimate, and goes away. Just a freak turn of mere risk-taking; still occasionally seen in third-rate shows.

EMBOLADO, 100.

ENCIERRO, 42.

ENGAÑO, cloth lure (cape or *muleta*).

ENMENDARSE, to shuffle back or sidestep as bull charges.

Opposite of *parar*. Maybe necessary if there is a *colada*; otherwise, bad fault.

ENTERRADORES, see MAREAR.

ENTRADA, bullfight ticket.

ESCARBAR, of bull, to paw and scrape ground. Sign of lack of bravery.

ESPADA (fem.) sword; (masc.) matador.

ESPONTÁNEO, amateur interloper who jumps into ring to have a go. Illegal, ruins the *lidia*, and may be direct cause of serious wound to matador (e.g. Miguel Angel, 1953, at Seville, who for some time was expected to die from a wound in the mouth). Waste no sympathy on the *espontáneo*. The crowd, who have paid to see skilled professionals work, nearly always shows its perversity by barracking police as they arrest the fool who has interfered with the show. The *espontáneo* may be brave enough occasionally, but he always appears in the first Act and uses a *muleta*, which the bull is not due to encounter till Act III. His defective passes also teach the bull to turn short and go for the body. No *espontáneo* has ever become a matador of any note.

ESTOCADA, 88–96. E. DESPRENDIDA, a bit below *todo lo alto*. E. TRASERA, too far back. E. DELANTERA, too far forward. E. PESCUECERA, in the neck. E. IDA, with plane of blade vertical instead of horizontal. E. TENDIDA, nearly horizontal instead of at 45°. E. TENDENCIOSA, a little *atravesada*. E. CONTRARIA, below *todo lo alto* but on far side of bull, through going in 'too close'; not blameworthy. ESTOCONAZO, 'a mighty thrust', implying power rather than elegance. ESTOQUE, sword.

ESTRIBO (1) stirrup; (2) ledge running round barrier a foot from ground, to help picadors to remount or fleeing toreros to vault the barrier. Passes are sometimes given sitting on the *estribo*; dangerous, Sánchez Mejías was killed thus in 1934.

FAENA, 'job of work', matador's solo work with *muleta*, Act III.

FAROL, 60–61.

FARPA, 101.

FESTEJO, any kind of entertainment, including bullfight.

FESTIVAL, amateur or charity *novillada*, with fighters in country clothes; not taken too seriously.

FILA, row of seats.

FOGUEAR, to 'fire' with explosive *banderillas*.

FRENTE, DE, 70–1, also used of *muleta* passes given face on, not edgewise.

FRENTE POR DETRÁS, obsolete pass in which bull charged at cape from behind man's back. Today often used loosely for the *gaonera*.

FUEGO, BANDERILLAS DE, 71–3.

GAONERA, 61.

GALLEANDO, 224, 231.

GARROCHA, wooden pole of pic, about 8 feet long without point.

GIRALDILLA, see LASERNINA.

GOLLETAZO, foul thrust into side of bull's neck. Admissible only to give quick death to accidentally injured and helpless animal.

GRADA, 30–31.

HULE, oilcloth, slang for operating-table.

IGUALAR, see CUADRAR.

INDULTAR, to reprieve (by petition of audience) bull that has shown quite exceptional bravery and nobility. Only about 25 cases recorded in last 100 years in Spain. Last case before 1955: 'Civilón', of Juan Cobaleda, 1936. 'Civilón' had brilliant record in bravery test as calf; full-grown, was so noble he would let anyone stroke him, and children play ring-a-roses round him and sit on his back (there are plenty of photos of this). Fought at Barcelona by El Estudiante in spring; when fighting was hottest, and Civilón charging picadors bravely, his *mayoral* called out his name from the *callejón*; Civilón halted in charge and went over to barrier to be patted. Was reprieved; same test repeated twice with same result, and he was permanently pardoned. Was still in *plaza* corrals when Civil War broke out in July; Red militiamen shot him. Latest case in Mexico: bull 'Ilustrado', of Villamarta, 1933; bought for stud. Latest in Spain, bull 'Desteñido', of Domecq, at Jerez de la Frontera, 1955. After long and laborious cure, owing to vile work by picador of César Girón (which only brought out bull's bravery all the more), life was saved. Domecq refused substantial offer for 'Desteñido' from a Salamanca breeder and retired the bull to his own ranch near Jerez, to serve as *semental*.

JABONERO, soap-coloured.

KIKIRIKÍ, 'cock-a-doodle-do', an *adorno* with *muleta*, swirling it in figure of 8 and making bull follow it as man trips slowly backwards.

LARGA, 52, 56–7, 60, 196, 231.

LASERNINA, 86.

LEVANTADO, 51.

LIDIA, ringcraft, strategy and *suertes* taken as a whole, and especially from viewpoint of suitability to conditions of given bull. Bad *lidia* can spoil a good bull; good *lidia* can correct defects in bull's style, and even, within limits, make a bull seem brave when it is not, or extract hidden bravery from an apparent *manso*.

LISTÓN, 17.

LOCALIDAD, bullfight seat or ticket.

MANDAR, 59, 109, 110.

MANO, of bulls, forefoot. MANO A MANO, fight with only two matadors.

MANOLETINA, 86, 193, 198.

MANSO, tame: (1) of cattle, domestic, not fighting (*bravo*) stock; (2) one of the *cabestros*; (3) of a fighting bull, 'less brave', or cowardly. M. DE SOLEMNIDAD, a 'copper-bottomed' *manso*, one normally 'fired'.

MAREAR, to daze or make giddy. Applied to objectionable and illegal practice of peones in giving *capotazos* to spin the bull round and round, as soon as their matador has registered some sort of prick or thrust, so that it will lie down for the *puntillero* to finish off. Audience always protests, but Presidents seldom punish this breach of rules. Such capemen are known as *enterradores* (gravediggers).

MARIPOSA, 61, 169-70.

MAYORAL, ranch steward or head cattleman.

MEDIA VERÓNICA, 60. M. ESTOCADA, thrust in which only half blade goes in; can be just as mortal and as rapid as a full one. M.E. LAGARTIJERA, trick invented by Lagartijo in killing; amounts to a half-thrust cleverly administered in just the right place but with lengthened arm. Used as term of praise by the ignorant, including some newspaper reporters. Can be justifiable with bull that is very *avisado*.

MEDIOS, LOS, central part of ring; bull 'weighs' heaviest here, i.e. will charge least readily unless it is very brave, in which case the *medios* are the best spot for a *faena*.

METISACA, 'put and take', thrust (not mere prick) in which the man never leaves go, but exits from *suerte* with sword still in his hand. Generally a defective thrust, for geometrical reasons.

MOLINETE, 86.

MONA, picador's greave worn under trouser.

MONOSABIOS, ring horse-servants in red blouses and caps. Duties: to pull fallen picador clear and help him remount; to look after horses, lead out any unserviceable or wounded ones, kill quickly any badly wounded, removing *peto* and harness, etc. Forbidden: to take any part in fighting, e.g. by doing *quites*, altering course of bull, or leading or forcing horse towards bull; breaches of these rules are common. Odd name ('clever monkeys') originated from similarly dressed troupe of performing monkeys that appeared in Madrid circus.

MONTERA, peculiar-shaped cap of foot bullfighters.

MORUCHO, 8 (was originally name of a thoroughbred race of cattle in Salamanca area).

MOZO DE ESTOQUES, sword-handler, matador's servant who looks after his fighting gear and personal affairs; generally acts as kind of factotum to the entire *cuadrilla*.

MULETA, 55, 76–7, 80–85, 108. MULETAZO, any *muleta* pass.

NATURAL (accent on last syllable), 77, 79, 80-1, 83-5.

NAVARRA, 60–1, 86, 209.

NOBLE (of bull), honest, going for the lure and not the man's body. See also SENTIDO.

NOVILLO, young bull over three years old; also, full-grown bull not suitable for major fight (see DESECHO). By regulations, must be under six. NOVILLADA, fight with *novillos*. NOVILLERO, junior or apprentice matador (see ALTERNATIVA).

OJO DE PERDIZ, 'partridge-eye', red ring round eye, especially of red bull. Classic Miura type, generally *manso* nowadays.

OLÉ!, quick shout of applause at fine piece of work.

ORTEGUINA, see MANOLETINA.

PALCO, box at bulling. Individual seats in boxes can be bought as a rule.

PALMAS, clapping.

PARAR, PARANDO, 59, 110. PARADO, 51, 53, 67.

PASE, pass (cape or *muleta*), see Chaps. 6, I, and 8 respectively. P. NATURAL, see NATURAL. P. EN REDONDO (DERECHAZO, PASE DE LA FIRMA), right-hand *natural*. P. CAMBIADO, backhander, bull exits on opposite side from *natural*. P. AYUDADO, two-hander. P. DE PECHO (breast pass), strictly a *p. cambiado por alto*. P. CAMBIADO POR BAJO, or TRINCHERAZO, slicing backhander with right, given low down but not bending knee; very powerful pass, was basis of Domingo Ortega's famous *faenas* of domination. P. ESTATUARIO (formerly called *p. de la muerte*), a *p. ayudado por alto* or two-hander over the top, given with feet together and simply lifting cloth over horns as they pass. P. DEL CELESTE IMPERIO, picturesque but now also obsolete term for same pass but with feet apart and following through with hands, thus *cargando la suerte*.

PASEO, PASEÍLLO, formal parade of toreros at beginning, after the *despejo*. *Alguaciles* lead, then matadors (senior man on left, junior man in middle, second swordsman on right), then foot *cuadrillas* of matadors, then picadors, finally *puntillero*, *monosabios*, sand-rakers and mule-team for drag-out. *Paseo* starts from horse-gate, crosses sand to below President's box, where all salute President, then breaks up, and those not due to fight first bull withdraw from ring. Band plays a *pasodoble* during the parade.

PATA, hindfoot.

PECHO, see PASE.

PEÓN, capeman, *banderillero*.

PETO, horse-protector, xi, 9, 52, 64–5.

PICA, the pic (GARROCHA plus PUYA).

PINCHAZO, prick, attempted sword-thrust which does not go in.

PITOS, whistles, opposite of *palmas*.

PODER A PODER, 69, 71, 197.

PRESIDENTE, official in charge of entire *plaza* during fight. In Madrid, high police official; in provinces, local governor or his deputy. Has power of arrest and fine or detention.

PUNTAZO, superficial horn-wound.

PUNTILLERO, 97.

PUYA, pic-point; PUYAZO, pic-thrust.

QUERENCIA, haunt or favourite spot preferred by bull in ring, either natural or acquired. Natural: door of bullpen; place where sand is cooler underfoot through leaky water-pipe, etc. Acquired: spot where bull has scored success by tossing man, killing horse, etc., or where it has happened to be left several times running after a *suerte*, through careless *lidia*; or, for a cowardly bull, some place on boards of barrier. Bull feels more at home in *querencia*, does not want to leave it, hence will not charge but stands waiting to hook. An acquired *querencia* always means trouble and danger; every effort should be made to get bull out of natural *querencia* and keep him out, and to make him forget an acquired one. A really nasty problem is a cowardly and *avisado* bull in *querencia* near bull-pen door; see Chapter 15, Interlude.

QUIEBRO, AL, 71, 182 (see also CAMBIO). Q. A CUERPO LIMPIO, offering one's body, without cape, as target for bull's charge, and then dodging this neatly by sudden sidestep or change of direction. ('*Cambio a cuerpo limpio*' would be contradiction in terms.)

QUITE, 52, 66–7, 146, 149. The rescue can be made with cape, or *a cuerpo limpio*, or by other means. Pedro Romero did a famous *quite* by pushing the man violently so that he fell over, and then taking the bull's charge on his own cape. I have seen *quites* done with thrown hats and other objects. A pursued peón often does a self-*quite* by throwing his cape one way and swerving the other way himself. Read 'jacket' for 'cape', and this *quite* is familiar to farm workers.

RABO, tail; cut in provincial rings as supreme token of triumph. This automatically deprives the first ear of all meaning.

RECIBIENDO, 91–2, 114, 184, 225.

RECORTE, 60, 196.

REDONDEL (also ALBERO, ARENA), see RUEDO, the standard word.

REJÓN, REJONEADOR, 99–103.

REVOLERA, 56, 60.

RODETE, darker ring that appears at base of bull's horn on completion of third year, and thereafter annually. Hence two rings mean four-year-old, three mean five-year-old, etc. Infallible means of telling bull's age, but often not clearly visible.

RUEDO, ring, the circular arena in which the bull is fought, bounded by *barrera*.

SALTO DE LA GARROCHA, pole-jump over charging bull, from in front, landing behind tail. Very spectacular, and dangerous. Performed in recent years by one modest *novillero* only (Pepe Calabuig), who was brilliant at it but not much good at anything else.

SEMENTAL, stud bull. Usual age for starting, three or four; useful life, about five years, but some last eight or ten. The famous 'Diano', of Ibarra (pure Vistahermosa main line) went on for fifteen years.

SENTIDO, craftiness, ability to distinguish man's body from cloth lure. Opposite of *nobleza*. Increases sharply with age.

SERPENTINA, 56, 60.

SOBRERO, spare bull kept as substitute for any rejected from ring.

SOBRESALIENTE, supernumerary matador, required by regulations when there are less than three matadors on the programme; also, matador retained by *rejoneador*. Usually a humble *novillero* in either case.

SOL, SOMBRA, SOL Y SOMBRA: Sun, Shade, and mixed Sun-and-Shade, the three divisions of seats in the *plaza*. *Sol* is the cheapest, being uncomfortably hot for most of the year, also because most of the fighting is done in the shade. *S. y s.* prices, in Spain, are nearer to Shade than to Sun ones. *Sombra* prices vary from **three** times as much as *Sol* in height of summer, to one-and-a-half times as much in early spring. In Madrid, *Sol* seats (Blocks 4–7) are acceptable up to mid-May as a rule; also, Block 3 of the mixed is really pure shade from July onwards; at same period, a seat in Block 4 (*Sol*) will give you shade for more than half the afternoon if it has a number below 30. In spring, Block 7 is very acceptable, but *tendido alto* with high numbers over 40 has view obstructed. The worst block in *Sol* is No. 6. Shade blocks are 9, 10, 1, and (least good) 2.

SORTEO, drawing lots, 35.

SUERTE, in general, 'luck'. Technically, 'hazard' in almost the billiards sense and also the ordinary sense: any pass or other action formally and deliberately performed with the bull (*suerte de varas*, the pic act). By extension, each of the three *tercios* or Acts of the fighting. To 'put the bull in *suerte*' means to lead it by cape-work or otherwise to the right place for it to charge the picador. SUERTE SUPREMA, 88. SUERTE CONTRARIA, in killing, when position is such that the man exits from the *suerte* towards centre of ring, instead of towards barrier (SUERTE NATURAL). Usually inadvisable, unless bull has a *querencia* on barrier, and a thrust *arrancando* is aimed at.

TABLAS, boards: (1) actual barrier; (2) adjacent territory as far as ten-yard line. All pic work takes place in (2) but should not be done *en tablas*, i.e. up against boards themselves.

TANDA, DE. Of picadors, regular, not reserve. Of *banderilleros*, the man or men whose turn it is to plant the sticks.

TAPARSE (1) said of bull that stretches muzzle forward while laying head back, making *descabello* almost impossible; (2) command by matador in Act 3 to his peones to stoop down behind barrier so as not to distract bull's attention.

TAURINO, 3.

TAUROMAQUIA, 3.

TEMPLAR, TEMPLANDO, 59, 108, 110, 227.

TENDIDO, 30; TENDIDA, see ESTOCADA.

TENTADERO, 39–41.

TERCIO, third: (1) one of the three 'Acts' of the fighting; (2) the ten-yard line, 62; (3) TERCIOS, territory from (2) to an imaginary circle two-thirds of the way in to the centre; part of ring in which most of the foot fighting develops.

TERRENO, terrain: (1) the different terrains of the ring, i.e. *tablas*, *tercios* and *medios*. (2) The 'man's terrain' and the 'bull's terrain'. The bull naturally feels more at ease in the open, and man safer near barrier; hence, if man is facing bull for any *suerte* other than the pic, his terrain is all of the ring that lies between the bull and the hither segment of the barrier, and the bull's terrain is all that lies beyond, from the bull to the farther segment of the barrier. (3) 'To tread the bull's terrain' means to advance into the area manifestly commanded by the bull, e.g. when challenging it from very close, say six feet or less. An 'invisible line', at which alone the bull will charge, and which demarcates this 'bull's terrain', becomes evident to an intelligent spectator after a little experience; naturally it is far clearer to the matador himself. Conversely, in every true pass, the bull invades the man's terrain. In the kill (normal style), the man must go into the very heart of the bull's terrain, hence the supreme risk of this *suerte*; but if done *recibiendo*, then the man does not invade but suffers invasion, and delivers the thrust at the moment when the two terrains coincide. These distinctions are of the first importance for a thorough understanding of the *lidia*.

TIEMPO, each tempo of a *suerte*, three in number: challenging, centre of *suerte*, and finishing off (*remate*). In passes or pics: the challenge and bull's attack, the encounter, and the bull's exit. In *banderillas* (other than *al quiebro*), the approach, the placing of the sticks, and the man's exit. In the kill (other than *recibiendo*): the man's entry, the *cruce* and thrust, and the man's exit. In *al quiebro* and *recibiendo*: the bull's attack, the man's action, and the bull's exit. Inefficiency in any one tempo spoils the whole *suerte*: in passes, the third tempo is as important as the second, for if the pass is not finished off properly, sending the bull through and away, it may hook round and catch the man; and in any case, the whole thing will look wrong. A UN TIEMPO, 94, 174.

TIENTA, see TENTADERO.

TOREAR, to 'torry', neologism which I have adopted from the poet Roy Campbell (himself an amateur picador) who has used it in print for twenty years: to play the bull with cloth lure or fight it from horseback. The verb 'bait', which I have seen on an English-language bullfight poster of La Línea, is unsatisfactory, suggesting as it does the goading of a tame animal to fury. Torrying of fighting bull or cow is different, being skilful evasion *and control* of attacks of a wild animal. TOREADOR, perfectly good old Spanish word, but now obsolete except in joke. The only correct word is:

TORERO, any bullfighter but especially matador.

TORIL, bullpen with door leading direct into ring.

TORO, bull. By Spanish regulations, over four and under seven years old, and of weight (for first-class rings) not less than 470 kg. (1,034 lb.) on the hoof. Mexican bulls are smaller. (Note: since this book, and especially the last chapter of it, was written, the authorities have again partly relaxed the regulation that had just been restored to force with such salutary effect. Their doing so at the petition of the ranchers alone, and not of the public or even of the toreros, was adversely commented on, and the results have been regrettable, so that the proper 470 kg. may be put back in force again; even 470 kg. is already 100 kg. less than the old minimum of 1928.)

TRAJE DE LUCES, bullfighter's gala uniform of coloured silk with gold or silver decorations or black embroidery. Peones do not wear gold.

TRAPÍO, fine handsome appearance and formidable presence of bull of good caste; indispensable condition for major fight, irrespective of weight.

TRASTEO, *muleta*-work in general. TRASTOS, sword and *muleta*.

UTRERO, three-year-old bull.

VARA (DE DETENER), pic, also pic-thrust.

VARETAZO, blow with shaft of horn. Can cause grave injury without bloodshed.

VERDAD, HORA DE LA, 88.

VERÓNICA, 57–60, 113, 162, 178.

VOLAPIÉ (originally *vuelapiés*, 'flying feet'), 94–6, 108.

ZURDA, left hand.